Biotechnology, Patents and Morality

This book critiques the decision-making process in Article 53(a) of the European Patent Convention. To date, such decisions have been taken at high levels of expertise without much public involvement. The book eschews traditional solutions, such as those found within legislative, judicial and patent office realms and instead develops a radical blueprint for how these decisions can be put to the public. By examining wide-scale models of participatory democracy and deliberation, this book fills a significant gap in the literature. It will be invaluable for patent lawyers, academics, practitioners and intellectual property and patent officials.

Maureen O'Sullivan, BA, BCL, LLM, PhD. Lecturer (Above the Bar) in Law, National University of Ireland, Galway. Chair, Vegetarian Society of Ireland. Fellow, Oxford Centre for Animal Ethics.

Routledge Research in Intellectual Property

Available:

Well-Known Trade Marks
A Comparative Study of Japan and the EU
Hiroko Onishi

Contemporary Issues in Pharmaceutical Patent Law
Setting the Framework and Exploring Policy Options
Bryan Mercurio and Daria Kim

Intellectual Property, Finance and Corporate Governance
Janice Denoncourt

Protecting Intellectual Property in the Arabian Peninsula
The GCC States, Jordan and Yemen
David Price and Alhanoof AlDebasi

Biodiversity, Genetic Resources and Intellectual Property
Developments in Access and Benefit Sharing
Charles Lawson and Kamalesh Adhikari

Pharmaceutical Patent Protection and World Trade Law
The Unresolved Problem of Access to Medicines
Jae Sundaram

Patent Pools, Competition Law and Biotechnology
Devdatta Malshe

Copyright Law and Derivative Works
Regulating Creativity
Omri Rachum-Twaig

The Patentability of Software
Software as Mathematics
Anton Hughts

Biotechnology, Patents and Morality

A Deliberative and Participatory Paradigm for Reform

Maureen O'Sullivan

Routledge
Taylor & Francis Group
LONDON AND NEW YORK

First published 2020
by Routledge
2 Park Square, Milton Park, Abingdon, Oxon OX14 4RN

and by Routledge
52 Vanderbilt Avenue, New York, NY 10017

Routledge is an imprint of the Taylor & Francis Group, an informa business

British Library Cataloguing in Publication Data
A catalogue record for this book is available from the British Library

Library of Congress Cataloging-in-Publication Data
Names: O'Sullivan, Maureen, 1967- author.
Title: Biotechnology, patents and morality : a deliberative and participatory paradigm for reform / by Maureen O'Sullivan.
Description: Abingdon, Oxon ; New York, NY : Routledge, 2019. |
Series: Routledge research in intellectual property | Based on author's thesis (doctoral - University of Edinburgh, 2018) issued under title: Morality patently matters : the case for a universal suffrage for morally controversial biotechnological patents. | Includes bibliographical references and index.
Identifiers: LCCN 2019013033 | ISBN 9780367181246
Subjects: LCSH: Biotechnology--Europe--Patents. | Patent laws and legislation--Moral and ethical aspects. | European Patent Convention (1973 October 5)
Classification: LCC KJC2751.B56 O88 2019 | DDC 346.404/68--dc23
LC record available at https://lccn.loc.gov/2019013033

ISBN: 978-0-367-18124-6 (hbk)
ISBN: 978-0-367-18127-7 (ebk)

Typeset in Galliard
by Taylor & Francis Books

This book is dedicated to Ciara, Conor and Randall, in line with a longstanding promise – and Isaac.

Contents

Table of cases

A & P TEA CO v Supermarket Corp, 340 US 147, 71 S Ct 127, 95 L Ed 162 (1950), 65

Animal Legal Defense Fund v Quigg (1991) 932 F 2d 920 (Court of Appeals, Federal Circuit), 63

Arizona State Legislature v Arizona Independent Redistricting Commission, 576 US, 135 S Ct 2652 (2015), 88

Association for Molecular Pathology v Myriad Genetics, Inc (2012) 132 Ct 1794 (Supreme Court), 23

C-34/10 *Oliver Brüstle v Greenpeace eV* [2011] -09821 (Grand Chamber), 24, 27, 43, 46, 47, 48, 49, 53, 57, 59, 68, 76, 100, 104, 119, 133, 148

C-364/13 *International Stem Cell Corporation v Comptroller General of Patents* EU:C:2014:2451, 24, 43, 49, 53, 59, 148

C-377/98 *Netherlands v Parliament and Council* [2001] ECR 1–070709 (ECJ), 20, 73

C-377/98 *The Kingdom of the Netherlands v European Parliament and Council* [2002] FSR 36, 20

C456-03 *Commission v Italy* [2005] ECR -5335, 26

Ciba-Geigy/Propagating Material (1979) C EPOR, 21

Diamond v Chakrabarty (1980) 447 US 303 (Supreme Court), 21, 23, 53, 55, 65, 70, 121

Edinburgh Patent Application No 949131742 (EPO Opposition Division), 24, 38, 56, 58, 77, 100

G2/06 *(Use of embryos/WARF)* (OJ EPO 2009, 306), 12, 17, 39, 40, 42, 43, 46, 59, 61, 76, 104, 133, 135, 154

G2/12 ("Tomatoes") and G2/13 ("Broccoli II") on 25 March 2015, OJ EPO 2016, 22

Harvard/Onco-Mouse [1989] OJ EPO 451, 32

Harvard/Onco-Mouse [1991] EPOR 525, 8, 25, 33

Howard Florey Institute-Relaxin [1995] 6 OJ EPO 388 (EPO Opposition Division), 31, 87

In the matter for an application for a patent by A and H [1927] 44 RPC 298, 14

In the Matter of an application for a patent by Rufus Riddlesbarger [1935] 53 RPC 57, 14

Table of legislation

Acknowledgements

This book is based on my doctoral research for which I was blessed with two outstanding supervisors, Professor Graeme Laurie and Mr. Gerard Porter, both at the University of Edinburgh. Without their excellent guidance and advice, this work may not have been achieved.

General introduction

Brief introduction to the European patent system

European patent law is intricate and multifaceted. Inventors have a dizzying array of jurisdictions from which to choose to protect their inventions. Patents can be granted by the European Patent Office under the European Patent Convention (EPC). Patents can be applied for in Geneva under the Patent Cooperation Treaty (PCT), which is an international treaty. Applicants can seek patents at national level and applications for EPC or PCT patents can be made at the national offices too. The latter can also be applied for at the European Patent Office (EPO).

At EU level, the Biotechnology Directive regulates some of the finer points of national patents when cases in which an interpretation of the Directive is sought are referred from national courts. At present there is no EU-wide patent but there is an agreement in place to introduce this protection at EU level under the EPC, creating a different jurisdiction. This is complicated somewhat by the fact that not all states have agreed to be a part of the patent system. Moreover, the establishment of the court system has proved contentious. By way of comparison with other jurisdictions that do not have multiple linguistic challenges, the European patent system appears to be ever more complex. All these procedural matters will be examined at the beginning of the book.

The emergence of morality and its inclusion in European patent law

In addition to these elaborate bureaucratic issues, the substantive law in Europe places a morality bar on controversial inventions – a prohibition which does not exist in other jurisdictions such as the US. Since the advent of biotechnology, this has assumed greater importance as the Boards and Courts have to deal with inventions which involve commodification of living matter or, indeed, destruction of human embryos.

The first European legislative instrument to broach the issue of morality predated the founding of the European Economic Community (EEC) and was embodied in the Strasbourg Convention which made morality an optional exception. When the EPC superseded the Strasbourg Convention this morality bar was made mandatory. Morality provisions have been included since then in both the Trade Related Aspects of Intellectual Property Rights (TRIPS) Agreement and the

EU Biotechnology Directive. Its meaning is somewhat obscure as legislators declined to endeavour to define morality leaving it instead to European institutions to debate. Morality, before the age of biotechnology tended to be invoked to restrict patents on gambling machines or abortifacients. The discovery of the DNA helix gave scientists the tools to start experimenting with genetic material and in order to fund their research and to profit from it they sought – and were granted – patents on these inventions.

Patent officials, asked to rule on morality when their expertise is in technical matters, arguably need a model which will assist them in the process through which they currently seem to muddle. Moreover, concepts of morality differ greatly across Europe.[1] This book focuses on this problem and seeks a resolution.

A tripartite nexus: biotech comes of age, patents proliferate and morality matures

As biotechnology developed, more and more patents were sought and granted amid controversies that life itself was being commoditised. Inventions which were sometimes more akin to discoveries also benefited from patent protection. The legal regime was more liberal in the US than in Europe because of the absence of a statutory morality bar in the former's patent legislation.

As noted, the EPC provides a morality bar for inventions that are otherwise patentable. If such inventions are within the morality exceptions, a patent cannot be granted. Yet there is no definition of morality which can guide patent officials who are obliged to apply it. Nor do the Boards of the EPO have a handbook to enlighten them. Currently, the case law does not predict how morality will be defined, as judges have little to guide them. In any case, morality by its nature evokes much disagreement, societal standards change over time and as a result of technological developments. How should issues relating to the morality bar, when a patent could be granted because the criteria are fulfilled but the invention potentially falls foul of Article 53(a) of the EPC, be decided? Article 53(a) provides that the invention must not offend against morality (or ordre public). The EPO has been criticised for not having achieved a satisfactory way of resolving this question.[2]

The application of the morality bar is thus problematic in terms of how this is decided and by whom. As everyone's conception of morality in a pluralistic world is likely to vary, an effective way of arbitrating between such potential polarities is important. Where decision-making is perceived by some critics as lacking in legitimacy as is the case in the interpretation of morality, much time will be spent in challenges to patent grants or revocations which could be avoided if such

1 This was acknowledged in the 'Travaux Préparatoires (EPC 1973)', IV/2767/61-E, 7, http://webserv.epo.org/projects/babylon/tpepc73.nsf/0/A79664CCCE197AC1C1257427004 (accessed 5 March 2019).

2 Amanda Warren-Jones, 'Identifying European Moral Consensus: Why Are the Patent Courts Reticent to Accept Empirical Evidence in Resolving Biotechnological Cases?' (2006) 28 EIPR 26.

processes were not so contentious from the start. This greatly increases potential cost of the patenting system too.

There is, of course, some academic support for the abolition or disregard of the morality bar but such a proposition is not advocated in this book. Rather, the focus of this work is on critiquing the existing decision-making process and recommending the adoption of an alternative – a blueprint which will be designed and discussed as the work progresses.

Outstanding disquiet: who gets to decide and how?

Traditionally, our legislators made important decisions for us in representative democracies but in an increasingly complex technological arena, patent officials determine whether biotechnological inventions are moral or immoral. This raises questions as to the quality of their decisions as there is no indication as to how they are qualified for such a task, nor do they have a set of principles which highlights the sort of inventions that would be subject to such scrutiny. Moreover, judges in early case law, such as *Plant Genetic Systems*,[3] were dismissive of some structures of public input such as opinion polls and surveys but the same courts did not outline how public opinion could be accommodated and hence excluded it.

The decision-making process for morally controversial biotechnological patent applications under Article 53(a) EPC is somewhat arbitrary as patent officials have to take decisions without guidance. Would judges, legislators or ethics committees be better suited to this task? As morality is a matter of societal-wide concern, the publics should have an input into such decisions, this work contends. This is especially important given the promise that patentable biotechnological inventions hold for curing disease, for instance, which is a matter of interest to us all.

Engagement on the issue of public debate is not currently being addressed because the EPO tends only to name what is not an acceptable way of listening to public concern.[4] Devices which seek to elicit public views such as opinion polls and surveys have not been accepted as evidence by the EPO.[5] The EPO tends to negate efforts by non-governmental organisations (NGO) to involve public voices;[6] perhaps rightly so. NGOs may not be better placed to elicit public views than officials at the EPO.

Arguably, the EPO already has a participatory process in that patent grants can be opposed and the opposition proceedings do allow individual representation. Controversial or unpopular decisions can therefore be contested but accessibility and deliberation fall somewhat short in this paradigm. This process is not adequate to address the normative claim of this book that when morality provisions are engaged by patent applications, public voices should be solicited, in a different way. This book examines a variety of possible solutions to the EPO's decision-

3 *Plant Genetic Systems v Greenpeace* [1995] EPOR 357.
4 *Plant Genetic Systems v Greenpeace* [1995] EPOR 357, 368–369.
5 Ibid.
6 Ibid.

making process, including judicial, legislative, patent office reform and the establishment of ethics committees.

None of these models of reform would achieve the wide-scale deliberation and participation that this work seeks to establish. There is some academic literature in which lawyers with expertise in the patenting of biotechnological inventions call for more public involvement and more transparency in the arbitration of this aspect of morality. This work develops a model of *how* the publics can be involved in ways that are meaningful in terms of the decision-making process.

This book does not advocate the harvesting of ill-informed public opinions. Instead, it will build a case to argue that when the morality bar in the EPC in the form of Article 53(a) EPC is engaged, the EPO should, instead of making unpredictable decisions behind closed doors which then may be challenged by a laborious number of processes, open the decision to education, deliberation and a subsequent vote. This process will elicit views from the 38 states[7] of the EPO. This draws on the approach pioneered in several Latin American countries which have established large-scale participatory democratic models. These involve frequent, direct votes on budgets and when those involved lack practical knowledge and education in the subject-matter at hand, local governments pay for their tuition and so equip them with the necessary skills. This book does not compare budgets and biotechnological inventions but, rather, gleans principles from participatory practices and seeks to apply them to certain EPO decision-making processes.

We currently lack a documented, functioning, adjusted and long-lived paradigm for the manner in which the patent system's decision-making process in the area of morality in biotechnological inventions can be opened up to public education, deliberation, participation and a vote. This is important because there is a body of thought which suggests that more democracy is desirable in this realm but does not develop this aspirational claim by showing how participation and deliberation can be combined in a complimentary fashion. The participatory budget has been able to adapt to changing circumstances on many occasions due to the flexibility of its participants and structure.

While it might be somewhat unorthodox to go to the Global South in search of a model of democratic innovation, the political climate in which participatory models of democracy emerged in Latin America features certain factors which may have been missing in Europe when democracy was first extended. At first sight what appears unconventional, at second sight may became logical and, indeed, modern. In Latin America, many recent constitutions enshrine participatory rights as they were gestated within a pre-existing international human rights framework. This contrasts with the formative period of other constitutions which were drafted within the nation state prior to the Universal Declaration of Human Rights and where the right to participate had not received consideration. The outer remit of what nowadays are regarded as human rights has expanded notably and has been influenced by international and regional bodies' declarations and conventions, activist judiciaries and socially minded legislatures.

7 Correct as of 5 March 2019: https://www.epo.org/about-us/organisation/member-states.html (accessed 5 March 2019).

A participatory paradigm for deliberative decisions

The right to participate is now identified as a human right and if meaningful public involvement is to be achieved, deliberation and participation should be combined. This may facilitate meaningful societal input. It is argued that in order to allay public concerns and to assist the EPO's duty as a public body to reach legitimate decisions, a much more robust and large-scale model is preferable to piecemeal, *ad hoc* paradigms.

The book will extract abstract principles from the participatory budget for reform of the decision-making process at the EPO. Features that can be generalised from the budget to the patent system are the Executive's role or potential role in organising and facilitating debate among the general public. Constructive deliberation and participation do not appear to spring up from grassroots levels spontaneously. In fact, mediation is important; otherwise debate can be fraught, polarising and can foster ill-will. The book will link the theoretical work on best practice in deliberation with the case study of the participatory budget. This will be in order to design a model for patent office reform in the fraught area of morally controversial biotechnological patents.

This book sketches a model for how a public awareness and educational campaign on issues of morality in biotechnological patent applications can be carried out. It also gives an example of how the publics can be involved and engaged widely through the use of outreach staff so that they not only deliberate but are also incentivised to participate. It will apply the principles from the discussions on deliberation and participation to aid in the drafting of a model of how participatory patents along with a plebiscite can be fashioned. It will also address some potential objections but will conclude showing that these can be addressed constructively and that an inclusive patenting system where issues of morality arise can be created.

While patent grants do require technical and legal skills, considerations of morality are potentially of interest to everyone. Even if publics are disinterested, the opportunity to participate should nonetheless be available as is the right to participate in referendums or, indeed, the right to vote. Expertise in scientific or regulatory matters does not mean expertise in ethical issues and at the level of ethics or morality, all views should receive equal airing, it will be contended.

It is argued that whenever the morality clause in Article 53(a) EPC is invoked a direct vote or type of referendum should be in place whereby the publics can decide whether the patent should or should not be granted. The EPO, as a public body, may actually be better placed to manage the practicalities and cost of organising such deliberative and participatory practices than a random array of special interest groups for whom the logistics (in terms of cost, time, travel and so on) may prohibit participation in opposition and appeals proceedings.

Radical reform of the triumvirate of patents, biotechnology and morality is currently untouched and this book makes an argument for a universal patent suffrage based on participatory practices which are explored to move beyond the theoretical to the practical. It therefore makes a contribution to knowledge in this area and fills a gap in the literature.

1 In search of a definition of morality in European Patent Law

1.1 Introduction

This chapter traces the origin and internationalisation of patent law, focusing on two European jurisdictions: the European Patent Organisation and the European Union. It first sets out the international instruments and shows that morality, which originally did not feature in the legislative framework, has now become a mandatory consideration for patent officials at the European Patent Office (EPO) (and in EU states) to weigh up where a patent application potentially raises this issue. It will discuss the historical origins of the morality clause and will show that the initial purpose was somewhat ambiguous and obscure. It also touches on international and European human rights legislation as it refers to the protection of intellectual property rights. The position of morality in the case law, especially at the EPO, will then be examined critically and I will show that its definition is uncertain, is in a state of flux and the current manner in which it is arbitrated undermines the principle of legal certainty. The aim of this book is not to achieve legal certainty: arguably, morality cannot be universally agreed but if arbitrated more effectively, its definition can be more legitimate.[1] Instead, it will argue for a model that is inclusive of a plurality of views to reflect that the patenting of morally controversial biotechnological inventions attracts a variety of opinions. It will seek to give these viewpoints a voice.

The following chronology will show that the nature of patent law has also evolved over time. The scope of protected subject matter has been expanded and simultaneously, morality limitations have increased as different ethical implications potentially arise with the changing nature of inventions. This is especially true where genetic frontiers are crossed and patent law has moved from a national to an international context. While there exists academic criticism of the decision-making process of the EPO,[2] little of this offers constructive proposals for reform. Many proponents of reform tend to confine their criticisms to proposing an alternative of one or the other following remedies: if legislation is not working,

1 And the focus is principally on procedural or input legitimacy.

2 Amanda Warren-Jones, 'Identifying European Moral Consensus: Why Are the Patent Courts Reticent to Accept Empirical Evidence in Resolving Biotechnological Cases?' (2006) 28 EIPR 26, 26–28.

some writers propose a judicial reform[3] and if the reverse is the case, then legislative clarity is suggested.[4] This book breaks this cycle and argues for reform from outside the system to address new issues which have emerged, such as the arbitration of morality across 38 signatory states of the European Patent Convention (EPC). Here public concepts of morality are notoriously difficult to discern. Yet the result is that morality is adjudicated on an *ad hoc*, unpredictable basis. The purpose of this chapter is to show that while this unpredictability is inevitable when adjudicating morality, the manner in which decisions are taken and by whom is currently controversial.

The next section provides a chronological account of patent law in order to trace its changes over the centuries and also, importantly, to note and analyse the inclusion of morality as a bar to the grant of morally controversial biotechnological patents.

1.1.2 Origins of patent law and its evolution until present times

The origin of the patent system is to be found in Venice and it was established by decree in 1449.[5] Initially, the aim of patent law was to encourage traders to introduce products and processes which were unknown in the state.[6] Letters patent, or open letters, were granted as proof of these privileges or monopolies and such letters were indicative of grants to individuals by the monarch.[7] In return for the monopoly, the grantee was obliged to disclose aspects of the product or process.[8] Originally, patents were only granted nationally and even though the aim has often been to prevent foreigners from dominating a given domestic market, in Venice, patents were granted in order to incentivise outsiders to innovate within the realm.[9] The balance between a private right in the form of a temporary monopoly and an obligation to effectuate public disclosure has, since the outset of the patent system, been a fundamental underlying principle. A justification for the monopoly granted in the patent system has been explained by highlighting the fact that the patentee is obliged to publicly disclose the invention so that the public can work the invention once the protected period has expired. Moreover, if the monopoly is broader than the contribution the invention makes to the art, courts can revoke the patent.[10] Modern practices such as opposition proceedings at the EPO show that this understanding has survived over the centuries even if such proceedings are not universal. Initially, the duration of the

3 George P Smith, 'Judicial Decisionmaking in the Age of Biotechnology' (1999) 13 Notre Dame JL Ethics & Pub Pol'y 93.
4 Oliver Mills, *Biotechnological Inventions: Moral Restraints and Patent Law* (Revised edn, Routledge 2010), Chapter 9 especially.
5 William J Flynn, *Patents since the Renaissance* (Booklocker Inc 2006) 8.
6 Ibid 9.
7 Tina Hart, Simon Clark and Linda Fazzani, *Intellectual Property Law* (6th edn, Palgrave Macmillan 2013) 9.
8 Ibid.
9 Ibid.
10 *Visx Inc v Nidek Co Ltd and others* (No 2) [1999] *FSR 405.*

grant was ten years, although Flynn notes that a patent was granted in Venice for a perpetual term in the sixteenth century.[11] This indicates that there has always been a tension as to the exact nature of a patent: whether it be a temporary monopoly or private property right and, indeed, there has been a fluctuation in the common understanding of this right over the centuries.

The Statute of Monopolies was passed in England in 1623 and its aim was the curtailment by Parliament of Crown monopolies. An exception to this general principle was set out in section 6 of the Act which guaranteed inventors an exclusive right over manufactured goods with a proviso that they should not be undermining of the law or the state and this requirement had moral undertones. It stipulated that they should not increase the price of commodities in the state, injure trade or be troublesome in some respect. This statute was the basis for English patents for centuries and these covered inventions of new products, machines and manufacturing processes. The focus was on stimulating industrial development rather than on inventors' rights.[12] It can be seen even in this early legal enactment that patent rights would be curtailed by the parameters of what was within the law and not go against the state's interests. For over a century after the enactment of the statute, it was ignored, however, and the royal prerogative and the Privy Council were used instead. The English Common Law and Chancery Courts eventually assumed jurisdiction over patent cases and this signified a shift away from a system of commodity monopolies to a patent system for inventions.[13] This also shows that the grant of patents has emanated from both legislation and precedent.

As will be seen by the end of this chronological exposé, the nature of patents is dynamic and their form is not impermeable. Nor, indeed, is the manner of their expansion in that they are creatures both of legislation and precedent but also of the executive which is charged with the task of applying morality bars whose definition remains elusive. Increasingly their parameters are decided by including the voices of objectors, such as Greenpeace, other non-governmental organisations and social movements,[14] which opposition proceedings facilitate.

1.1.3 Patent requirements

Generally speaking, inventions must be new, involve an inventive step and be capable of industrial application. The criteria for novelty stipulate that the invention has not been made public, taking into account prior art or the state of the art,[15] which comprises all prior knowledge in the given domain.[16] Neither can there have been any publication, which includes making available to the public either orally or in writing, by demonstration or in some other form of the invention prior to the application

11 Flynn, *op cit* 10.
12 William Cornish, David Llewelyn and Tanya Aplin, *Intellectual Property: Patents, Copyrights, Trademarks and Allied Rights* (8th edn, Sweet and Maxwell 2013) 123.
13 Ibid 35.
14 *HARVARD/Onco-Mouse* [1991] EPOR 525 attracted opposition from several NGOs.
15 Article 54(1).
16 Article 54(2).

filing date.[17] The requirement for there to be an inventive step provides that the invention must not be obvious to the ordinary skilled worker, in light of the state of the art.[18] The invention must also be useful in any type of industry, which includes agriculture.[19] If this last requirement is not fulfilled, there would be no benefit to society. Patent applicants must also disclose the invention, thus satisfying the public interest balance in this monopoly.[20]

Patents are negative rights which authorise the patentee to prevent others from using or exploiting the invention without permission[21] rather than a positive right to actually use and exploit the invention commercially. The grant of a patent does not amount to a licence to practise the invention. The use of the invention can be restricted or prohibited on ordre public or morality grounds nationally or internationally.[22] Even where exploitation is prohibited, this does not mean that the patent can be denied as patents are negative rights which restrict the actions of others. Patents currently last for 20 years from the filing date of the application in most jurisdictions and for most inventions.[23] The US used to employ a first to invent system but has relatively recently[24] altered this practice, bringing it closer to the European regime. As national rights, they are only valid in the jurisdiction where granted although as explained hereunder, the EPC's remit will be expanded under the unitary patent system.

As we shall see, attempts have been made for the last century at least to introduce an international regime and this endeavour is ongoing. The internationalisation aspect of the patent system is important for this book because it will show that the breadth of patent law has expanded considerably in the last 100 years and many actors have conflicting interests when it comes to patent grants. The inventions covered by patent law have also increased to include, for instance, biotechnological products and processes. The next section traces legislative developments which have expanded the scope and subject matter of patent law. It also notes the introduction of morality clauses in recent legislative enactments.

1.2 National to International Coverage: changes in protection in both form and substance

1.2.1 The Paris Convention for the Protection of Industrial Property 1883

The first endeavour to introduce an international patent filing system was the International Convention for the Protection of Industrial Property (1883), also

17 Article 56.
18 Ibid.
19 Article 57.
20 Article 83.
21 Enrico Bonadio, 'Biotech Patents and Morality after Brüstle' (2012) 34(10) EIPR 433, 435–436.
22 Ibid.
23 Article 63(1).
24 Leahy-Smith America Invents Act 2011, section 3.

known as the Paris Convention and this is administered by the World Intellectual Property Organisation (WIPO). This agreement created a union among contracting states which is advantageous for non-nationals seeking patents in other countries. The operation of a principle of national treatment means that nationals of other Member States must be treated equally to the host country with regards to patentability criteria. The priority period is 12 months from the date of filing in a signatory country. A priority period means that the applicant is not obliged to file for a patent in all designated countries at the same time. A second advantage is that the Convention allows inventors to exhibit their work before securing a patent and not fall foul of the novelty requirements in patent law which normally prohibits disclosure prior to the grant of a patent.

The Convention leaves the duration of the right to national law. It does not deal with many substantive matters of patent law such as the criteria for patentability but its scope covers patents and utility models along with a number of other intellectual properties such as industrial designs and trademarks. Countries can make further agreements among themselves as it has proved difficult to amend. It has a substantial number of contracting parties and was most recently amended in 1979.

No provisions on morality are included in this legislation. The issue of morality appears in other, later international patent laws that deal with substantive issues and is engaged most in the area of biotechnological inventions. Intellectual property rights also enjoy general protection under international human rights law as can be seen in the next section.

1.2.2 Universal Declaration of Human Rights 1948

The Universal Declaration of Human Rights provides for intellectual property rights, and offers protection for both material and moral interests which arise from authors' artistic, literary or scientific productions.[25] A number of other human rights instruments such as the European Convention on Human Rights (ECHR) also protect intellectual property rights[26] as does the EU Charter of Fundamental Rights.[27] No mention of morality is made in any of these instruments but in any case these rights are articulated in very general language and merely acknowledge the right without further details. Human rights law will be revisited at a later point in the book as it establishes a hierarchy of rights which may bring some clarity – or otherwise – to tensions which exist between private and public rights in the intellectual property realm.

25 UN General Assembly Resolution 217A(III), UN Doc A/810, at 71, Article 27(A), http://hrlibrary.umn.edu/instree/b1udhr.htm (accessed 5 March 2019).

26 According to Helfer, this is a recent trend in that the Court is now extending the property rights provisions to cover intellectual property rights, too. Laurence R Helfer, 'The New Innovation Frontier? Intellectual Property and the European Court of Human Rights' *Harvard International Law Journal* Vol 49(1) Winter 2008.

27 Article 17(2).

1.2.3 Strasbourg Convention 1963 – an optional morality provision

The Strasbourg Convention 1963 was the brainchild of the Council of Europe and came into force in 1980. It was open for membership only to Member States of the Council of Europe. Its main aim was to create common criteria for patentability, which were lacking in the Paris Convention. Article 1 of the Convention stipulates that in order to obtain patent protection, the invention must be susceptible of industrial application, be new and involve an inventive step. It signalled an attempt to harmonise patent law at an international level. It also spawned the EPC 1973 which was largely based on the Strasbourg Convention. While the latter had optional moral exclusions to patentability, the former's exclusions are mandatory showing that morality occupies an increasingly prominent place in patent legislative reform in Europe.

1.2.4 Patent Cooperation Treaty (PCT) 1970

The Patent Cooperation Treaty 1970 was drafted as an attempt to simplify the patent application process and it facilitates multiple national applications through the use of one procedure. An application is made to the patent or intellectual property office of a Member State, a regional office such as the EPO or at WIPO's office in Geneva. An international preliminary examination is carried out to give an opinion as to whether the invention is novel, involves an inventive step and is useful in industry. This opinion is non-binding, given that the criteria for patentability are not harmonised. This treaty is administered by WIPO and makes no reference to morality, perhaps reflecting that European institutions such as the Council of Europe and the EU have a broader approach to patenting, taking within their ambit ethical concerns which imbue this domain. Morality considerations are brought into account at national or regional level. The Patent Cooperation Treaty has 152 contracting parties at the time of writing.[28]

1.2.5 European Patent Convention 1973 – morality mandated

Negotiations for the drafting of a Convention on European patents took place throughout the 1960s and the intention was to establish a system which encompassed more countries than within the European Economic Community (EEC) which, at the time, had only six members. The EPO opened in 1978 and it grants "European" patents. In actuality, there is no such thing within the jurisdiction of the EPO as it merely provides a single office at which an applicant can lodge a patent application which is examined once. If one wishes to apply for a patent under the EPC one may file an application at the Irish Patents Office or other national office or at the EPO, and they act as a receiving office even though the EPO is the granting body. Similarly, the EPO acts as a receiving office for applications under the PCT and such applications can be filed, searched and examined

28 https://www.wipo.int/pct/en/pct_contracting_states.html (accessed 5 March 2019).

at the EPO. This allows patent applicants considerable flexibility and national patent or intellectual property offices may also act as receiving offices for WIPO. Any number of countries in which patent protection is sought may be designated and patentees therefore get a bundle of national patents rather than a European patent covering all contracting states. While examination is dealt with at European level, infringement proceedings take place at national level. This means that harmonisation is partial at best. Under the new patent system introduced in the EU which employs the EPC as its overarching legislation,[29] harmonised European patent protection will be available. Specialised patent courts are a feature of this reform, and this is detailed later in this chapter.

The European Patent Organisation has been established in conformity with the norms of the Vienna Convention on International Treaties 1969[30] and is a conventional intergovernmental organisation based on the EPC.[31] It has two principal branches: the EPO which occupies an executive role and the Administrative Council, which exercises a *quasi*-legislative function. It also supervises the Office's activities and takes charge of the Organisation's policy issues. Membership of the Administrative Council is almost entirely comprised of the directors of national patent or intellectual property offices,[32] giving a sense that there is a blurring between the executive and legislative functions. Regardless of the fact that the EPO lacks formal legislative powers, the Enlarged Board of Appeal (EBA) stated in the *WARF* case[33] rather controversially that the Administrative Council is the EPO's legislator.[34] In fact, in order to amend the EPC, a full diplomatic conference must be held in accordance with Article 172 EPC and the procedure to revise the Convention is quite complex.[35] The Boards of Appeal are bound only by the provisions of the Convention, under Article 23. The Administrative Council is vested with significant legislative and rule-making powers. It may amend the Implementing Regulations of the Convention[36] and has powers to authorise the EPO's President to negotiate agreements on its behalf.[37] These powers have been bolstered in revisions of the EPC which enable the Council to bring the EPC into line with European or international patent legislation.

Given that the governing legislation is so difficult to alter and that biotechnology is a rapidly advancing field, when the Biotech Directive came into force in the

29 The EU will employ the existing European Patent Convention rather than drafting a new law.
30 Article 5.
31 Article 4.
32 https://www.epo.org/about-us/organisation/administrative-council/representatives.html (accessed 5 March 2019).
33 G2/06 *WARF/Stem Cells* [2009] EPOR 15.
34 Ibid, 29.
35 Antonina Bakardjieva Engelbrekt, 'Institutional and Jurisdictional Aspects of Stem Cell Patenting in Europe (EC and EPO): Tensions and Prospects' in Aurora Plomer and Paul Torremans (eds), *Embryonic Stem Cell Patents: European Patent Law and Ethics* (OUP 2009) 247.
36 Article 33(1)(b) EPC.
37 Article 33(4) EPC.

EU, the Administrative Council incorporated the Directive's articles into the Implementing Regulations of the EPC as an interpretive aid, by way of a decision in 1999. The legitimacy of this sort of legislative enactment is questionable[38] for reasons of transparency and sovereignty as the jurisdiction of the EPO is greater than that of the EU. Therefore the ten non-Member States of the EU who are part of the EPO had their governing legislation amended without a formal amendment process taking place. Such legislative activity will often only attract attention if there is a subsequent negative consequence for any of the states in question, which does not appear to have been the case.

1.2.5.1 Patentable and non-patentable inventions, morality and other exemptions in the EPC

The revised text of the EPC under Article 52(1) now provides for the grant of patents for inventions regardless of the technology field, so long as they are susceptible of industrial application, are new and involve an inventive step.

This language is similar to the language authorising patent grants in many other legal instruments around the world. Article 27(1) Trade Related Aspects of Intellectual Property (TRIPS), discussed on p. 18, is echoed in these amended provisions which provide for patents on inventions in all technological fields. The Convention does not attempt to define invention but provides a list of things which are excluded, whether or not they would be regarded as inventions and interpretation is left instead, to the Boards. Pumfrey J in *Shopalotto.com's Application*[39] stated that it was not possible to provide a thorough definition of invention.

Excluded inventions are now listed in EPC 2000, the final version of which came into force in December 2007. Article 52(2) excludes from patentability a list of inventions, within the terms of (1). These include matters which have not been invented such as discoveries and patents are not available for computer programs or aesthetic creations. The list is circumscribed somewhat by Article 52(3), the terms of which utilises the term "as such" to narrow the remit of the exclusion.

The term "as such" has no specific legal meaning but has been used to restrict the ambit of the exclusion, especially in the sphere of computer programs where its interpretation has given rise to controversy. In T-1173/97 *Computer program product/IBM*,[40] the patent claims covered a computer program which could be directly loaded onto a computer and also a stored computer program product. The claims were rejected initially as constituting a computer program "as such". IBM argued that the EPC legislators had not wished to exclude from patentability all computer programs, meaning that the words "as such" had to be defined. The Board distinguished between computer programs without a technical character

38 Decision of the Administrative Council of the European Patent Organisation of 16 June 1999 (1999) OJ EPO 7, 437.

39 *Re ShopalottoCom Ltd* [2005] EWHC 2416.

40 T-1173/97 *Computer program product/IBM* [1999] OJ EPO 609.

which were not patentable and those which did have such features, which could be patented.[41] Despite the exclusion from patentability in the legislation, the Board concluded that computer programs were, after all, patentable,[42] thus circumventing the legislative constraints. Sterckx and Cockbain[43] note that IBM sought to override the exceptions and were heeded by the Board which conducted what they describe as an aberrant reading of the expression "as such" in Article 52(3) EPC by conflating the interpretation of Articles 52(2) and (3).[44] This shows that the text of the Convention has been interpreted controversially and in the biotechnological patent realm, the question of morality, ordre public and their definition are similarly the source of some polemic, as explored hereunder.

Article 53 enumerates the exceptions to patentability. This section states that European patents shall not be granted in respect of inventions whose commercial exploitation are contrary to either ordre public or morality. The assessment of this exploitation will not be made by the laws or regulations of contracting States.

The Working Party on the EPC in the Travaux Préparatoires opined that there is no European definition of morality.[45] They believed that arbitration of this issue should be left to European institutions but neglected to denominate which institutions had responsibility or, indeed, competence to carry out this task. A morality bar was included in the Convention because it already existed in the patent laws of several states but it was not defined in the same way in each one. For instance, Sterckx and Cockbain note that Belgian law does not have a morality or ordre public bar on patentability.[46] Other countries that do have morality provisions apply them very rarely but they would be engaged if the sole purpose of an invention were illegal, in which case a patent would be denied. However, patents may be granted on inventions where the exploitation is not allowed or is partially permitted. Examples would include patentable genetically modified organisms whose cultivation might be curtailed by national regulation or abortifacients with multiple uses such as for elective abortions or in cases of medical emergencies. The UK Patents Act of 1883 gave the Comptroller a right to refuse the grant of a patent the use of which would be contrary to law or morality[47] and patents have been refused on grounds of morality for contraceptive devices.[48] Such patents were refused even where the device did not claim to be a contraceptive.[49] Armitage and Davies observe that in their experience of practice at the Patent Office, under the 1949 Act, morality provisions were invoked almost exclusively on

41 Ibid.

42 Sigrid Sterckx and Julian Cockbain, *Exclusions from Patentability: How Far Has the European Patent Office Eroded Boundaries* (Cambridge University Press 2012) 82.

43 Ibid 78.

44 Ibid 80.

45 'Travaux Préparatoires (EPC 1973)' 16, IV/2767/61-E http://webserv.epo.org/projects/babylon/tpepc73.nsf/0/A79664CCCE197AC1C12574270049F447/$File/Art53eTPEPC1973.pdf (accessed 5 March 2019).

46 Sterckx and Cockbain, *op cit* 23.

47 Section 86, Patents, Designs and Trade Marks Act, 1883.

48 *In the matter for an application for a patent by A and H* [1927] 44 RPC 298.

49 *In the matter of an application for a Patent by Rufus Riddlesbarger* [1935] 53 RPC 57.

grounds of sexual morality.[50] The Working Party of the EPC also found that ordre public was similarly undefined and therefore lacked a uniform meaning.[51] Leaving these terms without definition is questionable as when they arise, the boards of the EPO have little guidance as to their application and this has created an inconsistent body of case law, which will be explored and critiqued later in this chapter.

Article 53(a) EPC is the focus of this book as its invocation has not clarified or resolved the problem of what is meant by morality in Europe. The EPC does not define ordre public or morality, in line with the recommendations of the Working Party. We shall see the development of the jurisprudence unfolding through legislative amendments and case law which endeavour to keep up with rapid technological change.

The EPO first published Guidelines for Examination in 1977 and these are regularly updated, the most recent edition being November 2018 at the time of writing.[52] These guidelines address the policy of Article 53(a) which provides that a fair test of what was considered moral could be judged by indications that the public in general would abhor the granting of a patent on a given invention.[53] How this was to be ascertained across the now 38 states was not articulated but will be explored further in this chapter.

Other exclusions to patentability are found in Article 53(b) and (c) which omit plant and animal varieties and conventional breeding techniques from patentability, along with surgical methods for treating humans or animals.

Additional changes brought about by EPC 2000 include the fact that Article 53(c) EPC now provides that methods for treatment of the human or animal body by surgery or therapy and diagnostic methods practised on the human or animal body are expressly excluded from patentability. In the previous version of the EPC, these were omitted for not demonstrating industrial applicability. What constitutes the state of the art has been extended by Art 54(3) EPC: this now includes the content of all European patent applications filed prior to the filing date of the instant application thus making obtaining a patent somewhat more difficult.

Post-grant amendments may also be made under the revised EPC as heretofore, these were permitted only as part of opposition proceedings. Patentees may request revocation of or limits on the patent under Article 105a EPC 2000. The next section details the application process along with procedures available for patent opponents.

50 Edward Armitage and Ivor Davis, *Patents and Morality in Perspective* (Common Law Institute of Intellectual Property London 1994).

51 'Travaux Préparatoires (EPC 1973)' 16, IV/2767/61-E http://webserv.epo.org/projects/babylon/tpepc73.nsf/0/A79664CCCE197AC1C12574270049F447/$File/Art53eTPEPC1973.pdf (accessed 5 March 2019).

52 https://www.epo.org/law-practice/legal-texts/guidelines.html (accessed 5 March 2019).

53 'Guidelines for Examination at the EPO', https://www.epo.org/law-practice/legal-texts/html/guidelines/e/g_ii_4_1.htm (accessed 5 March 2019).

1.2.5.2 Filing and oppositions

Anyone who wishes to apply for a patent has a number of options available. Classical European patents can be filed in EPO filing offices in Munich,[54] in the Hague[55] or in Berlin[56] or at national patent or intellectual property offices if permitted in the country where sought.[57] They can be filed in English, French or German or another language and translated into an official language.[58] After a novelty search relating to prior art is carried out, an Extended European Search Report is issued. The patent application is published as soon as possible after 18 months from the filing date. Although anybody may submit written observations regarding the patentability of the invention, there is no right of audience. Neither is there any official communication about any effect of the observations. There is, therefore, a right to be heard or, rather, a right to be read which does not necessarily encapsulate a right to be listened to, to get a response, a justification or an explanation. Moreover, as secrecy is a prerequisite for inventions prior to patent applications, scant opportunity exists for debates which engage society and this raises concerns about whether these quasi-regulatory decisions are legitimate.[59] A devolution of this decision-making process could, if managed appropriately, enhance the legitimacy of decisions on morality by being more inclusive of a broader spectrum of viewpoints.

An opposition procedure is provided for in Article 100 EPC 2000, Part V and this must be filed within nine months of the patent grant. Standing to oppose is open and this Article stipulates the grounds for opposition. The first is that the invention is not susceptible of industrial application, is not new and/or does not involve an inventive step or that the basic criteria are not fulfilled so the patent will not be granted. The next condition is that the invention is not patentable subject matter and such an invention should be excluded. The following ground for opposition is where the publication or exploitation of the invention would be contrary to ordre public or morality. The matter of ordre public and morality has been modified to reflect a bar where the invention is to be exploited commercially and these changes will be described hereunder. The other two grounds for opposition are insufficient disclosure of the invention and that the subject matter of the European patent extends beyond the content of the application. When opposition proceedings are commenced, the EPO's Opposition Division invites observations from the parties under Article 101(2). A number of outcomes may ensue which are that the patent may be revoked under Article 102, the opposition may be

54 Article 75(1)(a) EPC.

55 Ibid.

56 'Decision of the President of the European Patent Office Dated 10 May 1989 on the Setting up of a Filing Office in the Berlin sub-office of the European Patent Office' (1989) OJ 218, http://legis.obi.gr/espacedvd/legal_texts/anc_reg/en/ap_i_a10_2_1989_218.htm (accessed 5 March 2019).

57 Article 75(1)(b).

58 Article 14.

59 Charlotte Waelde, Abbe Brown, Smita Kheria and Jane Cornwell, *Contemporary Intellectual Property: Law and Policy* (OUP 2016) 373.

rejected or the patent may be amended and maintained after an oral hearing. Waelde *et al.* opine that opposition proceedings are valuable in that they permit input from groups who may wish to ensure that patent officials are balancing competing interests appropriately.[60]

The opposition proceedings do not address the concerns in this book of widespread public involvement adequately for a number of reasons. These include the fact that the bargaining powers of the parties are not equal – patent grants favour patentees and it requires much expertise to engage in these proceedings. Moreover, it is not a remedy available equally to all contracting states to the EPC simply because it is territorially bound – the opposition will have to appear physically which involves much expenditure both of time and money and favours those living locally. While this process is a limited form of participation, little deliberation takes place and different interpretations of morality are not articulated.[61]

1.2.5.3 Appeal procedures

Where a patent has been granted or refused, there are provisions in the EPC which facilitate the appeal of decisions to the EPO Boards of Appeal, giving further options to opponents of the patent grant. As will be seen in the case law analysis in this chapter, these are used frequently. Such appeals must be filed within two months of the decision. There is no appeal to the Court of Justice of the European Union (CJEU), given that such a decision would not bind all signatories to the EPC and, moreover, the CJEU lacks jurisdiction to reopen controversies relating to the examination of patents issued by the EPO.[62] The EPO and the CJEU operate in separate jurisdictions. Patents may also be granted by national patent offices. National courts, the final court of appeal of which is the CJEU, handle infringement proceedings so case law on this issue arises from time to time within the European Union. This will undergo some change as the unitary patent system gets underway and an extra layer or layers of procedure are added to this area.

Another appeal process was introduced by the revised EPC 2000, which facilitates petitions for review to the EBA of the EPO. Such appeals relate to procedural defects and questions of principle referred by the Boards of Appeal. Where the EBA accepts an appeal, proceedings before the Board of Appeal will be reopened. Appeals go from the Examination Division to the Technical Board of Appeal or the Legal Board of Appeal. These boards are composed of a mixture of technical and legal expertise but there is a deficit in the field of ethics which is surprising given that some of the appeals invoke Article 53(a) EPC.[63] Both these

60 Ibid.

61 Personal communication from David Thomas, solicitor, who acted for the British Union Against Vivisection in the *Harvard/Oncomouse* case.

62 G2/06 *WARF/Stem cells* [2009] EPOR 15.

63 An example of the lack of any reference to expertise in or knowledge of ethics or issues relating to morality within patent legislation can be seen in the recent job vacancy advertised for the appeal boards of the EPO: http://patentepi.com/en/vacancies/european-patent-office.html (accessed 5 March 2019).

boards can refer matters to the EBA. Furthermore, the President of the EPO may issue opinions on significant cases and seek clarification on particular areas of law from the EBA.

As stated above, the EPO administers the EPC through its Administrative Council, which also plays a legislative role. Of note is that the EPO's Working Party on Litigation advocated the establishment of a specialised court, which has already been done in the US in the form of the Court of Appeal for the Federal Circuit. This has also now been achieved in the EU and such courts are currently being established under the Unitary Patent and Unified Patent Court. The timeframe is currently somewhat delayed beyond 2018, due to uncertainties about the pending legal challenge before Germany's Constitutional Court[64] which the Court has now agreed to hear.[65]

Other international patent treaties had not achieved harmonisation of substantive patent provision and so the World Trade Organization (WTO) initiated the TRIPS Agreement in 1994. This treaty has continued the trend to include within its provisions a morality threshold, as can be seen in the next section.

1.2.6 Trade Related Aspects of Intellectual Property Rights (TRIPS) 1994

TRIPS is a substantial international treaty on intellectual property rights and patents are dealt with under Articles 27 to 34. Member States must make protection available for any inventions in all technological fields, regardless of whether the inventions are made locally or imported.[66] Exclusions are permitted and these include inventions, the commercial exploitation of which would raise ordre public or morality concerns.[67] Encompassed by this provision are the protection of human, animal or plant life or health and prevention of serious prejudice to the environment, so long as exclusions are not made only because the exploitation is prohibited by law in contracting states. The TRIPS Agreement contains morality provisions largely at the behest of European states[68] given that there already is a morality bar in pre-existing European patent legislation. As Europe maintains a commitment to morality's place within patent law, it would make sense for this bar to patenting to be as clear as possible but TRIPS does not add anything to the definition of morality or ordre public.

Exclusions from patentability may also be made for the treatment of humans or animals through methods of diagnosis, therapy or surgery. Animals and plants and conventional breeding techniques also fall within the exclusion criteria. Members shall, however, provide for the protection of plant varieties either by patents or by

64 https://www.unified-patent-court.org/news/status-unified-patent-court-project-19-december-2018 (accessed 5 March 2019).
65 http://www.ip-watch.org/2018/02/26/german-court-hear-unified-patent-court-challenge-epo-staff-questions-persist/ (accessed 5 March 2019).
66 Article 27(1).
67 Article 27(2).
68 Waelde *et al., op cit.*

an effective *sui generis* system or by any combination thereof. Signatories to TRIPS are obliged to adhere to core provisions of the Paris Convention.

1.2.7 Directive 98/44/EC on the legal protection of biotechnological inventions

Despite the existence of the EPC it was deemed desirable to introduce patent legislation at EU level. In 1988, the European Commission proposed a Directive in order to endeavour to harmonise the law on biotechnological inventions[69] as at the time, there was no overarching Union law to achieve this purpose. The EPC is broader than EU law, in that it currently covers 38 states and, in any case, its judgments are not binding on national courts. Initially morality did not play a role as the motivation of the Commission was to emulate the US and Japanese relatively permissive patenting regimes in order to increase European competitiveness.[70] However, European civil society activism and NGOs such as Greenpeace[71] and Friends of the Earth[72] mounted many campaigns against genetic modification and commodification of genetic material and the directive proved to be a controversial legislative proposal. In 1994, France introduced a bioethics law which prohibited the patenting of human genes on ordre public and morality grounds even if the invention satisfied patent criteria because the genes had been extracted from the human body and, therefore, isolated.[73]

In 1995 the European Parliament vetoed an early draft of the Directive[74] because MEPs had been concerned that ethical issues had not been given their due weight. Not all of the amendments they proposed had been accepted by the Commission when an amended draft was submitted to the Parliament in 1992.[75] The Parliament proposed further amendments, some of which were accepted by the Council and after a protracted period in which conciliation proceedings between the Council and the Parliament took place, the jointly produced text was vetoed by the Parliament.[76]

It may be that in the domain of intellectual property laws, the European Parliament is receptive to public opinion given that its members are directly elected. The Commission, by way of contrast, is the Union's executive branch and its

69 Directive 98/44 EC of the European Parliament and the Council of 6 July 1998 on the Legal Protection of Biotechnological Inventions.
70 Proposal for a Council Directive on the Legal Protection of Biotechnological Inventions (1988) COM 496, http://eur-lex.europa.eu/procedure/EN/100993 (accessed 5 March 2019).
71 http://www.greenpeace.org.uk/global (accessed 5 March 2019).
72 https://www.foe.co.uk/sites/default/files/downloads/policy-position-genetically-modified-crops-99968.pdf (accessed 5 March 2019).
73 P Lemaitre and J-Y Nau, 'La Directive Europeenne Sur Le Genome Humain Est Incompatible Avec Le Droit Francais, Selon Mme Guigou', *Le Monde* (9 June 2000) 9.
74 [1995] OJ C68.
75 (1992) COM 589 Final of 16 December 1992 (1993) OJ C44/36, http://Aei.pitt.edu/8656/01/31735055263507_1.pdf (accessed 5 March 2019).
76 Gerard Porter, 'The Drafting History of the European Biotechnology Directive' in Plomer and Torremans (eds), 13.

members are appointed by the Council of the European Union and not by nationals of Member States. The Commission promulgates trade and promotes harmonisation of the internal market. It proposes legislation which is voted on in a co-decision procedure by the Council and the Parliament. Notably, the EPO does not have such a direct connection within its jurisdiction. Aerts observes that the EPO lacks both a democratically elected body and judicial review[77] and he opines that patent law under the EPC lacks the democratic legitimacy of the EU and US.[78] It would appear that the Directive caused a lot more controversy than the EPC. Some reasons for this were that advances had been made in biotechnology, over two decades had elapsed between the two pieces of legislation, the issue of morality had been flexed and, moreover, genetic modification of plants and animals had stoked public interest in the European Union.[79]

Eventually, in 1998, a revised Directive was adopted after ten years of negotiation although it was challenged before the CJEU by the Netherlands,[80] Italy and Norway. The Netherlands contested the Directive on six grounds, those being that Article 100a of the Treaty was not the correct legal basis for the Directive and that there was a breach of the principle of subsidiarity. The third challenge was on the principle of legal certainty. Article 6 of the Biotech Directive provides that patents should not be granted where their commercial exploitation would be contrary to morality or ordre public. The Netherlands deemed that the language of the Directive is too general and equivocal and that there was insufficient guidance to determine when to apply this Article. The CJEU disagreed saying that the provisions of patent law which would apply where a patent was refused on morality or ordre public grounds were well known and were also present in the international legal instruments. These were not denominated by the court, however. Further claims included a breach of international law, a breach of the fundamental right to respect for human dignity and a breach of the procedural rules in the adoption of the Commission's proposal.[81] The Directive was upheld in 2001, yet eight Member States were referred to the CJEU in July 2003 for their failure to implement it and were threatened with fines.[82] It took until 2007 for all Member States to comply with the requirements.[83]

This legislation authorises patents on biotechnological inventions. Art 3(1) provides that patents are available for inventions which are new, involve an inventive step and are

77 Rob J Aerts, 'The Legitimacy of Patent Law-Making in Europe and the US-A Tentative Comparison' (2007) 38 IIC 165, 169.

78 Ibid 177.

79 No Patents on Seeds is a coalition of groups which have been campaigning on this issue for some decades, http://no-patents-on-seeds.org/ (accessed 5 March 2019).

80 C-377/98 *Netherlands v Parliament and Council* [2001] ECR 1–070709 (at para 12).

81 C-377/98 *The Kingdom of the Netherlands v European Parliament and Council* [2001] ECR I-07079.

82 State of Play of the Implementation of Directive 98/44/EC (last revision 15 January 2007), http://ec.europa.eu/internal_market/indprop/docs/invent/state-of-play_en.pdf (accessed 5 March 2019).

83 Ibid.

susceptible of industrial application. Patentability is assured where the invention consists of or contains or involves a process through which a biological material is created, prepared or utilised. Thus the legislation ensures that patents are available for living matter, which potentially raises issues of ethical concern in that some of these inventions may cross a threshold from the inanimate to the animate for the first time in EU law. Such patents had already been granted at the EPO since the mid-1980s[84] and were first upheld in the US in *Diamond v Chakrabarty*[85] in 1980, therefore, the terrain is not new. Nonetheless they continue to cause controversy among environmental groups such as Greenpeace[86] and Friends of the Earth.[87]

Art 3(2) of the Directive provides that biological material which has been extracted from its natural environment or generated through a technical process can be classified as an invention even if it once occurred naturally. This provision is controversial in that it blurs the distinction between invention and discovery. Drahos analyses this provision by commenting that isolated genes can be regarded as inventions because, regardless of the fact that they have been discovered, in their isolated and purified form, they can no longer be described as existing in nature. He observes that the sequences are the same and that all that has been changed is that some redundant codons have been removed.[88] Nonetheless, such tinkering renders the modified organism sufficiently novel to attract patent protection. Isolated biological material has had its properties identified but has not been genetically modified and the extent to which it fulfils the novelty requirement in patent law is unclear. Brabin comments that as genes are natural products, the information garnered by understanding the genes is, intuitively, a process of discovery rather than invention[89] and probably should not be patented. When the Directive refers to biological material which has been generated by a technical method it refers to a situation where cells have been replicated but not modified.

Article 4(1) stipulates that plant and animal varieties are not patentable because they are genetically fixed and would therefore fail the novelty test. Plants and animals that are genetically modified are, however, patentable. The definition of "variety" in relation to plants was to evoke some controversy before the enactment of this Directive[90] in cases heard under the EPC 1973 as amended[91] as the term is not defined either in the EPC or in the Directive. In *Ciba-Geigy/Propagating Material*[92] the EPO looked at the International Union for the Protection of New

84 http://ww.alt.no-patents-on-seeds.org/index.php?option=com_content&task=view&id=40 &itemid=42 (accessed 5 March 2019).
85 *Diamond v Chakrabarty* (1980) 447 US 303.
86 http://www.greenpeace.org.uk/global (accessed 5 March 2019).
87 https://www.foe.co.uk/sites/default/files/downloads/policy-position-genetically-modified-crops-99968.pdf (accessed 5 March 2019).
88 Peter Drahos, 'Biotechnology Patents, Markets and Morality' (1999) 21 EIPR 441, 443.
89 Charles Brabin, 'Intellectual Property Law in the Realm of Biology–Striking the Right Balance' (2014) 36 EIPR 687, 687.
90 *Ciba-Geigy/Propagating Material* (1979) EPOR vol. C.
91 *Lubrizol/Hybrid Plants* [1990] EPOR 173.
92 *Ciba-Geigy/Propagating Material* (1979) EPOR vol. C.

Varieties of Plants (UPOV) system when seeking to define "variety". Patent protection was possible only because the subject matter fell outside the UPOV definition of "variety" as the invention in question was generic so it related to more than one variety.[93] The Board read the provision narrowly and opined that as the patent claim which focused on the chemical treatment available was broader than a claim only to a plant variety, it was permissible. On this interpretation, more than one plant variety treated in this way can be patented, which broadens patent coverage by restricting the interpretation of the exclusion.

This outcome was criticised by Mills because importing nomenclature from one legislative instrument to another courts controversy as the purposes of the legislation may differ from those under consideration by the court.[94] A dictionary definition or expert advice may have been preferable.

Under Article 4(2), there is also a criterion that essentially biological processes for the production of plants or animals are not patentable. These are defined in Article 2 as comprising natural techniques of cross-breeding and selection. This provision is circumscribed, however, by Article 4(3) which provides patents for inventions using a microbiological or technical process or products resulting from such processes. The issue of essentially biological processes has given rise to controversy between the EPO and the European Commission. In 2015, the EBA of the EPO considered granting patents for products which were brought about as a result of essentially biological processes so the product of a non-patentable technique could avail of patent protection.[95] The Directive is silent as to whether these products are patentable but the Commission has issued a Notice, indicating that products resulting from essentially biological processes are not patentable.[96] Even though the EPO is not bound by this notice, it works closely with the EU and has announced its intention to stay proceedings in all examination and opposition cases involving animals or plants produced by essentially biological processes.[97]

Patents are not available for the human body or parts thereof in their natural state or where one of its elements is merely discovered under Article 5(1). Article 5(2), however, confirms that patents are available for elements of the human body which have been isolated or produced by a technical method. Full or partial gene sequences are included, regardless of whether they possess identical structures to their natural counterparts.

This section specifies that propagation or replication of biological material which does not strictly involve invention can be patented so a reward for expertise

93 Mills, *op cit* 70.

94 Ibid.

95 G2/12 ("Tomatoes") and G2/13 ("Broccoli II") on 25 March 2015, [2016] OJ EPO 28.

96 Commission Notice on Certain Articles of Directive 98/44/EC of the European Parliament and of the Council on the legal protection of biotechnological inventions (2016/C 411/03), http://eur-lex.europa.eu/legal-content/EN/TXT/?uri=CELEX%3A52016XC1108%2801%29 (accessed 5 March 2019).

97 'EPO Stays Proceedings in Certain Biotechnology Cases', http://www.epo.org/news-issues/news/2016/20161212.html (accessed 5 March 2019).

and specialised labour is permissible. Where technical processes have been applied, the biological material will have been replicated. Despite the legislative authorisation of this technology, the European Group on Ethics expressed qualms about the patentability of this isolated material.[98] Protection for such material has also stoked controversy in the US, as will be shown.

This interpretation of this aspect of patent law first came to light in the US Californian Supreme Court case of *Moore v Regents of the University of California*.[99] In this case, Moore was a cancer patient who found out that without his consent, his doctors had carried out research on his tissue samples and had gained lucrative contracts for this work. Moore was unsuccessful in his claim under the tort of conversion in which he sought a share in the profits of this research. The majority of the court opined that his oncologists had earned their reward and hence were entitled to be compensated for their labour and expertise. Moore, however, was the mere source of the cells in the court's view and he would receive nothing for this part of his claim, although he did recover for the absence of consent and breach of fiduciary duty. In this case, his cells had been propagated in the laboratory but not modified and were, arguably, a discovery rather than an invention.

Patents on isolated genes will no longer be granted in the US since the Supreme Court decision in *Association for Molecular Pathology v Myriad*[100] in which Justice Clarence Thomas denied a patent on an isolated segment of DNA, opining that it was a natural product rather than an invention. Some change must have been made to the organism in order to attract patent protection, in his judgment. No method or process claims had been made in this case as the methods employed were not novel, so his judgment referred only to the product. Had the processes employed in making the invention been novel, they would have been patentable but they were well known. This case represents a surprising turn in US patent adjudication, considering that an earlier Supreme Court in *Diamond v. Chakrabarty*[101] had pioneered the extension of patents to living organisms and everything under the sun in the courts. Given the legislative specifications in European laws, which permits patents in such circumstances, neither the EPO nor the CJEU are likely to follow suit and so patents on isolated cells are likely to be more easily granted in Europe.

The Directive, like the EPC also precludes patentability of some inventions on certain grounds. The Directive's parallel provision to Article 53(a) EPC is to be found in Article 6(1), which denies the patentability of inventions whose commercial exploitation would conflict with ordre public or morality. Similarly to the EPC, such assessment should not be made just because it offends a law or regulation.

98 European Group on Ethics in Science and New Technologies, 'Ethical Aspects of Patenting Inventions Involving Human Stem Cells, Opinion No. 16' (2002) para 2.3, http://ec.europa.eu/european_group_ethics/docs/avis16_en.pdf (accessed 5 March 2019).

99 *Moore v Regents of University of California* (1990) 51 Cal.3d 120.

100 *Association for Molecular Pathology v Myriad Genetics, Inc* (2012) 132 Ct 1794.

101 *Diamond v Chakrabarty* (1980) 447 US 303.

Interpretations of the Directive are binding when the CJEU pronounces on the Directive and this occurs where there has been a referral for clarification from a national court. Examples of such referrals include the *Brüstle*[102] case from the German Federal Court of Justice and *International Stem Cell Corporation* from the UK High Court.[103] Interpretations of the Directive may vary at national level, especially if the enacting regulations do not conform strictly to the text of the Directive. Due to differing jurisdictions the jurisprudence of the EPO and the CJEU may, in the future, diverge somewhat – or significantly, especially with the creation of the unitary patent system, discussed below, and the fact that not all EU members are full participants in this new process. Moreover, the future of this system may be affected if the Brexit process is completed.

The Directive clarifies the morality and ordre public provisions further by means of a non-exhaustive list of what cannot be patented, although rapid advances in technology means that the wording of the Directive will continue to be unclear.

Art 6(2) provides, in relation to paragraph 1 that processes for the cloning of human beings are not patentable. This does not indicate whether the products resulting from such processes are patentable although a cloned human being could not be patentable by virtue of Article 5.1 of the Biotech Directive, especially if read in conjunction with Recital 40 which prohibits modification of the germ line genetic identity of human beings. The *Edinburgh* patent which was granted by the EPO in 2002 caused much controversy before its amendment because it had the potential to cover human cloning.[104] The situation in Europe contrasts somewhat with US patent law practice in which process patents which potentially[105] or overtly[106] cover human cloning have been granted by the USPTO. The status of the products of such techniques is uncertain. Since 2011 no patents can be granted in the US on "human organisms"[107] but the scope of such terminology is unclear. In Europe, the processes may be unpatentable but could be legal, giving rise to products which may be patentable depending on the drafting of the claim and the admixtures of DNA. However, a second prohibition follows and prohibits patents for processes that would facilitate the modification of human beings' germ line genetic identity.

This provision presumably seeks to deny patents on inventions where heritable traits have been introduced to human beings possibly also from other species. Whether this would apply to animals modified with a large percentage of human DNA is not clear – we do not possess a definition of what constitutes a human being. Given that definitions such as "chimera" and "hybrid" have been added to by German researchers who have coined the term

102 C-34/10 *Oliver Brüstle v Greenpeace eV* [2011] ECR I-9821.

103 C-364/13 *International Stem Cell Corporation v Comptroller General of Patents, Designs and Trade Marks*, Judgment of the Court, Grand Chamber, 18 December 2014.

104 *Edinburgh Patent Application* No. 949131742 (EPO Opposition Division).

105 University of Missouri U.S. Patent No. 6,211,429.

106 Tufts University, U.S. Patent No. 6,781,030.

107 Leahy-Smith America Invents Act 2011, section 3.

"chimbrids"[108] to denote genetically modified living beings which do not fit neatly into either category, this section could do with further clarification.

The next subsection in the legislation prohibits patents on uses of human embryos for industrial and commercial purposes. The principal source of human embryos are surplus embryos which have been created for IVF treatment. At present, their fate varies depending on the jurisdiction. In the UK, for example, it was reported in 2012 that nearly two million embryos had been destroyed since IVF began,[109] whereas in Ireland their destruction is not permitted so they languish indefinitely in an icy limbo. In the exploration of the case law hereunder, the matter of morality and how it impacts on patenting inventions using these embryos will be scrutinised.

In a further restriction on patentability relating to animals, patents will not be granted on methods which modify the genetic identity of animals where this would probably cause them to suffer unless there are significant benefits for people or animals. Any animals resulting from these methods similarly cannot be patented.

Subsection (d) is a statutory enshrinement and modification of the *Harvard/ Oncomouse*[110] balancing test, elaborated below in the case law section. The balance between the interests of animals and human beings has been enshrined in the Directive and altered to reflect that substantial benefit is now required to outweigh potential suffering to the animal. Previously, the interests of animals were not taken so seriously and, for instance, the Technical Board of Appeal in *Harvard/ Oncomouse*[111] opined that the suffering of animals and environmental risk would have to be weighed up against the usefulness of the invention to mankind. Thomas and Richards are critical of the Opposition Division's assessment of morality and ordre public[112] when it said that in order to assess what would be acceptable, legislation is the best guide.[113] The rationale was that if animals were used in medical experiments then that would indicate that few people would object to their patentability. However, they dispute this claim, saying that public views are much more nuanced and that while the public may approve of experimentation for specific purposes, the modification of animals to cause cancer and death would probably not be viewed in the same way.[114] In any case, they also point out that there was very little public knowledge about the Oncomouse when the patent application was made and, therefore, it had neither chance nor motive to form an opinion about the ethics of the invention or any related patent.[115]

108 Jochen Taupitz and Marion Weschka, *CHIMBRIDS – Chimeras and Hybrids in Comparative European and International Research: Scientific, Ethical, Philosophical and Legal Aspects* (Springer Science & Business Media 2009).

109 Andrew Hough, '1.7 Million Human Embryos Created for IVF Thrown Away' *The Telegraph* (31 December 2012).

110 T 0315/03 *Transgenic Animals/HARVARD*, decision of 6 July 2004.

111 *Harvard/Onco-Mouse* [1990] EPOR 501, at point 5.

112 David Thomas and Georgina A Richards, 'The Importance of the Morality Exception under the European Patent Convention: The Oncomouse Case Continues' (2004) 26 EIPR 97, 102.

113 *Harvard/Onco-Mouse* [1990] EPOR 501, para 9.3.

114 Thomas and Richards, *op cit* 102.

115 Ibid 120.

Therefore, the principle upon which the Opposition Division relied is unclear. Animals' interests will now be given more consideration but how the necessary calculations will be made is not predictable. If there is a shift in the way in which we treat some animals from welfare to rights, this may have a significant effect on interpretations of morality in this domain and, consequently, on whether particular inventions are patentable. This may be relevant to some classes of animals, given that there is currently a legal initiative to have all apes in captivity in New York State recognised as persons, through the use of habeas corpus.[116] The Director of the Non-Human Rights Project, Steven Wise who is an attorney has said that although he has not been successful to date, he will not give up until he is. Should some animals be recognised as persons, morality may take on a bigger role although such rights are unlikely to extend to the animals most used in experiments which are mice.

Article 6 of the Directive is bolstered by Recital 38, which adds that processes whose use offends against human dignity, examples being processes to produce chimeras from germ cells or totipotent cells of humans and animals, are also excluded from patentability. The discourse on human dignity is increasingly permeating patent cases given invocations of the EU Charter of Fundamental Rights which, unusually, positions dignity (Article 1) before life (Article 2) in the denominated rights. The CJEU has clarified that Article 6(2) leaves no discretion regarding the unpatentability of processes and uses which it sets out.[117] Of note is that plants are omitted from this list, although patents on genetically modified plants have, on occasion, been interpreted restrictively by the CJEU.[118] Moreover, groups such as Greenpeace regularly challenge the grant of such patents because of concerns such as commodification, risk to the environment and human health.[119]

The Biotechnology Directive was devised at a time of significant change in European patent granting practice in that the European Commission wanted to ensure competitiveness with other markets and biotechnological research was increasing. Moreover, biotechnology is a very fast-moving field and shortly after the passage of the Directive, the isolation of human embryonic stem cells, which could greatly advance medical therapies, became possible.[120] No mention was made at the time of human embryonic stem cell technologies in the Directive which left this to the courts to resolve. The reticence to enshrine a lot of detail in legislative instruments is at least in part due to the difficulties involved in revising regional legislation. Porter points out that much debate has ensued about Article 6(2)(c) and

116 Nonhuman Rights Project, http://www.nonhumanrightsproject.org/ (accessed 5 March 2019).

117 C456–03 *Commission v Italy* [2005] ECR I-5335.

118 *Monsanto Technology LLC v Cefetra BV and Others* [2010] ECR I-6765.

119 *Plant Genetic Systems v Greenpeace* [1995] EPOR 357.

120 JA Thomson, J Itskovitz-Eldor, SS Shapiro, MA Waknitz, JJ Swiergiel, VS Marshall, and JM Jones, 'Embryonic Stem Cell Lines Derived from Human Blastocysts' *Science*, Vol. 282, Issue 5391, 1145–1147, http://science.sciencemag.org/content/282/5391/1145.full (accessed 5 March 2019).

how inventions involving these cells should be treated under the legislation. This has taken place in legal, ethical and policy fields.[121] Yet the means of guarding morality in the legislation is not clear.

In the wake of the introduction of the Biotech Directive in the EU in 1998, the EPC was amended to align many of its provisions closely with the Directive.

1.2.8 Amendment to EPC 2000

The EU Directive has now been integrated into EPC 2000, and this was done by means of a Decision of the Administrative Council of the EPO in 1999. Article 53 of the EPC 2000 has been aligned with 27(2) of the TRIPS Agreement, as it was not previously fully compliant. Nor should it have been, necessarily, given that the EPO, along with Serbia which is a member of the EPO but not of the WTO, are not signatories to TRIPS.[122]

Articles 5 and 6 of the Directive have been incorporated into the EPC 2000 as Rules 28 and 29. The Rules provide that under Article 53(a) EPC, Rule 28, patents will not be granted on methods for the cloning of human beings. Patents will also be denied for processes which facilitate the modification of human beings' germ line genetic identity. Neither will patents be granted for any uses of human embryos for industrial or commercial purposes. Animals will not be subjected to patented methods which modify their genetic identity if this would cause them to suffer without a significant medical benefit accruing to people or animals. No animals resulting from these methods can be patented.

Rule 29 denies patents on the human body at any of its formation or developmental stages. This extends to discoveries of any of its elements and this includes sequences or partial sequences of genes. Elements extracted from the human body or elements which have been generated by a technical method and this may include gene sequences and partial sequences may be patentable even where structurally they are identical to natural elements. Disclosure of the industrial application of gene sequences of partial sequences must be made in the patent application.

These provisions align the EPC more closely with the text of the Directive and while the European Patent Organisation and the EU operate within separate legal orders, such voluntary legal approximation shows a desire for the two regimes to coincide in their decisions.

There has been a shift in the scope of the ordre public or morality exclusions to patenting from publication or exploitation of an invention to a focus on commercial exploitation, meaning that these exceptions have been narrowed. The patent or intellectual property office may approve an invention but its commercial exploitation may offend. Yves Bôt, the Advocate General in *Brüstle*[123] defined

121 Gerard Porter, in Plomer and Torremans 5.

122 EPO membership can be viewed at this link: http://www.epo.org/about-us/organisation/member-states.html, and Serbia has observer status at the time of writing at the WTO: https://www.wto.org/english/thewto_e/whatis_e/tif_e/org6_e.htm#observer (both accessed 5 March 2019).

123 C-34/10 *Oliver Brüstle v Greenpeace eV* [2011] ECR 1-9821.

industrial or commercial purposes as being a matter of large-scale production that was out of proportion to the applied treatment.[124] However, precise definition may not be so clear and a fine line may have to be drawn to differentiate between exploitation and commercial exploitation in future case law. It is likely to be drawn where the invention presents no advantage to the embryo itself.

The purported purpose of the "ordre public" exception has been up to recently to deny protection for inventions which are likely to provoke riot or public disorder or which would lead to criminal or other offensive behaviour.[125] This exception was much more circumscribed than morality until a decision in 2013 in which human rights considerations were invoked to invalidate parts of a patent grant under the heading of ordre public rather than morality.[126] This will be explored further in the case law, below.

This legislative alignment, as heretofore mentioned, is controversial. Moreover, courts from varying European jurisdictions are not bound by each other's judgments so such homogenisation of European patent law does not have any ramifications in terms of precedent. With the introduction of the new European patent system, discussed hereunder, there will be a further jurisdiction to consider and although the governing legislation is the EPC, the court system will be novel and specialised.

1.2.9 Patent Law Treaty 2000

This treaty is administered by WIPO and its aim is to simplify and streamline formal procedures for patent applications, both at national and regional level. Although dated from 2000, this treaty entered into force in 2005 and it harmonises patent procedures and formalities for filing, obtaining and maintaining patent protection. It does not concern substantive patent law and therefore does not deal with moral issues. The then-Director General of WIPO, Dr. Kamil Idris, indicated when the treaty was completed, that he now wished to commence the harmonisation of substantive law and work towards a unitary global patent protection[127] showing the ambition of a globalised patent protection.

In addition to international patent harmonisation, protection within regional organisations such as the EU and the EPO is also progressing.

1.2.10 An EU-wide patent

1.2.10.1 Precursors

Despite the fact that the EPC covers 38 European states in which all EU Member States are included, and the Biotech Directive also applies to all EU members, so

124 Ibid, Opinion of Advocate General 113, ECLI:EU:C:2011:138.
125 EPO Guidelines for Examination, Part C, Chapter IV, Para 4.1.
126 T 0149/11 of 24 January 2013, *Method and Device for Processing a Slaughtered Animal or Part Thereof in a Slaughterhouse.*
127 Reported in Out-Law, http://www.out-law.com/page-694 (accessed 5 March 2019).

there is no shortage of legislation, the goal of introducing an EU-wide patent has been ongoing for decades. Many efforts have been made so as to simplify the process in Europe. An early precursor of current reform was the Draft Convention for a European Patent Law in 1962. According to Ilardi,[128] one of the concerns expressed about this legislation was whether non-Member States could avail of it, showing that there was a goal to create an international, or at least a regional patent system. This initiative culminated in work carried out on the EPC in 1973 and the Community Patent Convention 1975. The latter document was ultimately not adopted although it was signed by all EU Member States and sought to create a community patent system. It involved a single application to the EPO and aimed to harmonise the granting of patents throughout the EU. The centralised litigation procedure, which involved the setting up of a European Court to deal with patent appeals, would have created a single community patent and not a patent which is subject to national laws. However, it was unpopular due to its high cost. The aim of introducing EU-wide legislation survived this Convention's demise, as will be shown.

1.2.10.2 Unitary Patent Protection

Efforts to introduce legislation did not abate and a unitary patent protection has now been approved. This legislation[129] promises to enhance patent protection among participating Member States by creating a unitary patent which binds everyone with the intention of fostering innovation and enhancing the internal market. A European patent with unitary effect will also prove much more cost effective than the current system, according to Recital (5) of the Regulation. This is disputed in the literature, however by Sir Richard Kitchin who has said that the appeals process could result in litigants having to appear in more than one jurisdiction. He believes that costs will be inflated by the new system.[130] McMahon also argues that the unitary patent package is likely to augment rather than reduce the complexity in the patenting process, given that there are now four overlapping European regimes under which patents may be sought.[131] Procedural aspects are dealt with in further legislation which regulates principally translation and compensation along with the identification of who is responsible for litigation costs.[132]

128 Alfredo Ilardi, *The New European Patent* (Hart Publishing 2015) 4.

129 Regulation (EU) No 1257/2012 of the European Parliament and of the Council of 17 December 2012 implementing enhanced cooperation in the area of the creation of unitary patent protection, http://eur-lex.europa.eu/legal-content/EN/TXT/?uri=CELEX:32012R1257 (accessed 5 March 2019).

130 Quoted in Justine Pila and Christopher Wadlow, *The Unitary EU Patent System* (Hart Publishing 2015) 4–6.

131 Aisling McMahon, 'An Institutional Examination of the Implications of the Unitary Patent Package for the Morality Provisions: A Fragmented Future Too Far?' IIC 2017 48(1) 42.

132 Regulation (EU) No 1260/2012 of the European Parliament and of the Council of 17 December 2012 implementing enhanced cooperation in the area of the creation of unitary patent protection, http://eur-lex.europa.eu/legal-content/EN/TXT/?uri=CELEX:32012R1257 (accessed 5 March 2019).

The establishment of a unified court points to the perceived desirability of legal certainly and harmonisation. The unitary patent is classified as property. The reform includes legislation which sets out the procedural aspects of the establishment of the courts' structure and affirms that the CJEU retains jurisdiction to ensure harmonisation and compliance with European Union law, under this agreement.[133] The courts will have a plethora of legal instruments to consider from the abovenamed regulations to national patent law, the EPC – a surprising inclusion given that this is not part of EU law – and, of course, EU law itself. The court retains the power under Article 45 to close the proceedings to the public, should it so choose. This marks a departure from the principle of justice being done in public and being seen to be done. It also deals with remedies and appeals.

The new European-wide patent will not change anything regarding the definition of morality in the legislation as the EPC is employed. However, specialised courts may have some effect on interpretation. Mills argues that such courts tend to favour patent holders and to be quite pro-patent[134] and it is notable that the courts are set up, under Article 15, to provide for judges with legal qualifications but also technical ones.[135] The technical judges are not required to have a grounding in morality so how Article 53(a) will be competently applied is unclear. As the courts are still in the process of being established, no evidence-based assessment can currently be made about outcomes and any predictions are therefore speculative.

The above chronology of doctrinal elements of patent law highlights a number of factors. The first is that patent law has expanded its breadth significantly in the last century as can be seen from the introduction of several international and regional agreements. Secondly, the subject matter covered by patent law has increased and now includes living organisms of plant, animal and human origin. Finally, the nebulous concept of morality (and ordre public) has been incorporated into several legal instruments such as the EPC, the Biotech Directive and the TRIPS Agreement. Its definition, as indicated, has not been without difficulty during the legislative process. The interpretations of the provisions on morality in the boards of the EPO and the courts of the EU are now explored in order to examine whether or not judicial exposure and examination has brought clarity to this domain.

133 Agreement on a Unified Patent Court and Statute of the Unified Patent Court 2013/C 175/01, http://www.upc.documents.eu.com/PDFs/2013-02-19_Agreement_Unified_Patent_Court_JOUE_ 2013-06-20.pdf (accessed 5 March 2019).

134 Mills, *op cit* 45.

135 Agreement on a Unified Patent Court and Statute of the Unified Patent Court 2013/C 175/01, http://www.upc.documents.eu.com/PDFs/2013-02-19_Agreement_Unified_Patent_Court_JOUE _2013-06-20.pdf (accessed 5 March 2019).

1.3 European case law on morality and ordre public

1.3.1 At the EPO

This section of the chapter will explore case law on the interpretations of morality and ordre public and will highlight the fact there is an awareness at the EPO that there is not a uniform standard of morality. On occasion, nonetheless there are assumptions that the majority of Europeans will feel the same way about particular inventions where the Boards refer to concepts such as "universal abhorrence", as explored in this section. This book will show that ordre public and morality are not easily defined and are not uniformly understood in different states. At times the EPO conflates the two standards and at others, they are treated separately. As courts struggle to decide the issues, morality and its judgment has come under several headings. Therefore, looking for solutions to identified problems within the legislation may be somewhat redundant and judicial interpretation may prove equally unsatisfactory. This section will analyse the case law critically in this light.

1.3.2 The drafting intentions of the EPC

As already noted, in the Travaux Préparatoires of the EPC,[136] the definition of "ordre public" was found to differ, depending on the jurisdiction. It was defined widely in the Netherlands but in other states, while the concept existed it was not deemed to be important. The Working Group considered excluding it or else defining it but the latter option could have violated national laws. Ultimately the bare term was included without further embellishment.[137] Similarly, morality was not delimited as no universal concept existed within the EPO's reach and this was to be left for European institutions to work out.[138] These institutions were not named, nor was the issue of their jurisdiction considered.

The following selection of cases will show that there have been a number of different interpretations of morality and ordre public in Article 53(a) EPC where references have been made to various standards or tests by which these criteria can be applied. They do not add up to a coherent formula because of the lack of principles on which such decisions are based. There is also an appreciation of a public voice when the Boards refer to concepts such as universal abhorrence[139] and universal outrage[140] but no path has been charted for how these views can be ascertained or accommodated and this is the focus of this book.

136 In section 2.2.5.1.

137 'Travaux Préparatoires (EPC 1973)' 16, IV/2767/61-E http://webserv.epo.org/projects/babylon/tpepc73.nsf/0/A79664CCCE197AC1C12574270049F447/$File/Art53eTPEPC1973.pdf (accessed 5 March 2019).

138 Ibid.

139 *Lubrizol/Hybrid Plants* [1990] EPOR 173.

140 *Howard Florey Institute-Relaxin* [1995] 6 OJ EPO 388 (EPO Opposition Division).

1.3.2.1 Morality: universal abhorrence (plants)

In an early case decided under the EPC, *Lubrizol/Hybrid Plants*,[141] an application was made to the EPO for a patent on processes to develop hybrid seeds speedily. The claim was refused by the EPO on the grounds that the processes were essentially biological and these were unpatentable within Article 53(b) EPC. The rationale for this exclusion from patentability is that the processes involve traditional techniques such as cross-breeding and therefore are not novel. Had microbiological processes been used, there would have been potential for patentability. An appeal with amended claims was made and was successful as the Board of Appeal deemed that the processes invoked in the patent claim were not essentially biological but instead involved specialised techniques. Neither were the plants considered to be varieties due to the fact that they were not stable and were therefore novel.

An opposition was mounted to the patent and the Opposition Division held in this case that the Article 53(a) exclusions of morality and ordre public only applied to cases where the invention was universally regarded as abhorrent. This was the first case in which Article 53(a) was applied to plants. How universal abhorrence would be assessed is not clear from the case. Sparse guiding principles give courts much leeway but such cases do not appear to serve in helping to establish any precedent in the area either. This case evoked relatively very little controversy and decisions involving animals and human genetic material rather than plants stirred more public debate until the wide-scale cultivation of genetically modified plants became possible in the mid-1990s.[142]

1.3.2.2 Morality: balancing test (animals)

In *HARVARD/Oncomouse*[143] a patent was granted by the EPO on transgenic animals which had been bred for use in researching cancer. The mice in question were genetically engineered to contain a gene which would greatly increase their susceptibility to cancer. The lineage of this case is that the United States Patent Trademark Office (USPTO) granted a patent on this same subject matter to the president and Fellows of Harvard College in 1989. Both a product and a process claim were made to the EPO and it is the former application which caused the controversy. It was initially rejected by the EPO on a number of grounds and with reference to Article 53(a), the Examining Division deemed that the EPC was not an appropriate forum for regulating potential problems associated with genetic modification. However, the Technical Board disagreed and engaged in a weighing-up exercise which sought to balance risk and suffering of the animals on the one hand with the benefits to humans on the other, thus elucidating Article 53(a)

141 *Lubrizol/Hybrid Plants* [1990] EPOR 173.

142 Maureen O'Sullivan, 'Governing Against the Grain?: Overseas Perspectives on the UK Government's Impending Decision on the Commercialisation of GM Crops' (2004) 16 ELM 16.

143 *Harvard/Onco-Mouse* [1989] OJ EPO 451.

by means of a balancing test.[144] The case was remitted to the Examining Division which decided in the applicant's favour.

Matters did not rest there, however. Objections raised included that patenting life was immoral when the life had been created solely in order to suffer. Thomas, who represented the British Union Against Vivisection in the case and Richards point out that the case focused on morality rather than ordre public and observe that arguments under this umbrella included animal welfare and religious objections about patenting life-forms. The objections on animal welfare grounds include a belief that it is wrong to genetically engineer animals and furthermore, the financial incentive through the patent monopoly is a double wrong, in their view.[145] This case occurred before the enactment of Article 6(2)(d) of the Directive and its subsequent incorporation into the amended EPC, Rule 28(d) in which the balance between the interests of humans and animals is now weighted less towards humans than before. The Examining Division held any potential suffering was outweighed by benefits to human beings and there was, therefore, no impediment to patentability. The application did not fall within the bar to patenting animal varieties as the claim was made in relation to non-human mammals, which was much broader. This decision does not seem to be very logical in that the ban on patenting varieties can be avoided by developing processes that apply to a much wider scope of organisms.

With regard to the Examining Division's treatment of animals, its decision reflects the law's general approach – that they are regarded as property and patent law does not consider whether they have rights. Protection of their interests is based on concepts of welfare and this may be problematic if an application were to be made for a patent on a so-called "higher" mammal, such as an ape or cetacean whose intelligence is now receiving closer attention than before in light of animal rights activism. The Examination Division noted that patenting higher organisms had encountered ethical objections in the US[146] but no further heed was paid to this.

One of the problems with this test, according to Bagley, is that the Examining Division did not define morality, nor did it articulate why it chose the factors that it did, rather than any others. Morality is contentious. Of course, the Examining Division was following instructions from the Technical Board[147] but the case has not served to clarify what constitutes morality. Opposition proceedings were commenced invoking Article 53(a). The Opposition Division indicated that legislation was the best guide to applying morality, saying that if one wanted to ascertain what was considered right or wrong in European society, the legislation rather than public opinion polls should be consulted.[148] As already mentioned, public

144 T19/90–3.3.2, https://www.epo.org/law-practice/case-law-appeals/pdf/t900019ep1.pdf (accessed 5 March 2019).

145 Thomas and Richards, *op cit* 99.

146 T 0315/03 *Transgenic Animals/Harvard* of 6 July 2004, http://www.epo.org/law-practice/case-law-appeals/recent/t030315ep1.html (accessed 5 March 2019).

147 Margo A Bagley, 'Patent First, Ask Questions Later: Morality and Biotechnology in Patent Law' (2003) 45 WM & Mary L Rev 469, 521.

148 *Harvard/Onco-Mouse* [1991] EPOR 525 [9.3].

opinion on the uses of animals in different situations can be quite specific: while it may approve testing on animals where there is a recognised human benefit, it does not mean that all suffering would be tolerated.

The case was eventually resolved in 2001 when the claim was amended and restricted to transgenic rodents which contained an additional cancer gene rather than non-human transgenic mammals on grounds of Article 53(a). The opponents filed an appeal and the claim was restricted even further by the Technical Board of Appeal in 2004 to cover only transgenic mice[149] given that not all rodents were considered to satisfy the morality test in Article 53(a) and Rule 23d(d) EPC, whereas mice are standard laboratory test animals.[150] Such differences between boards on what is deemed to be acceptable shows that outcomes are unpredictable and making applications which are subsequently restricted suggests that there needs to be vigilance about overly broad initial claims. A troubling feature of this case and others like it is that the granted patent was in force for the intervening time before it was greatly curtailed and perhaps it would be wiser to extend the law incrementally rather than restrict it as a result of opposition proceedings. Moreover, public voices are all but absent in such prolonged processes.

1.3.2.3 Morality: morality sidelined?

Other patents have since been granted on animals with the EPO ruling in *Leland Stanford/*Modified Animal that patents were not excluded on grounds of moral controversies surrounding the nature of the technology. In the view of the EPO, genetic engineering does not, as a technology, raise any moral issues. The Opposition Division declined to act as a moral censor[151] although Article 53(a) obliges it to give morality and ordre public its due weight. Given the fact that genetic engineering is a new technology, perhaps it should have exercised more restraint in weighing up the issues, although it was also bound by the law. Of note is the fact that the law in this realm is now experiencing a process of constitutionalisation whereby it is being infused with ethical norms derived from the EU Charter of Fundamental Rights and also the European Convention on Human Rights, which will be explored later in this chapter.

In *Upjohn's Application*[152] the invention was for a mouse which had been genetically modified to provide a model for research into stimulating hair growth. The mouse would suffer baldness as a result of the transgene. The examiners' main objection related to the lack of inventive step as regards the invention as a whole but they also found a breach of Article 53(a) on moral grounds. One of the modified genes which had been engineered into the mouse was an oncogene which could be deleted without affecting the breadth of the main claim. Upjohn duly redrafted the application to exclude the oncogene and the patent was

149 T 0315/03 *Transgenic Animals/HARVARD* of 6 July 2004.
150 Ibid.
151 *Leland/Stanford Modified Animal* [2002] EPOR 2.
152 Re Upjohn's Application, No. 89913146.0.

granted.[153] This shows a change in policy and treatment of animals in that in this case, unlike in *Harvard/Oncomouse*, the oncogene was taken out of the claim in order for it to be allowed.

How the balancing test was applied is not clear except that greater cognisance of potential animal suffering is becoming common and the interests of animals is likely to receive more serious consideration than before. However, there still are no further morality guidelines on these issues and decisions are, therefore, unpredictable. We lack a framework of principles on how we ought to treat mice or animals with greater cognitive skills, such as apes. Without guidance, the legislation does not really clarify controversial issues. Tests will depend randomly on the knowledge of board members or in opposition proceedings, on the interest groups that are able and willing to take part. The application of morality and ordre public provisions in Article 53(a) is hardly satisfactory and, of course, it does not address at all the plurality of views on morality that exist, or would exist if there were more public knowledge. The next case alludes to public voices in this domain but struggles to find an appropriate means of accommodation.

1.3.2.4 Morality: risk of harm – polls and survey evidence

In *Plant Genetic Systems*,[154] the EPO found itself grappling with applying concepts of morality in a case involving genetically modified crops which had been engineered to be resistant to a glutamine synthetase inhibitor. Greenpeace had opposed the patent, claiming that the use of herbicides would be increased by the company seeking the patent and that there were also unknown risk factors associated therewith.[155] The EPO held that challenges to patentability based on morality would only be entertained if there was demonstrable actual evidence of harm to society. Greenpeace's challenge was unsuccessful in the Opposition Division and they then appealed to the Technical Board of Appeal. The Board stated that, in order to engage Article 53(a) EPC, it would require verifiable data that these crops posed a risk to the environment before it would consider applying the Oncomouse balancing test. It is not clear in any case how a test balancing the rights of humans and animals would be applied to a different set of species. Moreover, data on risk is very difficult to acquire especially when the technology is novel and has not been tested over an extended time. Such stringent conditions could not be satisfied, they set a very high bar and so the patent was duly granted.

The Board in *Plant Genetic Systems*[156] stated that morality signifies an opinion that there is right and wrong behaviour and these can be distinguished by deeply rooted European cultural norms, for the purposes of the EPC. Under Article 53(a), where the exploitation (before the amendment of 2000) of inventions does not

153 Mills, *op cit* 61.
154 *Plant Genetic Systems v Greenpeace* [1995] EPOR 357.
155 http://www.independent.co.uk/news/UK/greenpeace-warns-of-threat-from-crop-patent-deal-1565928.html (accessed 5 March 2019).
156 *Plant Genetic Systems v Greenpeace* [1995] EPOR 357.

conform to these norms, the patent grant cannot be made on moral grounds.[157] At very least, the refusal of the grant of a patent would be difficult to justify with any certainty, given this hazy guidance. The Board went on to postulate that a singular version of culture could be identified within European society and civilisation and that this metaphorical sieve would enable the separation of the patentable wheat, as it were, from the morally unacceptable chaff under Article 53(a) EPC.[158] This conceptualisation of particular culture is problematic: it is unlikely that even within any society there is to be found a unitary belief system or a single moral standard. It would have been useful had the Board articulated clearly what that version was so it could guide future cases but it did not do so because perhaps it cannot do so. In any case, national courts are not bound by decisions of the EPO or its boards so consistency cannot be established through precedent. Viens says that this clashes with the reality of the pluralism which pervades both the European Union and its Member States.[159] This applies on an even wider scale to the 38 states of the EPO's jurisdiction. McMahon indicates that states are normally deferred to on morality issues within both the EU and the ECHR systems[160] and that this should also infuse proceedings of the EPC.[161] Moreover, how can established moral norms inform how people will view new technologies, such as biotechnological inventions? Public opinions might be completely unpredictable so, arguably, assumptions should not be made.

The Board disregarded the fact that an elevated level of moral distaste for such inventions was present in Europe. It opined that survey evidence and opinion polls indicating disapproval of patents on genetically modified organisms would not be relied upon in order to assess overarching European morality.[162] Such polls and surveys can be unreliable and often people gain their information through media which may not represent the full facts. There may be more reliable methods for ascertaining public views but these were not explored.

1.3.2.5 Morality: universal outrage

The concept of universal outrage was relied on by the EPO in the next case, *Relaxin/HOWARD FLOREY INSTITUTE*[163] to circumscribe the parameters of the morality bar. Here, the patent application related to a protein produced by women in childbirth which helps to relax the uterus. The patent was granted by the EPO and was subsequently opposed by individuals associated with the Green wing of the European Parliament. They challenged the patent on a number of grounds including novelty, inventive step, morality and ordre public. They

157 Ibid 366.
158 Ibid, Reasons for the Decision, 368.
159 AM Viens, 'Morality Provisions in Law Concerning the Commercialization of Human Embryos and Stem Cells' in Plomer and Torremans, *op cit* 88.
160 McMahon, *op cit* 64.
161 Ibid 63.
162 *Plant Genetic Systems v Greenpeace* [1995] EPOR 357.
163 *Relaxin/HOWARD FLOREY INSTITUTE* [2000] EPOR 235.

asserted that the subject of the application was a discovery and not an invention and therefore did not qualify for patent protection. Given that the subject matter of the patent was a human gene, the opposition included claims that the grant was tantamount to slavery and that human dignity was offended.

The challenges were unsuccessful as was the opponents' subsequent appeal. The EPO found that while the gene itself was a discovery, the process of isolation and characterisation was patentable. They did not regard the gene itself as representing life but rather described it as a chemical entity taking part in biological processes.[164] What this does show is that there is a significant dichotomy on how genetic material is viewed: for some it is synonymous with life itself and for others it is a chemical entity which, if novel, may be patentable. Each viewpoint represents a standpoint on a wide moral spectrum. The EPO stipulated that Article 53(a) EPC should only prevent the grant of patents which would universally be considered to be outrageous without indicating how this could be assessed. The dismissal of public concerns and the setting of opaque standards to define morality delineated by the use of words such as universal brings the adjudication of morality into disrepute because the manner in which a successful claim can be constructed is unclear. As a process for opposition is established in the legislation, its use should be transparent.

1.3.2.6 Morality – a case of doctrinal confusion?

The *Relaxin* overwhelming consensus test is judged by Mills to be more practical than the balance of interests test by the Examining Division in *Onco-Mouse*[165] although it is unclear how such consensus could be established. A balancing test is certainly more difficult to apply especially when considerations such as human health, animal cruelty and disease prevention are all in play. However, it is also difficult to keep abreast of changes in public opinion and, for example, patents on animals created solely for testing cosmetics would be unlikely to be granted given the ban on such use within the EU since 2013.[166] At present we lack mechanisms to weigh up such balances. In any case, how can we make judgments about what the majority of people think when there is acceptance that Europe does not have a uniform standard of morality? Moreover, the majority of the publics are unlikely to have known much about the *Relaxin* case or other patent cases which engage the morality bar.

Legislative harmonisation regarding patentability criteria and the place reserved for morality within the patent system has been advocated.[167] A difficulty with legislating for morality is that the public views of what it means are likely to

164 Ibid Part IV http://www.epo.org/law-practice/case-law-appeals/recent/t950272eu2.html (accessed 5 March 2019).

165 Mills, *op cit* 62.

166 Directive 2003/15/EC of the European Parliament and of the Council of 27 February 2003 amending Council Directive 76/768/EEC on the approximation of the laws of the Member States relating to cosmetic products.

167 Mills, *op cit* 80.

change. Moreover, society is unlikely to have a unitary view. Legislation freezes a time-specific definition which, as society evolves, may quickly become redundant but fossilised nonetheless. An examination of court judgments shows that this area is very unpredictable. Arguably, it is a realm outside of law and so legal certainty cannot apply. Moreover, if we leave decision-making to the judiciary, many judges study law at schools which do not even teach jurisprudence, so they may be unfamiliar with varying theories of law or the place or even existence of higher order norms.[168] A positivist will have difficulty arbitrating morality which is not articulated clearly and may rely on instinct or just side-line the matter altogether, especially where its definition proves elusive.

While the cases just examined have focused on different legal provisions, the subsequent case law will show that predictability on the scope of the morality bar has not improved over time.

1.3.2.7 Morality parameters: narrowing or broadening?

The *Edinburgh* patent,[169] granted after the introduction of the Biotech Directive, concerned the isolation, selection and propagation of animal transgenic stem cells. The main issue focused on whether the patent extended to human embryos. The Opposition Division held that the exclusion from patentability on morality grounds has to be interpreted broadly so as to include not only the commercial or industrial use of human embryos but also the human embryonic stem cells obtained by destroying human embryos. They also stated that reliance must be made on principles of human dignity, personal integrity and autonomy. The patent was amended so as to exclude human embryonic stem cells. The Opposition Division eventually held that while the original application violated Article 53 (a) EPC, the amended claims did not. Even though the patent was initially wrongly granted, it must be opposed in order to potentially be revoked. If there were widespread public input on such applications, it is less likely that overly broad patents would be granted as many more perspectives could be accommodated. This might help all participants to appreciate that there is a multiplicity of considerations in these patent applications.

168 There exists in most legal systems a hierarchy of norms in which some laws supersede others in terms of their legality or force. A classic example would be where a Constitution, such as the Irish Constitution, claims to be the supreme law of the state, making all other laws, such as legislation, subordinate to its provisions. As the Constitution in question also comes from the people, any cession of sovereignty such as accession to an international treaty, must be agreed by way of referendum, as the law is deemed ultimately to emanate from the people. The EU's portal on national legal orders is informative in this respect. In the case of other supra legal systems, each will have their own hierarchy, not all of which align and some of which are in a state of evolution. The European Union, and the CJEU in particular, has since the introduction of the Lisbon Treaty commenced a process of considering laws in conjunction with provisions of the EU Charter of Fundamental Rights relating to human dignity, as shall be seen in the discussion of the *Brüstle* case, in particular, on pp. 46–49.

169 *Edinburgh Patent Application* No 949131742.

1.3.2.8 Morality and human embryos: a more restrictive approach?

The boundaries of morality, which had been stretched to accommodate living matter, including plants and animals, as noted above, were further tested in the context of human embryos in G2/06 *Stem Cells/WARF.*[170] In this case, the Examining Division heard a claim for a patent sought by the Wisconsin Alumni Research Foundation. The Foundation developed the first techniques to isolate human embryonic stem cells in 1998 and the application concerned primate embryonic stem cells.[171] All the claims which could encompass human embryonic stem cells were invalidated on grounds of immorality as human embryos were described in the application as indispensable starting materials and their use would be for industrial purposes. The only source of the cells were pre-implantation embryos.[172] *WARF* asserted that it was necessary to "use" embryos to create the claimed invention which would have resulted in their destruction. The Examining Division equated the use of an embryo as starting material for the generation of a product of industrial application with the industrial use of this embryo. The refusal to grant the patent on grounds of immorality was an expansive interpretation of Rule 28(c) (formerly Rule 23(d)(c)) EPC which provided that European patents should not be granted on inventions concerning uses of human embryos for industrial or commercial reasons. This broke with the convention of reading Article 53(a) restrictively as set down in the Guidelines for Examination to the EPO[173] which states that this provision should only be invoked rarely. The patenting of human embryonic stem cells has evoked a previously unseen level of controversy.

Several questions were referred to the EBA in 2005, seeking clarity on whether Rule 28(c) EPC applied retrospectively to an application which had been filed before the rule was enacted and if so, whether the patenting of such claims was forbidden under Article 53(a) EPC. It was also sought to ascertain whether it was relevant if other methods which did not involve the destruction of human embryos had become possible after the filing date. The President of the EPO proffered an opinion on the questions and contrary to the practice to date in which Article 53(a) had been interpreted narrowly he believed that this would undermine the spirit of the morality exclusions enshrined in this Article.

The EBA found that patents are not available for products which could only be prepared by a method involving the destruction of a human embryo which was the source of the products. A later technical development would not affect this decision.[174] The EBA made it clear that patenting itself was not regarded as being

170 G2/06 *WARF/Stem Cells* [2009] EPOR 15.

171 University of Wisconsin Stem Cell & Regenerative Medicine Center, the Thomson laboratory, faculty website, available at https://stemcells.wisc.edu/node/217 (accessed 5 March 2019).

172 T1374/04 *WARF/Stem Cells* [2006] EPOR 31.

173 Guidelines for Examination in the EPO, http://www.epo.org/law-practice/legal-texts/ guidelines.html (accessed 5 March 2019).

174 G2/06 *WARF/Stem Cells* [2009] EPOR 15.

contrary to ordre public and morality, rather it was the performing of the invention that offended.[175]

This interpretation of the morality bar is quite complex. The EBA's commentary suggests that the grant of the patent is inconsequential yet a patent gives rights to exclude others which brings it into moral terrain. Moreover, it is unlikely that it would be universally agreed that patenting human embryos is morally acceptable so long as the performance of the invention is not allowed. Patents are defined as property rights. The principles to which the EBA is referring are not clear and in such an ethically fraught area, it is problematic that decisions of magnitude are made that appear to be *ad hoc*. Golden observes that in the US, the issue of the provision of public funding for human stem cell research is more controversial than whether to issue or enforce patent rights[176] and that this is due to differences in the legislative provisions in the US, as compared with Europe.[177] While US jurisprudence has developed moral utility[178] bar, this is not enshrined in legislation. Furthermore, this restriction has not been applied in cases of biotechnological inventions.

Plomer describes the task of the examiners when trying to decipher the meanings of ordre public or morality[179] in relation to inventions as a continual puzzle and she questions whether they are supposed to look for the morally reprehensible factor in the nature of the invention, the patenting process itself or the commercialisation of the invention,[180] thus making a threefold puzzle. In *WARF*, she states that the prohibition pertained to the nature of the invention rather than to the patenting aspect. In her view, the performance of the invention rather than the patenting raises the controversy in this case, in the eyes of the court[181] and this would mean the actual destruction of human embryos for industrial or commercial purposes in the creation of the invention rather than possession of exclusive rights to prevent others from doing likewise. This demonstrates that opposition to the invention and to the patenting thereof are often mixed up and this is manifested also in the courts. She alludes to the systemic conflict within laws of the EU which pertain, respectively, to legislation which allows destructive and commercial use of human embryos on the one hand, and those which prohibit patents on associated inventions on grounds of immorality, on the other.

Undoubtedly the examiner's task is daunting. While this study does not advocate ethical training as a panacea for the lack of representation of public voices in the patenting process, neglecting to offer officials instruction on what constitutes morality and ordre public when the bar must be applied does not ease

175 Ibid paragraph 41.
176 John M Golden, *WARF's Stem Cell Patents and Tensions between Public and Private Sector Approaches to Research* (SAGE Publications 2010) 318.
177 Ibid 315.
178 *Lowell v Lewis* 15 F. Cas. 1018 (1817).
179 Aurora Plomer, 'Towards Systemic Legal Conflict: Article 6(2)(c) of the EU Directive on Biotechnological Inventions', in Plomer and Torremans, *op cit* 178.
180 Ibid.
181 Ibid.

interpretation. Some endeavours could be made to draw up guidelines or a non-exhaustive list of principles. Moreover, arguably patents on morally controversial biotechnological inventions raise distinct issues from those which relate to allowing the creation of the invention. While this distinction will be explored further in the next chapter, the matter of who develops the invention – whether this be a publicly funded body or a private corporation incentivised by potentially lucrative patents – may make a difference to public approval.

1.3.2.9 Arbitration of morality: who should be responsible?

It is questionable whether patent offices are the appropriate place in which morality can be defined, although members of the office believe that it is their responsibility to do so. Treichel, from the Directorate of International Legal Affairs of the EPO, has asserted that it is the responsibility of the office to use its judgment on the matter of morality and this can be done by the incorporation into patent law of higher-ranking norms. As one of the paramount concerns of the Biotechnology Directive is the protection of human dignity, G2/06 should be perceived as an essential step in the constitutionalisation of European patent law. This case identified these norms as respect for human dignity and the banning of the commercial exploitation of human embryos.[182]

It would be helpful if it were made clear how patent officials are to determine such norms. Mills argues that governments should delineate the boundaries of morality[183] but societal views change a lot faster than legislative endeavours. As legal definitions will trail scientific advances,[184] perhaps legislation does not offer a solution. Nonetheless, the view has been expressed that it is the legislator's role to determine the moral consensus and this is reflected in Rule 28(c). These provisions have been described as unquestionable and unqualifiable binding bans given that they emanate from the legislator's own moral judgment.[185] Although the incorporation of the Implementing Regulations into the EPC has added some clarity to the question of morality, such provisions are still open to interpretation and must be questioned and, indeed, qualified depending on the case. Perhaps the legislature rather than the individual legislator relying on his moral judgment, should decide this matter: to suggest otherwise, as does Treichel,[186] implies that personal rather than representative, democratic opinion suffices to arbitrate the meaning of morality for everyone.

While there is some discussion in the academic literature that the current set up is not satisfactory, there are few suggestions for other decision-making practices. Should decisions be handed over instead to ethics committees which may be composed of a group of individuals trained to consider an abstract public good?

182 Pierre Treichel, 'G2/06 and the Verdict of Immorality' (2009) 40 IIC 450, 450.
183 Mills, *op cit* 57.
184 Treichel, *op cit* 459.
185 Ibid 466.
186 Ibid.

This question will be explored in more detail in the next chapter but, briefly, some ethics committees may contain within their ranks corporate lobbyists and also house extremist views so they may not represent an ethical or an independent standpoint. It is doubtful in a pluralistic world whether such a standard could be useful, especially given that morality at the frontiers of law and technology is fast-moving. Furthermore, Waelde *et al.* express concern that the role of moral arbiter may be subverted by an unelected administrative group that could judge the ethics of new technologies,[187] identifying this as in contravention of the UK's policy of significant investment in stem cell research. They ask whether it is satisfactory for these policies to potentially be frustrated by the EPO showing that there are tensions between national policy and processes which occur at the upper echelons of patent decision-making at the European level. Beyleveld and Brownsword did suggest the establishment of an ethics committee to hear any opposition on moral grounds with a right of appeal to the ECtHR over 20 years ago but this has not occurred.[188] What is clear is that the application of the morality bar at present by the EPO and its boards is the subject of criticism and it is arguable that the decision-making process needs refinement.

There is no definition of human embryo in the Directive, other European or international legal instruments and where such definitions exist at a national level, they tend to vary. Bearing this in mind, an alternative to legislative reform would be a case-by-case evaluation if such reform had difficulty keeping up with advances in science. Given that there is no consensus on morality across European countries, it does seem odd that an unequipped body is setting moral standards on the patentability of biotechnological inventions for all citizens without guidance, training or significant consultation.

1.3.2.10 Morality beyond WARF *at the EPO*

The *WARF* case was recently applied in *Technion/Culturing Stem Cells*[189] where a patent was refused on an experiment which used publicly available established cell lines that once involved the destruction of a human embryo. The patent was not granted because even though the established cell lines had involved an earlier rather than a recent destruction of an embryo, such time shifting was not permitted to be used to evade the restrictions in *WARF*. *Technion*, therefore broadens the ambit of *WARF* and shows consistency in its treatment of the human embryo across varying time frames. Regardless as to whether the invention involves the present or past destruction of a human embryo, it will not be patentable.

187 Waelde *et al, op cit* 515.

188 Deryck Beyleveld and Robert Brownsword, *Mice, Morality and Patents: The Onco-Mouse Application and Article 53(a) of the European Patent Convention* (Common Law Institute of Intellectual Property 1993) 68–70, 89–90.

189 T 2221/10 *Culturing Stem Cells/TECHNION* of 4 February 2014.

Mahalatchimy *et al* observe that *Technion* has made law emanating from the EPO and the EU in this realm more uniform.[190] Evidence on the methods to obtain human embryonic stem cells that do not involve prior destruction of human embryos must now be part of the patent claims. What is missing in the judgment, however, is a definition of a human embryo which means that law at the EPO currently diverges from the judgments of the CJEU in *Brüstle*[191] in which human embryos were defined and later redefined in *International Stem Cell Corporation*.[192] This redefinition reflected that parthenotes were not, after all, to be classified as human embryos as while they could commence the process of embryonic development, there are not able to complete it. Nordberg and Minssen observe that *WARF* and *Technion* oblige patent applicants to verify that source material involving the destruction of a human embryo has not been used and that therefore the morality bar is not engaged. They say that this conflicts with the traditional narrow construction of exceptions in the EPO's jurisprudence and also in the intention of the drafters of the EPC. They point out that exceptions should be invoked against the applicant rather than being treated as a positive requirement.[193]

Clearly the application of the morality bar is in a state of flux at the EPO and, as shall be noted in section 1.3.2.11, is similarly evolving at the CJEU. The departure from a narrow application appears to have surfaced in the area of the use of human embryos. Moreover, courts have now built up a broader understanding of the multidisciplinary nature of the issues which controversial biotechnological inventions raise and these include not only law, technology and science but also questions of morality on which there has been little guidance. The next section will show how the criteria to satisfy ordre public have quite recently been dramatically broadened in a case which also concerned the use of a human being, albeit not in embryonic form.

1.3.2.11 Ordre public: the EPO's new morality?

Ordre public is terminology which has traditionally been poorly defined and, as previously noted, does not have universal meaning within Europe. It is rather odd to take this untranslated expression from private international law and act as if it can have universal application across 38 states in the area of patenting without clear definition. Some efforts have been made to signal what it might mean,[194]

190 Aurélie Mahalatchimy, E Rial-Sebbag, AM Duguet, A Cambon-Thomsen and F Taboulet, 'Exclusion of Patentability of Embryonic Stem Cells in Europe: Another Restriction by the European Patent Office' (2015) 37 EIPR 25, 27.

191 C-34/10 *Oliver Brüstle v Greenpeace eV* [2011] ECR I-9821.

192 C-364/13 *International Stem Cell Corporation v Comptroller General of Patents, Designs and Trade Marks* (Grand Chamber) 18 December 2014.

193 Ana Nordberg and Timo Minssen 'A "Ray of Hope" for European Stem Cell Patents or "Out of the Smog into the Fog"? An Analysis of recent European case law and how it compares to the US' IIC 2016 47(2) 138–177, 168.

194 Beyleveld and Brownsword, *op cit* 68–70, 89–90.

and even where ordre public is equated to public policy concepts, this ignores the fact that it will inevitably differ from state to state and that it is a creature of civil law jurisdictions somewhat uncomfortably transplanted. Legal transplants can be of problematic application, not least when they are undefined and applied to a new area without adjustment or adaptation. In *Plant Genetic Systems*[195] the Board noted that the drafters of the EPC had acknowledged that there was no European definition of ordre public (and they said the same about morality).[196] The EPC Working Party also recognised this matter and in the Travaux Préparatoires of the EPC,[197] it was accepted that this concept varied according to different countries. The Working Party was of the opinion that interpretation of the meaning of ordre public should be a matter for European institutions[198] (as, indeed, should the notion of morality).[199] The identity of these institutions was not indicated. The Technical Board of Appeal in *Plant Genetic Systems*,[200] described ordre public as covering public security and individuals' physical integrity within society along with environmental protection.[201] In some cases, such as *Oncomouse*[202] the Technical Board did not distinguish between morality and ordre public and while boards of the EPO often conflate the two, there are some exceptions,[203] as examined later in this section.

Attempts have been made to add clarity to some of the nomenclature of the European patent legislative instruments. For example, the UK Banks Report has advocated that ordre public should be interpreted to mean public policy and public order[204] but the parameters of these concepts in the realm of morally controversial biotechnological patents is not clear. The UK Intellectual Property Office's recent patent examination guidelines[205] gives clear guidance on how to apply principles of morality based on the case law but ordre public receives barely a mention. Moreover, these reports are at national level. Warren-Jones correctly claims that the terms ordre public and morality have been treated abstrusely by the

195 *Plant Genetic Systems v Greenpeace Ltd.* [1995] EPOR 357.
196 Ibid 366.
197 'Travaux Préparatoires (EPC 1973)' 16, 7–8, http://webserv.epo.org/projects/babylon/tpepc73.nsf/0/A79664CCCE197AC1C1257427004 (accessed 5 March 2019).
198 Cf. Document IV/2767/61-E, 7.
199 Cf. Document IV/2767/61-E, 8.
200 T356/93 *Plant Genetic Systems/Gutamine synthenase inhibitors* [1995] 8 OJ EPO 545, 557–560.
201 Ibid paragraph 5.
202 T 0315/03 *Transgenic Animals/HARVARD* of 6 July 2004.
203 Amanda Warren-Jones, 'Finding a "Common Morality Codex" for Biotech—a Question of Substance' (2008) 6 IIC 638.
204 Banks Report, Report of the Committee to Examine the Patent System and Patent Law, HMSO 1970.
205 IPO, 'Examination Guidelines for Patent Applications Relating to Biotechnological Inventions in the Intellectual Property Office' (2016), https://www.gov.uk/government/uploads/system/uploads/attachment_data/file/512614/Guidelines-for-Patent-Applications-Biotech.pdf (accessed 5 March 2019).

EPO Appeal Boards, despite there being an appreciation of a difference in their meaning.[206]

It would be helpful if the Boards were to develop a practice of referencing previous cases if they are guided by their obiter dicta. Otherwise, the endeavour to make sense of their interpretations is arduous. Despite the fact that ordre public is often used in a public order sense, Beyleveld and Brownsword contend that if an invention could harm human beings, the provisions on ordre public would raise an issue as to whether principles of justice, freedom and freedom from interference were contravened.[207] Given the established practice of the EPO in referencing morality when Article 53(a) is engaged, T 0149/11 as explored hereunder has not helped to make the interpreter's task any easier.

In a recent case at the EPO, *Method and device for processing a slaughtered animal or part thereof in a slaughterhouse*,[208] ordre public rather than morality became the focus of the Appeal Board's interpretation of Article 53(a) in a case which concerned a patent application for a means and instrument to process slaughtered animals. The Board distinguished between the invention which would be made regardless and its exploitation which was the concern of the patent. The application related to an invention for both a method and device for processing a slaughtered animal or part of a slaughtered animal in a slaughterhouse. The controversy in this application arose because the application required that at least one observer be positioned at the slaughter line. This was understood by the Board to mean that such a person would comprise part of the patentable invention, although the inclusion of a human being in the patent application, on reading the case, appears to have been inadvertent. Nonetheless, the patent was not granted and it is clear from the EPC that human beings cannot be patented. Moreover, given the recent constitutionalisation of law in this area, patent arbitrators are increasingly aware of the need to take human dignity issues into consideration. The patent application should have been drafted with greater care to avoid the inference.

What is exceptional about this case is that in upholding these objections to the patent, the Board associated human rights violations as being contrary to ordre public rather than the broader category normally used of morality. Moreover it was also associated with the protection of fundamental values and rights such as the right to life, physical integrity and human dignity. The European Convention on Human Rights was invoked, and ordre public was found to be underpinned by fundamental rights and freedoms contained in this legislation. Reference was made to rights of integrity, liberty and the prohibition of slavery within the EU Charter of Fundamental Rights which came into force in the EU in 2009 with the enactment of the Treaty of Lisbon. However, these are extraordinary references, given that EU legislation is not binding in the EPO's wider remit. It would suggest that the EPO lacks a set of principles within its jurisdiction and, therefore, considers it

206 Warren-Jones, 'Finding a "Common Morality Codex" for Biotech', 641–642.

207 Beyleveld and Brownsword, *op cit* 47–52.

208 T 0149/11 of 4 January 2013, Method and Device for Processing a Slaughtered Animal or Part Thereof in a Slaughterhouse.

appropriate to search outside. While it may be considered a positive development to seek out a moral compass in an area imbued with ethical issues, ideally, if the EPO lacks principles, it should surely draft its own. Principles written for one purpose may not transplant smoothly into another system, especially where its jurisdiction is broader than that of the EU. The Travaux Préparatoires of the EPC acknowledged the multiple moralities existing within European states, it was decided not to define morality in the EPC, institutions were supposed to provide guidance and yet, 40 years later the EPO still grapples with its dearth of written values. Clearly some precision is needed but importing evolving values from another legal system may well add to the confusion in this area rather than quietening it.

This case also signifies a vast expansion in the potential scope of ordre public as heretofore it had been confined to devices likely to disrupt public order and its ambit was therefore narrow. The case thus blurs the lines between ordre public and morality, especially given that morality was the banner under which cases such as *WARF* concerning human embryos was decided. What it also signifies is that patent law at the EPO is becoming increasingly constitutionalised and infused with higher order norms of ethics and morality. These influences are emanating from the Council of Europe's Convention on Human Rights and the European Union's Charter of Fundamental Rights. While it is not undesirable for the EPO to seek a moral compass, clarity as to its guiding principles and how these have been reached would be welcome.

The section has shown that morality and ordre public under Article 53(a) EPC (as amended) are not easy to adjudicate and, in the absence of principles, the Boards have struggled and produced a body of case law which is inconsistent. This book is not arguing for the delineation of morality and ordre public by a legislative body: such a task may not foster clarity as technology advances rapidly and the law struggles to keep pace. It is more concerned with how decisions regarding patents on morally controversial biotechnological inventions are taken and by whom. The next section explores the issue of morality as it arises under the Biotech Directive and the case law which this legislation has spawned. Unlike the EPO, the CJEU has not made ordre public the focus of any of its case law in biotechnology to date.

1.3.3 Morality in the case law of the CJEU

The CJEU in recent years has considered its first important case on equivalent provisions in the Biotech Directive as it is the final court of appeal from national courts under the Biotech Directive. The *Brüstle*[209] case was the first case in which the CJEU decided on the patentability of certain inventions under the Directive. The EU in relative terms, is a late-comer to the realm given that the Biotech Directive was passed in 1998 so other patent legislation, such as the EPC, predates it by more than 20 years. In *Brüstle*, the court considered Article 6(2)(c) of the

209 C-34/10 *Oliver Brüstle v Greenpeace eV* [2011] ECR I-9821.

Directive on a referral from Germany's Federal Patent Court. Greenpeace initially had argued before the German courts that the patent was invalid because it breached the terms of the Directive, Article 6(2)(c) which prohibits patents on uses of human embryos for industrial or commercial purposes. Greenpeace was partly successful at first instance but on appeal, the action was stayed pending the aforementioned referral. The court sought answers from the CJEU on the meaning of the term human embryo in Article 6(2)(c) of Directive 98/44/EC. The court questioned whether all developmental stages of human life were included. It also sought to ascertain whether unfertilised human eggs into which had been transplanted a mature human cell nucleus and parthenotes were to be classified as human embryos. It further asked whether stem cells obtained from blastocysts were included and it queried the meaning of industrial and commercial purposes. The court also enquired as to the patentability of technical teaching where the human embryo was not included with the technical teaching in the patent claim, although the patent was for a product or process which involved the destruction of a human embryo.

Prior to its judgment, Advocate General Yves Bôt issued an opinion. In essence, clarification as to what constitutes a human embryo for the purposes of the Directive was sought. The Advocate General opined that a Community-wide definition of human embryo is necessary in order to deter forum shopping for a favourable regime,[210] effectively recommending a constitutionalisation[211] of the status of the human embryo through the mechanism of patent law. This has not even been achieved by the jurisprudence of the European Court of Human Rights (ECtHR) in its interpretation of the right to life, and it has shown restraint in the extent to which it is willing to circumscribe this right.[212] The Advocate General showed no such reticence. He reasoned that as both totipotent cells and blastocysts can develop into human bodies, they come within the definition of embryo. Pluripotent cells cannot develop into a complete human body but they arise in the blastocyst and give rise to foetal or adult cells. If a prior destruction of the embryo is necessitated by the technical process, the invention should be unpatentable even where the use of the embryo is not mentioned. Bôt also indicated that while in some countries, the human embryo is considered to exist from fertilisation, in others, implantation is the embryonic threshold.[213] In a somewhat conservative approach, he considers that it is illogical to deem that legal status should only arise with nidation or implantation. He brings some clarity to what may be considered as use for industrial or commercial purposes, indicating that the meaning of the use of embryos for industrial or commercial purposes would involve a large production, which would be out of proportion to the quantity of

210 *Brüstle v Greenpeace eV*, Opinion of the Advocate General.

211 The term "constitutionalisation" is meant here to indicate that the CJEU is taking it upon itself to develop, in the absence of a written constitution, constitutional norms within the EU's legal order. These norms rank higher than legislative instruments.

212 *Vo v. France* [CG], No. 53924/00 para. 82; *Evans v UK*, No. 339/05 para. 46; *A. B&C. v Ireland* [2010] ECHR 2032.

213 *Brüstle v Greenpeace eV*, Opinion of the Advocate General 67.

operations performed *in utero* on an embryo to cure a defect or to increase its possibility of survival.[214]

The CJEU held that human embryo under Article 6(2)(c) of the Directive 98/44 includes any human ovum after fertilisation, any non-fertilised human ovum into which the cell nucleus from a mature human cell has been transplanted, and any non-fertilised human ovum whose division and further development have been stimulated by parthenogenesis. The CJEU left it to the referring court to decide whether pluripotent cells taken from a blastocyst would constitute a human embryo, leaving open a very wide interpretation of patent exclusion. Human embryos used for scientific research will also be excluded from patentability and patents will only be permitted for therapeutic or diagnostic purposes which are applied to the human embryo and are useful to it.

The CJEU confirmed in *Brüstle*[215] that commercial exploitation would be defined in accordance with the recommendation of the Advocate General, so adjudication comes down to a question of scale – in this case, at least. A parallel patent application to the EPO resulted in a revocation of the patent in opposition proceedings for insufficient disclosure.[216] The EPO has chosen to incorporate the principles from the CJEU's decision into its guidelines for examination,[217] signifying an ongoing tendency to approximate its laws to those of the EU. The EU's reading of morality provisions is not restricted by guidelines recommending that the provisions of the Directive be read narrowly. The EPO, despite such restrictions is choosing to align its principles with those of the CJEU, in cases concerning human embryos at least. Whether such voluntary convergence continues remains uncertain and will undoubtedly depend at least in part on what material or matter the patent application covers.

The inherent tensions in the Directive between promotion of investment and the protection of the dignity of the person are evident. These points of conflict are unlikely to abate because on the one hand, biotechnology is a growing industry and promises cures for currently untreatable diseases and there may be a moral imperative to encourage its growth. On the other hand, many aspects of European law are becoming increasingly constitutionalised with more and more references to the European Charter of Fundamental Rights and the European Convention on Human Rights. If a more conservative era in the framing of the rights of the human embryo emerges at the European or supra-national level, these instruments may be used to rein in biotechnological exploration and their patents under a morality banner. Who makes these decisions and how they are taken will be an important consideration.

214 *Brüstle v Greenpeace eV*, AG113.

215 C-34/10 *Oliver Brüstle v Greenpeace eV* [2011] ECR I-9821.

216 *Brüstle*, EP1040185 (28 June 2013). See generally EPO Press Release, 'EPO Revokes Patent in the *Brüstle* Case' (11 April 2013) http://www.epo.org/news-issues/news/2013/20130411a.html (accessed 5 March 2019).

217 Guidelines for Examination in the European Patent Office (EPO Guidelines), November 2016 edition, Part G, Chapters II–17 to 18 on Rule 28(c).

Subsequent to the judgment in *Brüstle*, the understanding that parthenotes should be classed as embryos has been overturned in *International Stem Cell Corporation*[218] which was a reference from the UK High Court. Parthenotes are not now considered to come within the definition of human embryos because while they can commence embryonic development, they cannot complete the process.

1.3.3.1 Commentary

The *Brüstle* decision has been criticised for seeking to establish a European-wide definition of human embryos through patent law.[219] Nordberg and Minssen argue that by basing the exception to patentability on human dignity, the CJEU equates, for the purposes of patent law, a life in being with a fertilised ovum.[220] O'Sullivan also indicates that the decision leaves an area of ambiguity in that embryos which have been created through SCNT/therapeutic cloning are unlikely to have capacity to develop into a human being and, regardless of the fact that these are totipotent, they are still likely to be excluded from patentability.[221] This area is currently unsettled.

It remains to be seen whether this construction of human life informs other areas of the law involving the right to life, such as abortion law or the status of embryos left over from IVF processes. Harmon *et al* criticise *Brüstle* opining that what is essentially a moral question was reframed as a legal one and the CJEU thereby failed to engage with what it was being asked.[222] Tensions may emerge in the jurisprudence of the new specialised patent courts if and when cases are appealed to the CJEU if there is uncertainty as to the extent to which patent law is to be influenced by human rights discourse. Moreover, to date the EU has not acceded to the European Convention on Human Rights and it will not aid harmonisation if separate definitions of human life in all its stages emerges through EU patent law combined with human rights concerns. Moreover, it remains to be seen whether life and dignity acquire different meanings under the EU Charter and the European Convention on Human Rights.

The case law at both the EPO and the CJEU indicate that there is no consensus about what constitutes morality and ordre public in the EPC or the Biotech Directive. Given that technology is advancing rapidly and new ethical issues arise regularly, some academic commentary criticises the paucity of public input. The critique envisages more public involvement than our representative system of politics allows. The European Parliament does engage robustly with ethical issues

218 C-364/13 *International Stem Cell Corporation v Comptroller General of Patents Designs and Trade Marks* (Grand Chamber) 18 December 2014.

219 Nordberg and Minssen, *op cit* 144.

220 Ibid 152.

221 Ella O'Sullivan, 'International Stem Cell Corp v Comptroller General of Patents: The Debate Regarding the Definition of the Human Embryo Continues' [2014] EIPR 36 (3) 155, 162.

222 SHE Harmon, Graeme Laurie and Aidan Courtney, 'Dignity, Plurality and the Unfinished Story of Brüstle v Greenpeace' [2013] ELR 38(1) 92, 96.

related to biotechnology but the debate does not engage the wider publics. It could be argued, of course, that public voices are not heard more often because of lack of interest but awareness is not high because there is a paucity in the provision and transmission of information. Criticisms of the lack of public involvement are explored in Chapter Four, yet few writers elaborate on an alternative model that would address this critique in a thorough manner. This matter encapsulates the normative quest of this book: to adjudicate effectively the decision-making process of such patents prior to grant so that pluralistic public voices are engaged. This may cause oppositions, appeals and post-grant challenges to be reduced – or not: its effect may be unpredictable. It is also aimed to achieve a more holistic approach towards what Europeans truly consider to constitute morality within the context of this work. This, I will argue, can be achieved using the executive body in the form of patent office officials to engage public opinions and to initiate an educative process on the advantages and disadvantages of patenting biotechnological inventions. This book focuses on the process of such engagement and not the outcome.

The publics do care about moral issues and this is evidenced by public and individual participation in opposition proceedings, which is permitted under Article 99(1) EPC.[223] However, at present these views do not have a broad means of expression. To highlight the disengagement between what might constitute public opinions and those of patent attorneys, in a recent publication on the matter of Article 53(a) in opposition proceedings, the authors, both of whom are European patent attorneys and practitioners or lecturers, denied that this article subsection is invoked much in opposition proceedings and declined to cover it in their book.[224]

This juxtaposes in an interesting way with the actual evidence of the case law, above. Moreover academic commentary, such as the following by Crespi who has written extensively on the issue of morality in European patent law, shows that the morality bar to European patents, in EPC Article 53(a). He indicates that this article has for a long time been invoked by green, animal rights groups and other campaigners in opposition proceedings to certain patents which had been granted by the EPO.[225] The case law supports Crespi's claim and shows that the publics, embodied by environmental, animal rights and other campaigners regularly challenge patents to which they are opposed. The practitioners' observations demonstrate their lack of knowledge of higher order norms. For them, administrative efficiency may trump moral content but this interpretation of the law is *illegitimate*. Morality bars to positive law are in a sense part of the constitutional order whether they be written or not and cannot be sidestepped without creating a crisis of legitimacy. While one can sympathise with patent attorneys not versed in ethics

223 For instance in the *Harvard/Oncomouse* case.

224 Marcus O Müller and Cees AM Mulder, *Proceedings Before the European Patent Office: A Practical Guide to Success in Opposition and Appeal* (Edward Elgar Publishing 2015) 47.

225 R Stephen Crespi, 'The Human Embryo and Patent Law: A Major Challenge Ahead?' (2006) 28 EIPR 569.

who are responsible for administering the morality bar which overarches the granting of the patent, ignorance of same cannot be used to deny its status.

1.3.4 Conclusion

This chapter has carried out a chronological account of the introduction and development of patent legislation. It has noted the internationalisation of patent law and the expansion in the subject matter which it covers. The inclusion of mandatory provisions of morality and ordre public within patent legislation such as the EPC and the Biotech Directive (along with TRIPS) was traced. The confusion surrounding how to define morality and ordre public was palpable from the documentation: while it was agreed that there was no European definition of morality or ordre public, no attempt was made to bring clarity to the area. Instead, European institutions, whose identities were not revealed were to be charged with applying these vague principles. The buck, essentially, was passed to the boards and courts which had to grapple with a fast-moving technological field, a paucity of legal – and moral or ethical – guidance. Little publicity ensued over plant patents but when patents were granted on animals and sought on human embryos, public voices became more audible. This chapter has examined relevant case law in this context, focusing especially on the interpretation of morality (and ordre public), principally at the EPO and its boards but also in the CJEU. This chapter has sought to demonstrate that morality is not currently being arbitrated appropriately, due to inherent uncertainty in the application of this norm for two reasons. The first is that it lacks definition and the second is that those charged with its administration do not have a grounding in its meaning or how it should be applied. Moreover, there is little space for public input and it may be argued that little interest has been shown. However, many NGOs, other groups and individuals take part in opposition proceedings suggesting that among the knowledgeable, public interest is keen. The question as to how to accommodate a multiplicity of views and make decisions on the basis of these views is an ongoing research problem. The normative focus of this work is to broaden possibilities for public involvement as much as possible.

Having identified the problem in this chapter through a doctrinal approach to the legislation and case law, the next chapter will explore morality further in the context of its locus in the patent system. It will consider academic commentary on aspects of the legislation and case law from the perspective of public input. It will also investigate the calls for more public inclusion. Its principal task will be to analyse whether traditional processes of reform can produce a better manner of adjudicating morality in morally controversial biotechnological patent applications.

2 Patent moralities and their traditional adjudications

A critique

2.1 Introduction

The last chapter charted the history of patent law, noting its internationalisation and the increasingly important role that morality plays in patent legislation. However, it also highlighted that morality is not well defined and that judgments are unpredictable, leading to legal uncertainty. This book assumes that the morality clause will be retained in patent legislation and any advocacy of its abolition is outside the scope of this book. This work does not delve into whether morally controversial biotechnological patents should or should not be granted. It is not a moral treatise which seeks to find the right answer to questions of morality in patent legislation. It is concerned rather with developing a robust process for reaching decisions that are inclusive of a plurality of viewpoints and so rejects any fatalism which might assert that change from without is not possible. It discusses who should have the right to have an input into these decisions, drawing on literature which deals with public involvement in decisions of magnitude. It is argued that the populace in general should be involved in patent grants and refusals when the morality bar under Article 53(a) EPC has been triggered. It bases this normative claim on a number of premises which include the following.

The European Patent Convention (EPC) mandates a morality bar and yet does not postulate what morality actually is or how it comes to be decided that the patent application potentially falls within this exclusion. A clear set of principles could address this in part, but this is not the proposal of this book for reasons which will emerge in this chapter. At present, officials at the European Patent Office (EPO) must assess morality in a vacuum of definition and yet, as executive or administrative officers they are no better versed in ethics and what it may entail than society in general. Nor do I advance a proposal for ethical training, which will be explained in this chapter, too. Morality is a subject of much debate in a pluralistic world and this book argues for a decision-making model which will better accommodate a multiplicity of views. It is not a quest to develop expertise among a cohort of decision-makers but, rather, the book seeks to represent as broadly as possible the plurality of viewpoints that exist, or would exist with sufficient information, on matters of morality in controversial biotechnological patents. This chapter will critique the utility of the "usual solutions" in the context of these patents, concluding that in order to facilitate inclusivity, such solutions do not go far enough.

This chapter seeks to achieve a number of tasks. It will distinguish between general moral issues raised by biotechnological inventions, which sometimes get mixed up with the more specific matter of the morality bar in Article 53(a) which refers only to the role of morality in the patenting process. Next, it will consider whether morality constraints can simply be ignored and concludes that this is not possible. It then highlights the current outlet that public voices have to express concerns about morality, holding that this can be expanded. Subsequently, I explore and critique traditional remedies such as legislation, precedent and patent office practices to show that the various branches of government are poorly equipped to adjudicate morality and that ethics committees will not provide an adequate solution either. If arbitrating morality is left to the legislature, it risks fossilising this changing standard where laws are drafted too tightly and if too loosely, then it falls upon the courts to decide the matter. Judges tend not to relish being foisted with this responsibility and often chide legislatures for their inaction. For instance, in the US case of *Diamond v Chakrabarty*[1] the court noted that the legislature had not pronounced on whether patent law extended to micro-organisms and they regarded this as a matter best decided by Congress. Furthermore, judges may be obliged to grapple with scantily drafted legislation, such as in the *Brüstle*[2] case where the term "human embryo" was not defined in the Biotech Directive. Consequently, the understanding that parthenotes constituted human embryos was overturned two years later in *International Stem Cell Corporation*[3] where this part of the decision was deemed to have been erroneously made. Sometimes it is believed that ethics committees could step into this breach but they may just dominate the process or else be sidelined by only being afforded an advisory role. Ethicists often are in search of an objective good but they can play a valuable role in helping to identify which applications raise novel moral issues.

Finally, this chapter also shows that citizens are increasingly being included by governments in their own governance and so many conventional paradigms of law-making are undergoing a process of change. This will be explored in subsequent chapters but briefly, the human right to participate is being utilised in a number of policy arenas to include different interest groups in matters which concern them, such as under the Aarhus Convention and this, I will argue, can *and should* be expanded further. This chapter explores some paradigms that point to a more deliberative and participatory approach to resolving dilemmas in the ethical realm which, if well designed can assist in the resolution of ethically fraught issues. In doing so I propose to build a nexus between the adjudication of morality within the patent system and public input, which will be explored in more detail in Chapter Four.

1 *Diamond v Chakrabarty* (1980) 447 US 303.
2 C-34/10 *Oliver Brüstle v Greenpeace eV* [2011] ECR I-9821.
3 C-364/13 *International Stem Cell Corporation v Comptroller General of Patents Designs and Trade Marks*, (Grand Chamber) 18 December 2014.

2.2 Untangling morality of the invention and morality in patent grants

Before exploring the entwined skeins of morality and patenting in Article 53(a) EPC, it may be useful to identify some of the moral issues which pertain to biotechnological inventions prior to their coming within the ambit of the patent system. Ethical aspects of the *creation* of biotechnological inventions sometimes get confused with the morality bar in the granting of the patent. As morality is difficult to define objectively, no consensus as to which model of morality should predominate is likely to be reached either when dealing with inventions or patenting such inventions. It is argued by some that biotechnological inventions are not just another small, almost routine extension of human ingenuity but, rather that they touch core questions regarding what it means to be human itself before the patent system is ever engaged. Habermas has written on the fact that biotechnology raises moral issues that are novel and which go to the ethical core of humanity's understanding of itself.[4]

Discussion of these broader issues is outside the scope of this book but where morally controversial biotechnological inventions are allowed and patents applied for, the morality bar in Article 53(a) EPC will be engaged. Sandel has also said that advances in genetic and other technologies will force us to consider matters which we do not normally contemplate relating to nature's moral status and of the manner in which we should behave towards the world.[5]

The matter of how society is to decide such issues and whether patents should be granted on morally controversial biotechnological inventions is fraught: even where there is awareness of advances in science and technology – and the issues are so complex that they are not at the forefront of public consciousness – society is divided and decisions tend to get made by scientists and technocrats, largely out of the public eye. For example, at the Asilomar Conference in 1974, it was scientists who declared a six-month moratorium on genetic engineering – the issue did not come into the wider realm of public consciousness for some two more decades nor did it fall into a tailored regulatory framework.[6] Snead has commented that Descartes had excluded moral questions from modern science so that the natural world could be investigated freely. This has led some scientists and philosophers to disregard these questions altogether.[7]

Despite difficulties in defining morality, it operates as a bar to patentability in European patent law and therefore cannot legitimately be ignored. The current manner in which it is being adjudicated is inadequate and, thus, various approaches will be examined hereunder.

4 Jürgen Habermas, *The Future of Human Nature* (Taylor & Francis 2005) 14–15.
5 Michael J Sandel, *The Case against Perfection* (Harvard University Press 2009) 9.
6 Paul Berg, 'Meetings That Changed the World: Asilomar 1975: DNA Modification Secured' (2008) 455 Nature 290.
7 O Carter Snead, 'Science, Public Bioethics, and the Problem of Integration' (2009) 43 UC Davis L. Rev. 1529, 1590.

There has been considerable blurring of the lines between the morality of allowing research into biotechnology and concerns relating to morality provisions in patent legislation. However, the nature of such ethical issues is unclear and the extent to which these matters can be accommodated within patent law is similarly obscure. Laurie observes that on the one hand lies disquiet about technological and scientific advances in themselves and on the other about the patents granted over their products and processes but these separate matters frequently get conflated.[8]

The decision as to whether to grant a patent is a moral issue but courts and patent examiners are constrained in that their task is to administer the law with little guidance. The scientific progress will continue, either more or less robustly but it is unsatisfactory to deal with moral issues in this indirect way because patent law is ill suited to regulating morality.[9] Moreover, the actors charged with applying the morality bar tend to have a technical or legal background and no training in ethics so even the ability to identify applications which engage Article 53(a) EPC is not assured. The profile of judges in the new courts being set up in the EU under the Unified Patent System will not differ so the adjudication of morality is unlikely to become any more straightforward.

Another way of viewing the matter is to accept the interconnectedness of the technology and the patents. Laurie says, in relation to Article 6 of the Directive on the legal protection of biotechnological inventions that if its true ethical core is respect for human dignity, then this cannot be sidelined. He believes that we are utterly perplexed about the issues.[10] Whilst the patent system cannot be expected to regulate morality, it does not have to be used to provide incentives for research which commoditises humanity.[11] Mills also separates the creation of the technology which raises its own morality issues from the patent grant as the patent applies to an invention which already exists and has therefore been permitted. However, denying patent protection for such inventions may serve to regulate indirectly by de-incentivising the creation of such inventions in the first place.[12] This would not be a very satisfactory way of dealing with ethical issues as inventions may be encouraged by one set of policies and then discouraged by another. A more transparent and streamlined process would be preferable.

Not everyone would agree with Mills' views. For instance the court in *Diamond v Chakrabarty*[13] said that denying patents on biotechnological inventions would be unlikely to end the research as much had already taken place in the absence of patent protection. The court stated that legislative or judicial intervention in the patent realm would not stop scientific investigation.[14] However, the dictum in

8 Graeme Laurie, 'Patenting Stem Cells of Human Origin' [2004] EIPR 59, 61.
9 Ibid, 64–65.
10 Ibid.
11 Margo A Bagley, 'Patent First, Ask Questions Later: Morality and Biotechnology in Patent Law' (2003) 45 WM & Mary L Rev 469, 545.
12 Mills, *op cit* 10–11.
13 *Diamond v Chakrabarty* (1980) 447 US 303.
14 Ibid.

Diamond was delivered over 30 years ago and in the US there have been fewer restrictions on patenting biotech inventions because US patent law lacks a general morality bar. In Europe, the inclusion of a morality bar in patent legislation means that there is an extra step to traverse when inventors seek patents.

Whilst concerns about the morality of the invention tend to question whether scientists *should* engage in research because they *can*, the ethical issues which arise in patenting morally controversial inventions include the incentivisation of this research and the granting of monopoly rights to exclude others from using the invention.

Among anti-patenting activists, there are two different positions which are sometimes conflated and these are, respectively, opposition to genetically engineering higher life forms and granting patents over these entities.[15] However, whilst these two positions are interconnected, there is still a dichotomy between permission for the technology for research purposes and the use of the patent system for its encouragement.

The EPC, however, does not separate morality from patentable biotechnological inventions. The legislation is not Cartesian in the sense of side-lining non-scientific matters (as did Descartes)[16] as it brings together important issues which arise in different disciplines, for instance law, science and ethics. Patent grants raise ethical concerns due to the enactment of legislation such as the Biotech Directive and the associated amending legislation of the EPC. Whilst expertise in patent law and some knowledge of biotechnology is necessary to apply the law correctly, the issue of how morality is arbitrated is important because some patents will not be granted if they do not pass this test. Patent officials, however, do not really have the skills to apply the morality bar. At very least, they should have a satisfactory means of knowing which patent applications in the biotechnological realm flag up ethical issues. This could avoid controversies such as the granting of the *Edinburgh* patent,[17] explored in Chapter Two.

Morality in patent grants is of interest to all members of society, I contend.[18] The allocation of patents in this area is an important means of incentivising biotechnological research which promises cures for serious diseases. Whether monopolies are justified for particular inventions is not always clear and

15 Rebecca Dresser, 'Ethical and Legal Issues in Patenting New Animal Life' [1988] Jurimetrics 399.

16 O Carter Snead, *op cit.*

17 *Edinburgh Patent Application* No.94913174.2.

18 It may be that publics should also be consulted about whether the invention should be created or not. In that context, UNESCO has recently established Bioethics Ireland which is a branch of its European Division. One of its goals is to extend education to all levels of society under the auspices of the Universal Declaration on Bioethics and Human Rights: https://unescobioethicsireland.eu/ (accessed 5 March 2019). As this unit is based at my university, NUI Galway, I am part of the research group and recently (25 May 2017) gave them a presentation on deliberation, participation and biotech patents. The book, however, focuses on Article 53(a) EPC and, therefore, a detailed analysis of participation in the realm of whether biotech inventions should be *created*, is outside of its scope.

therefore, the manner in which such decisions are made is important. This book argues that the decision-making process should be broadly based to represent as many viewpoints as possible. However, given the complexity of the area, it may prove difficult to articulate concerns in a satisfactory way, especially within patent law.

The grant of a patent over an invention and the use of a public incentivisation scheme is a profoundly moral matter in its own right. Whilst society may or may not be satisfied with permission being given for creation of biotechnological inventions, the matter of commercial exploitation is now the primary concern of the morality bar within the EPC: narrowed from its original scope which extended to publication and exploitation of the invention.[19] It may be that the patent system is the first frontier at which those who are opposed to the morality of the invention can make their voices heard, even if they are not always listened to. This has the effect of potentially hindering the purpose of the patent system which is to encourage invention and not to regulate moral issues which could already have been decided. However, no right – and patents are classified as property rights in much legislation – is absolute and restrictions on rights are the norm, although these should be clear. Moreover, the patenting of morally controversial biotechnological inventions raises separate moral issues. Perhaps an adequate forum for discussion of technological advancement should have been provided at the advent of the creation of these inventions. There are now deeply conflicting interests and the forums in which the matter is being flexed is the EPO and its boards and courts within the EU. Various solutions to this dilemma have been proposed, as can be seen in the next section.

2.2.1 Can morality provisions in patent law just be ignored?

One solution would be to excise all references to morality from patent law. This is not the proposition of this book because I believe that the morality bar serves a distinct purpose discrete to issues relating to patenting morally controversial biotechnological inventions. This includes questions over whether we should commercialise inventions which we allow to be created, whether they should be monopolised, whether we should incentivise such research through the patent system and, more generally, whether living organisms should be the subject of a patent grant, even if the latter point is already moot. There are also controversies over the granting of patents on isolated DNA which has not been modified,[20] even though this is permitted by the legislation.[21]

Lawyers are often keen to assert that patent law is not a realm into which morality should intrude and that the grant of a patent is a purely administrative exercise. Once the criteria are achieved, the grant can be made. In this view, issues

19 *Brüstle v Greenpeace eV* [2011] ECR I-9821.

20 James Boyle, *Shamans, Software, and Spleens: Law and the Construction of the Information Society* (Harvard University Press 1996).

21 Biotech Directive, Article 5.

of morality should be decided at the research stage[22] and not later. However, monopoly grants or awards of property rights frequently attract academic criticism and patents do not differ in this respect.[23] Patents on morally controversial biotechnological inventions raise various ethical issues such as monopolies and patenting living organisms. Moreover, morality is enshrined in European patent law and must be given its due weight. Sterckx and Cockbain have said that the EPO is required to apply the morality bar by the EPC and that this bar is so essential to the EPC that it was included in the Trade-related Aspects of Intellectual Property Rights (TRIPS) Agreement, Article 27(2) TRIPS and also in Article 6(1) of the Biotech Directive.[24] To those who object to morality provisions within patent law and who believe that these should instead remain on the outside, they argue that the only legal forum in which the ethics of biotech patents is assessed on a case-by-case basis is within the patent system.[25]

Nonetheless, it could be asserted that as the issue of European moral exclusions from patentability has not been clarified, patents should be granted and can always be invalidated later by boards, national courts or by the new EU patent courts.[26] This approach was taken in the *Edinburgh* case[27] in which a patent was granted controversially as it potentially covered human embryonic stem cells. It was opposed and subsequently amended to exclude such cells. The approach of patenting promptly followed by subsequent queries has been strenuously criticised where it operates more often in the US as the bars to morality are fewer, although the moral utility doctrine has been invoked in the past to refuse patents on inventions which were injurious to the sound morals of society.[28] This doctrine no longer tends to be cited since *Juicy Whip, Inc. v Orange Bang, Inc*[29] in which the Federal Appeals Court held that inventions which could deceive some members of the public would not be unpatentable on moral utility grounds, given that Congress had chosen not to pronounce on the matter. Some patent grants generate calls for legislative reform by Congress along with queries as to how such patents had been issued at all. According to Bagley, the US has resisted this urging over the last three decades, only ceding slightly in 2011 when it amended the Patent Act to prohibit the granting of patents on human organisms.[30] This may lead to a situation in the near future in which Congress may have to debate retrospectively whether patents on biotech inventions such as human-animal chimeras, or

22 Bagley, *op cit* 513.
23 William J Flynn, *Patents since the Renaissance* (Booklocker Inc 2006) 17, 20.
24 Sigrid Sterckx and Julian Cockbain, *Exclusions from Patentability: How Far Has the European Patent Office Eroded Boundaries* (Cambridge University Press 2012) 289.
25 Ibid 300.
26 Aurora Plomer, 'Human Dignity, Human Rights, and Article 6(1) of the EU Directive on Biotechnological Inventions' in Aurora Plomer and Paul Torremans (eds), *Embryonic Stem Cell Patents: European Patent Law and Ethics* (OUP 2009) 225–226.
27 *Edinburgh Patent Application* No 949131742.
28 *Lowell v Lewis*, 15 F. Cas. 1018 (1817).
29 *Juicy Whip, Inc v Orange Bang, Inc* (1999) 185 F 3d 1364 (Court of Appeals, Federal Circuit).
30 Bagley, *op cit* 474–475.

previability foetuses which have been created only to be destroyed in order to research disease, should have been granted. Where legislation restricting patent grants is introduced, it is not retrospective and patents on controversial subject matter, which have already been granted, will stand.[31]

Suggesting that a provision of the law be ignored because it is ill-defined is a non-remedy and instead, the core problem with the system as it currently operates is that patent office officials are not equipped to carry out the task with which they are charged. Morality is becoming an issue of constitutional importance within patent law. Arguably, constitutional law should derive from the people who, in representative democracies, are sovereign. Instead, one finds that it is the judiciary who are extending the consideration of constitutional rights to some morally controversial biotechnological patent applications. Some cases have begun to cite human dignity concerns when dealing with human embryos and, indeed, parthenotes[32] although the breadth of the definition of human embryo in *Brüstle*[33] was curtailed in *International Stem Cell Corp*[34] within two years. The European Convention on Human Rights together with the EU Charter of Fundamental Rights bring other dimensions to patent law, especially as more cases involving human embryos are coming before the courts.[35] It is notable that the status of the human embryo varies greatly in different European countries and none of the legal instruments define its parameters. This shows the plurality of viewpoints which has not been helped by the fact that the Court of Justice of the European Union (CJEU) has not been very comfortable admitting that it is dealing with moral rather than legal issues in this terrain.[36] This also indicates that the judiciary do not appear to find the application of ethical matters an easy task. Nonetheless, Sterckx and Cockbain point out that the morality bar in Article 53(a) EPC is a higher ranking legal norm than the provisions of Article 52(1) EPC and where there is conflict, the former should prevail.[37]

This suggests that as morality trumps an otherwise valid patent, then the latter must bow on the triggering of the former. Ignorance of the law will not, in the adage, be an excuse to the existence of a hierarchy of norms. Leapfrogging over problematic applications of the law rather than dealing with them directly is not best practice and in any case, under the EPC, the EPO has no option in this matter.

The morality test encompasses a variety of approaches taken by the EPO in its evaluations of the Article 53(a) patent eligibility bar, as seen in the last chapter.

31 Ibid 516.
32 C-34/10 *Oliver Brüstle v Greenpeace eV* [2011] ECR I-9821.
33 Ibid.
34 C-364/13 *International Stem Cell Corporation v Comptroller General of Patents, Designs and Trade Marks*, (Grand Chamber) 18 December 2014.
35 G2/06 *WARF/Stem Cells* [2009] EPOR 15; C-34/10 *Oliver Brüstle v Greenpeace eV* [2011] ECR I-9821.
36 SHE Harmon, Graeme Laurie and Aidan Courtney, 'Dignity, Plurality and Patentability: The Unfinished Story of Brüstle v Greenpeace' [2013] ELR 92, 100.
37 Sterckx and Cockbain, *op cit* 243.

Llewelyn and Adcock observe that the EPO finds the definition and application of morality a fraught issue. As the Office's main concern is granting patents for inventions which meet specific criteria, perhaps it could be argued that morality is too vague a concept for it to apply. Yet it is mandated to consider morality and is clearly uncomfortable with this task.[38]

Kass characterises as a weakness in the relationship between science and society that patents presuppose the benefits that accrue from inventors' innovations to the publics and whilst they are well designed for supporting innovation, they are ill suited to controlling or regulating it.[39]

This suggests that patent offices are not well placed to bar patents which are morally controversial when their function is to grant patents that fulfil certain technical criteria. One should not forget the general principle of not being a judge in one's own cause and as patent offices are funded by the patents they grant and renew, it may be that impediments to patents are read narrowly. Bagley asserts that patent applicants and their attorneys are fundamental to the creation of patent law and policy and argues that the US has an approach of patenting first and questioning such grants later. She also separates out the distinct issues of encouraging research and then granting a patent for inventions which this research may produce. The grant of exclusive rights by the government on controversial inventions raises separate moral issues but Congress, the United States Patent and Trademark Office (USPTO) and the courts have been relatively inactive in delimiting boundaries. This means that biotech patent applicants, namely scientists or researchers, influence greatly decisions over what gets patented.[40]

Clearly, morality when specifically included in legislation cannot legitimately be ignored. First of all, law and morality, as the legislation stands, are not separate because of the specific provisions of Article 53(a) EPC. Secondly, morality cannot be sidestepped and later invoked to revoke patents of dubious validity because it exists as a bar to controversial applications. Third, morality occupies a higher rank[41] than the patentability criteria of novelty, inventive step and usefulness in industry. Despite difficulties in interpretation, its place must be respected. There is evident discomfort in its application by patent officials and by the judiciary. However, this does not preclude the seeking of a better means of arbitration and of seeking to define morality and ordre public. Who does so and how this is done are the primary research questions in this book.

2.2.2 Opposition on morality grounds: public voices

European opposition to patents on biotechnological inventions, including animals continues and derives from a number of different premises. Various positions

38 Margaret Llewelyn and Mike Adcock, *European Plant Intellectual Property* (Bloomsbury Publishing 2006) 283.

39 Bagley, *op cit* 189.

40 Ibid 509.

41 This point is acknowledged by Sterckx and Cockbain, *op cit* 243 and Pierre Treichel, 'G2/06 and the Verdict of Immorality' (2009) 40 IIC 450.

include those who believe that patenting animals is inherently wrong because it offends moral values.[42] Antoine Goetschel, a former prosecutor appointed to protect animal welfare in Switzerland has questioned who represents the interests of genetically modified animals.[43] Professor Andrew Linzey of the Oxford Centre for Animal Ethics advocates a Christianity-based respect for God's creations[44] and this includes the rights of animals. Some NGOs such as Greenpeace[45] and Friends of the Earth[46] advocate an instrumental view of morality and focus on potentially negative consequences that both such engineering and patenting would have on the environment and on the economy. Of note is that the above positions are represented by privileged individuals or NGOs and it is currently difficult to discern public views. Morality provisions have been used as a broad vehicle to challenge patents in controversial areas such as environmental risk,[47] stem cell research[48] or experimentation on animals.[49] Furthermore, it is feared that genetic diversity will be lost and there is a concern that risk calculations are difficult, if not impossible, to make.[50] However, the response from patent advocates has been robust and they observe that humans have a long history of objectifying animals for their own purposes – buying and selling them at will and using them to satisfy several human needs and desires.[51] As aforementioned, however, the approval of the use of animals for one purpose does not mean that all uses of animals would gain public approval[52] and biotechnology raises different moral issues such as the genetic engineering of animals to suffer, for instance.[53]

The morality provisions within the patent system are the vehicle through which NGOs can exercise their opposition to patents which, in their view, should not be granted.[54] Morality and ordre public are a broad umbrella, as can be seen from the sample of positions in the previous paragraph. Sommer asserts that European opposition to patent grants is often mounted by Greenpeace and other special interest groups or organisations and this is borne out in the case law. Their efforts

42 For instance, Cruelty Free International (Formerly the British Union Against Vivisection) opposed the grant of a patent in the *Oncomouse* case.
43 Leo Hickman 'The Lawyer Who Defends Animals' *The Guardian* (5 March 2010).
44 Andrew Linzey, *Christianity and the Rights of Animals* (Wipf and Stock Publishers 2016).
45 Greenpeace, http://www.greenpeace.org/international/en/campaigns/agriculture/problem/genetic-engineering/ (accessed 5 March 2019).
46 Friends of the Earth, http://www.foe.org/projects/food-and-technology/genetic-engineering (accessed 5 March 2019).
47 *Plant Genetic Systems v Greenpeace* [1995] EPOR 357.
48 G2/06 *WARF/Stem Cells* [2009] EPOR 15.
49 Re Upjohn's Application, No. 89913146.0.
50 Ulrich Beck, *World Risk Society* (Polity Press 1999).
51 Dresser, *op cit* 411–413.
52 David Thomas and Georgina A Richards, 'The Importance of the Morality Exception under the European Patent Convention: The Oncomouse Case Continues' (2004) 26 EIPR 97, 102.
53 T19/90 *Harvard/Onco-Mouse* decision of 3 October 1990.
54 Oliver Mills, *Biotechnological Inventions: Moral Restraints and Patent Law* (Revised edn, Routledge 2010) 12–13.

are often either wholly or partly successful in that some patent applications have either been withdrawn or modified.[55] There is much to be said for the relative openness of this process at the EPO. The logistics of participation are, nonetheless, problematic unless individuals or groups seek out education and are able to fund themselves. Such opposition is very costly monetarily, temporally and also in terms of expertise. Without substantial resources, participation is a paper-based right only. There is a disparity of means between grantors, grantees and objectors. Patents must be opposed in order to face revocation and this process is onerous for the challenger.

It has been suggested that if patent office examiners and patent courts were allowed to access surveys and opinion polls which deal with issues of "morality", this would identify whether or not European publics understand the technology sufficiently for them to have formed an opinion.[56] Some effort could then be made to address any knowledge gap. However, discussion and public awareness of such issues is not uniform across Europe. Kure points out that there is no such public discussion in new EU Member States regarding the patentability of human embryonic stem cell (hESC) lines. Patentability is discussed only within the relevant scientific community in these countries. Yet, the scientists do not publish papers on patentability and neither are patent lawyers overly focused on the area.[57] Public voices are not universally engaged and often the media are an important but not necessarily accurate source of information. Wider public discussion of the issue of morality would enhance its understanding and the various positions which people hold. In order to partake in challenges to patents, a considerable grounding in a variety of disciplines is required.

In further proceedings, a post-grant challenge can be mounted by members of the public within nine months of the publication of the EPO's grant of the patent. The EPO is still constrained, nonetheless, by the lack of clarity in relation to morality exceptions in the applicable legislation. The dicta from various judgments are not of much assistance. They do not really establish a comprehensive precedent or consistent interpretation of the legislation. Whilst the statutes are quite general – and this may provide a desired flexibility, on the one hand – on the other, it can result in unpredictable interpretations which may be either too broad or narrow and these are epitomised by the various tests such as balancing, unacceptability, and public abhorrence under the EPC.[58]

Viens argues that on the issue of patenting stem cells, there is an array of moral theories available to guide this practice and that there is no agreement among reasonable people on which approach is better.[59] His comments describe a

55 Tine Sommer, 'Patenting the Animal Kingdom?: From Cross-Breeding to Genetic Make-up and Biomedical Research' (2008) 39 IIC 139, 141.

56 Warren-Jones, 'Identifying European moral consensus', *op cit* 27.

57 Josef Kure, 'Human Embryonic Stem Cell Research in Central and Eastern Europe: A Comparative Analysis of Regulatory and Policy Approaches' in Plomer and Torremans, *op cit* 77.

58 Bagley, *op cit* 541.

59 AM Viens, in Plomer and Torremans, *op cit* 89.

plurality of perspectives which have not been aired widely. Regardless as to the extent to which these views differ, it will be shown that well managed public education and debate tends to soften polarities and facilitates mutual comprehension of and respect for such differences.[60] Whilst opposition and appeal procedures broaden the decision-making process to other influences, the processes involved are onerous for the challenger.

By way of contrast with the European regime, the US lacked a post-grant proceeding which would facilitate public intervention in patent grants until the America Invents Act 2011. However, this does not include morality as a criterion for a patent challenge. Bagley, writing before the enactment of this Act but in words that are still relevant, given this ethical lacuna, believes that, in addition to some other reform, Congress should adopt such a scheme as it would at least facilitate some public input, allowing for the registration of opposition.[61] This would be especially useful given that at present, the public lack standing to challenge a patent's validity in court, as set out by the Court of Appeals for the Federal Circuit in *Animal Legal Defense Fund v Quigg*.[62] It remains to be seen whether the new courts to be set up in the EU evolve to resemble their specialised US counterpart or whether they retain their engagement with the essence of Article 53(a) as expressed, more or less, in Article 6 of the Biotech Directive.

It has been recommended by Harmon that the EPO recognise that there are different interests at stake which should be identified and their underlying values understood. There needs to be a way of measuring the extent of society's reaction to the commercialisation of given inventions. Heed should be paid to the views of several interested stakeholders that genes are humanity's heritage. He notes, however, that although it is improbable that the EPO will adopt a tough and analytical approach to Article 53, which could engage stakeholders in the patenting process, he would expect it to do a number of things. First, to: (i) acknowledge and articulate competing interests and their underlying moral theories; (ii) arrive at a means of measuring society's abhorrence to the commercialisation of opposed products/processes; and (iii) use its moral compass to formulate a comprehensible and cross-jurisdictional commercialisation morality.[63] This book takes Harmon's prescription further by developing a model of how such stakeholders can be engaged by accommodating a plurality of viewpoints within a deliberative and participatory structure. The EPO can develop their skills in administering debate rather than deciding moral matters for signatories across 38 states. It is the contention of this book that as morality in a pluralistic world cannot be defined in a manner that will represent public views, publics rather than patent officials should have the opportunity to make up their minds on whether patents should be granted when they

60 Amy Gutmann and Dennis Thompson, *Why Deliberative Democracy?* (Princeton University Press 2004).

61 Bagley, *op cit* 544.

62 *Animal Legal Defense Fund v Quigg* (1991) 932 F 2d 920.

63 SHE Harmon, 'The Rules Re-Engagement: The Use of Patent Proceedings to Influence the Regulation of Science (what the salmon does when it comes back downstream)', 2006 IPQ 378, 403.

trigger the morality threshold. How this can be achieved is the subject of Chapters Three, Four and Five. Before embarking on this normative quest, more conventional methods will be assessed against a benchmark of whether they do better at reflecting the multitude of potential public voices in this realm.

The next section will consider whether traditional methods of reform would be useful in resolving the problem of how to arbitrate morality in controversial biotechnological patent grants and whether publics can be given an input.

2.2.3 Traditional methods of reform

In this chapter we have seen already that there is a legal obligation to deal with the question of morality and ordre public: they cannot be sidelined. It has also been made apparent that their definition is not easily made and, moreover, opposition proceedings have shown that there are keen public voices, which often manifest interest through NGOs, which wish to be heard. It has been suggested that courts rather than legislatures could adjudicate the issue of morality more effectively. Smith believes that a balance needs to be struck between deliberative democracy and activism from the bench, expressing a scepticism about the legislature's ability to deliver in this arena and claiming that reliance on legislation will necessarily lead to delays.[64] Some traditional mechanisms for reform including the judiciary, legislature, patent offices and ethics committees will now be scrutinised.

2.3 Would specialised courts better address the issue of morality?

This book has shown that there is a lack of clarity in the decisions emanating from the EPO on the issue of morality and ordre public. Arguments have been made for the establishment of specialised courts which already exist in the US.[65] Some academics hold that we should seek to achieve a better model with a European patent court staffed with professional judges.[66] With the introduction of the Unitary Patent System this will soon become a reality in most countries in the European Union if, indeed, it is established. This section will look at judicial and academic commentary in the US about the role of judges in this realm, noting the establishment of a court which handles patent appeals. It will then comment on some features of the new patent court system in the EU and can only speculate as to morality's role in the regime.

2.3.1 The US

Whilst judges in specialised courts will have considerable expertise in patents and biotechnology, they may not be experts in ethics and even if they do have training

64 George P Smith, 'Judicial Decisionmaking in the Age of Biotechnology' (1999) 13 Notre Dame JL Ethics & Pub Pol'y 93, 117–118.

65 Ibid.

66 Plomer, *op cit* 225–226.

in concepts of the public good, these would not necessarily reflect opined that it was urged to arbitrate issues which should more properly be decided by the legislature, given its resources for research into such matters.[67]

Judges often do not feel equipped to make such decisions without legislative guidance and can be particularly ill prepared in seeking to apply the law to new technologies. The US Supreme Court in *Diamond* went on to say that the legislative process could strike a balance between competing interests and that such matters lie in the domain of our elected representatives. Congress and the Executive, rather than the courts, should be involved in this decision-making.[68]

In the context of such reflection, it is somewhat strange that the court did not exercise judicial restraint and refer the matter back to the legislature but it chose not to follow this course. The majority of the court in *Diamond v Chakrabarty* adopted a very modernist approach to the issue of patents and genetic technology. This was especially notable in the language of Mr Justice Douglas, when he talked about inventions of benefit to humankind, pushing back scientific frontiers.[69] Hence the debate as to where responsibility should lie and how the balance of power should be honed continues without resolution nearly 40 years later. It has been suggested that, in order to aid their deliberations, the judiciary could rely on expert evidence and witnesses. However, Smith has commented that non-expert judges and juries can hardly be competent to appoint experts as they lack the knowledge to assess their credentials and he observes that not all experts are equal.[70]

Judicial activity in the US differs somewhat from Europe, given that patent rights there emanate from the Constitution. The legislator's inaction has been criticised, where laws become outdated and new ones are not enacted to deal with emerging issues and Smith suggests that the solution to this problem may lie within the power of the courts. He advocates that judges' interpretation should be steered by reason, fairness, common sense, and comparison. He advocates the creation of a law of biotechnology based on precedent where principled decisions can be made and predictability assured. Otherwise, in his view, science will be the driver of the direction in which biotechnology will evolve and law's role will be solely reactive. He does believe that other disciplines should have some input but does not elaborate as to the form this may take.[71] The moral utility doctrine, which in the past was used for inventions considered, among other things to be, immoral[72] has not been invoked to date in any court cases involving biotechnological patents.

It has been argued that the judiciary shares with the legislature the responsibility for law-making, in the common law tradition. In this view, the courts' task is to find an equilibrium in their approach between interpreting existing statutes in line

67 Ibid 318.
68 Ibid.
69 *A & P TEA CO v Supermarket Corp,* (1950) 340 US 147, 71 S Ct 127, 95 L Ed 162.
70 Smith, *op cit* 105.
71 Ibid.
72 *Lowell v Lewis,* 15 F. Cas. 1018 (1817).

with modern standards of justice and delegating law-making responsibilities to legislatures, where appropriate. Their role is not just of interpretation but also of policy formulation and it has been argued that it is especially important that courts embrace this multifaceted role, as the citizenry is deemed by him to be unsophisticated.[73] This raises an important question: why is the citizenry ignorant and is this immutable or susceptible to change? What role do government and other parties play in their education? Are judges not also citizens? Judges may also lack competence in technology and policy formation. Education in such matters that this book advocates will benefit the judiciary as much as citizens in general but it will not give them any more expertise in *arbitrating* morality than anyone else. Morality in a pluralistic world will require public input in its arbitration to ensure representativeness and to avoid paternalism. However, education will broaden everyone's knowledge of different perspectives and rationales for various viewpoints. Elitist democracy – a system in which only experts decide on broad-ranging issues in the belief that the populace in general are ignorant and disinterested – often prevails where government is secretive and does not give easy access to information.

The US patent system is now more specialised in that it set up the Court of Appeals for the Federal Circuit (CAFC) in 1982. This court replaced the Court of Claims and the Court of Customs and Patent Appeals and it reviews appeals from USPTO decisions and is also able to craft uniform interpretations of any statutory provisions. Although the CAFC appears averse to making patent policy in the absence of statutory authority, it is quite comfortable in the role of statutory interpreter.[74] This court does seek to harmonise the application of patent law and is considered to be "decidedly pro-patent".[75] It has jurisdiction to hear all patent appeals. It will be instructive to compare the new specialised EU court system with its American counterpart in due course, should it go ahead.

2.3.2 *Europe*

With the setting up of specialised courts within the EU, the regime in Europe will become much more intricate. Sir David Kitchin, a Lord Justice of Appeal in the Court of Appeal of England and Wales also believes that it will become more patent-friendly[76] and it may, therefore, not prioritise the issue of morality and ordre public.[77] He has the following to say about the new court structure in the EU, in a commentary that highlights the increased complexity of the new system. That four different patent regimes will now co-exist. Each set of rules differ from national patents, to European patents outside the scope of the Unified Patent Court (UPC), and those within, and unitary patents. This will pose significant

73 Smith, *op cit*
74 Bagley, *op cit* 542.
75 Mills, *op cit* 45.
76 Justine Pila and Christopher Wadlow, *The Unitary EU Patent System* (Hart Publishing 2015) 4–6.
77 A point also raised by McMahon, *op cit* 65.

challenges for businesses. Should one lose a patent case, appeals will be heard in Luxembourg. Such bifurcation can greatly advantage patentees.[78]

It remains to be seen whether the new EU courts follow the tendency but experience is likely to prove to be a good teacher. The operation of specialised courts and how they will work in practice in the EU is thus unpredictable. Recent academic work raises some concerns. For instance, Pila and Wadlow contend that non-specialised courts such as the CJEU are better positioned to take EU Treaties and laws into consideration when applying patent legislation[79] and it has also been argued that patent law should not be applied in a restrictive manner, in isolation from other relevant laws such as those associated with rights and freedoms.[80] Moreover, as already argued, morality cannot be sidelined as it is a higher-order norm within European patent law. Pila and Wadlow say of the new patent courts in the EU that they will circumscribe the oversight of the general law and policy on European patents and that this restriction is intentional.[81] They call for the supervision by a generalist court of patent subject matter,[82] given that new thresholds between nature and invention are arising. Thambisetty argues that patent courts often develop in a peculiar manner due to the highly specialised subject matter and the fact that more time is now dedicated to litigating intellectual property. Specialised courts often add to an extension of the scope of patent rights,[83] and this is likely to occur in the new court system in the EU, given that many judges will have technical expertise but lack of training in ethics and complainants and respondents are likely to be confined to a relatively small cohort of biotech corporations, university researchers and NGOs of various colours.

The granting of patents involves a balance between private rights and the public interest. Specialised courts are likely to narrow the remit of the morality bar further and how this will interplay with the increasing constitutionalisation of patent law is unpredictable at present. This section has shown that courts are not best placed to deal with ethical issues which arise in morally controversial biotechnological inventions. As the judiciary struggle to apply the morality bar consistently, the next section explores legislative options for resolving this ongoing dilemma.

2.4 Legislative clarity

Given that courts can make this area quite unpredictable, an alternative approach to the problem of arbitrating morality is legislative reform. As the legislature is elected directly and has more research tools at its disposal it may be better placed to regulate complex areas, rather than the judiciary.

78 Pila and Wadlow, *op cit.*

79 Ibid 23.

80 Sivaramjani Thambisetty, 'The Institutional Nature of the Patent System: Implications for Bioethical Decision-Making', in Christian Lenk, Nils Hoppe and Roberto Adorno, *Ethics and Law of Intellectual Property* (Ashgate 2007) 257.

81 Pila and Wadlow, *op cit* 23.

82 Ibid.

83 Thambisetty in Lenk *et al., op cit.*

One of the problems with relying on the legislature in its traditional framework to stabilise norms was identified by Von Savigny, who opposed the codification of law in nineteenth-century Europe. Such codification had increased vastly during that era and he believed that this phenomenon would lead to rigidity in the law – clearly not desirable in a fast-moving technological field. In Von Savigny's view, one of the main functions of legislation is to help to clarify uncertainties. However, the law may not be able to clarify easily uncertainties about morality. Legislation may still become detached from its societal roots and as lawyers acquire an increasing monopoly over legal knowledge, the more removed from society it becomes.[84] This is especially true in the realm of law connected with science where terminology is highly specialised and decisions are effectively made by technocrats who tend not to have a grounding in matters of ethics. For instance, if the judgment relating to parthenotes being classified as human embryos[85] in *Brüstle*[86] had been legislatively enshrined, departure would have been much more difficult and certainly not amenable to rectification with the stroke of a pen once the error in the scientific knowledge was realised. Once written down, according to Von Savigny, rules could no longer evolve in a fluid way. As he conceptualised law as an expression of the spirit of the people, and therefore reflective of culture, written law would cease to be connected to society, the conduct of whose members it regulated. The increase in codification also facilitated the rise of political power, where society's functions become divided.[87]

Patent laws' evolution has attracted more and more regulation over the years in Europe in the form of treaties such as the EPC, the Biotech Directive, the amendment to the EPC and also the inclusion of patent law within a trading environment, epitomised in the TRIPS Agreement. The scope and subject matter have also become extended. New specialised courts are being set up. Von Savigny's ideas illuminate the extent to which the legislative process can become removed from society[88] and are of relevance to this book in the articulation of morality in public law and policy. In the US in the area of biotechnology patents, the legislature is underactive,[89] leaving important decision-making to the courts whereas in Europe, the courts and patent offices grapple with a concept of morality, the definition of which causes much disagreement.

Once the courts or legislatures of various jurisdictions act, the executive body in the form of patent offices simply administer and apply the law. In the US, in order to address this lacuna, it has been suggested by academics who think that there should be some consideration of morality, that Congress could restrict the enforcement of a granted patent on a case-by-case basis. An example is given of

84 Roger Cotterrell, *Sociology of Law* (Butterworths 1992).

85 When it was subsequently decided that, as parthenotes can commence but not culminate the process of development, they should not be classified as human embryos.

86 C-34/10 *Oliver Brüstle v Greenpeace eV* [2011] ECR I-9821.

87 Cotterrell, *op cit.*

88 Von Savigny did, of course, advocate a more common law approach which this book eschews but his views are useful in the critique they provide of bureaucratisation.

89 Smith, *op cit.*

government limits on the enforcement of medical process patents against medical practitioners.[90] Another way in which Congress could engage in regulating the issuance of patents in this area would be to have a pre-grant procedure to evaluate any potential ethical impact. It could oblige the USPTO to consult a designated evaluator, such as an ethics advisory committee, either within or outside of the USPTO. Then, if the applicant did not receive notice of an objection within a specified period of time, the patent would be granted.[91] Alternatively, Congress could assess the eligibility of a patent on an *ad hoc* basis. These measures could help enshrine the notion of government as being truly representative of the people, rather than the current patent system of governance by experts for whomsoever they choose to benefit,[92] in Bagley's view.

Despite the fact that biotech patent grants have often been controversial, the first draft of the Biotech Directive focused solely on harmonising the legal criteria for patentability, those being: novelty, inventive step and industrial application, without paying heed to ethical concerns which are, in essence, higher-order norms which must take precedence within the European legal system. A consideration and articulation of the hierarchy of norms should have been carried out and this was not done. Since the coming into force of the Lisbon Treaty, questions of morality framed in the discourse of human dignity, are beginning to permeate the jurisprudence of the CJEU.[93] The Biotech Directive predates the Lisbon Treaty and it distinguished inventions and discoveries. The former was considered patentable and the latter not, although isolated biological material which had been propagated independently would be patentable, even if genetically identical to its source material.[94] Even though there is more legislative guidance in Europe, the problem remains as to how to arbitrate the question of morality and of note is that of late, the CJEU has taken a proactive turn.

Negotiations over the introduction of the Biotech Directive took place over a ten-year period and many viewpoints were accommodated during this time. However, as Porter points out the inclusion of a morality clause to assuage controversies over patenting of biological materials has not managed to quell doubt and debate.[95] He also describes the different viewpoints: whereas the Commission's focus was commercial, the Parliament advised on ethical and moral issues and the Economic and Social Committee was concerned with ensuring that the human body would not be commercialised.[96] Subsequent cases have shown that the interpretation of various terms is not clear and several patent applications have been curtailed as potentially encompassing human beings.[97] Whilst much debate occurred, the forums are highly specialised and do not create much space for a

90 Bagley, *op cit* 535.
91 Ibid.
92 Ibid.
93 In the *Brüstle* case, for example.
94 Porter, in Plomer and Torremans, *op cit* 9.
95 Ibid 10, 11, 14.
96 Ibid.
97 Ibid 25.

public voice, education or understanding. Moreover, as Van Overwalle points out the Biotech Directive was the harbinger of the fact that patent law can now cover living matter.[98]

Regardless of extensive debate, the option of not extending patent protection to morally controversial biotechnological inventions was never really considered so a full range of options were not truly available. Whilst it is true that the European Parliament is a representative and democratically elected body of the European Union, it is the only one[99] and ultimately functions alongside the Commission, which initiates legislation and the Council with which it works in the co-decision-making procedure in the law-making process. Neither the Commission nor the Council are democratically elected. Citizens can petition Parliament through a citizens' initiative but the level of public input envisaged in this book is considerably more grassroots. Widespread public input, a model of which is elaborated in Chapter Five, could address this issue succinctly by utilising a more ground up approach, spearheaded by government ensuring an integration between publics and patent offices.

In the US, by way of contrast to the legislatively active European Union the legislature has largely left patent law to the courts. Despite the judges' stated wishes in *Diamond v Chakrabarty*[100] that Congress pass appropriate legislation, the legislature did not speak directly on the issue of patents on living matter. It did not explicitly exclude human beings from the scope of patentable subject matter under §101. Instead, politicians stepped in to restrict the patentability of human organisms through the appropriations power by enacting the Weldon Amendment which does not permit the use of federal funds, provided for the operation of the USPTO, to be used for the issuance of patents on human organisms. This has now been made a permanent part of the patent statute,[101] but up until 2011; this legislation had to be renewed every year. Statutory criteria could be drawn up to define what being human actually constitutes as no statutory or constitutional source currently provides a definition of humanity[102] and this matter is not necessarily self-evident.

Similar legislative inertia can be found in Europe in some instances, even though there is a much more developed legislative regime both within the EU and at the EPO. In the CJEU, the court, possibly echoing *Diamond v Chakrabarty*, stated in *R v Ministry of Agriculture, Fisheries and Food, ex p Compassion in World Farming*[103] that agricultural inventions may raise ethical issues not seen in other

98 Geertrui Van Overwalle, 'Legal and Ethical Aspects of Biopatenting' in Peter Drahos, *Death of Patents* (Lawtext Publishing 2005) 215.

99 European Parliament, at your service, http://www.europarl.europa.eu/atyourservice/en (accessed 5 March 2019).

100 *Diamond v Chakrabarty* [1980] 447 US 303.

101 Leahy-Smith America Invents Act 2011, Section 3.

102 Ryan Hagglund, 'Patentability of Human-Animal Chimeras' (2008) 25 Santa Clara Computer & High Tech LJ 51.

103 *R v Ministry of Agriculture, Fisheries and Food ex p Compassion in World Farming Ltd* Case C-1/96 [1998] ECR I-1251.

areas. These relate to whether it is acceptable to seek better agricultural practices and products through gene manipulation. The court observes that its task to interpret the legislation and as Parliament has not distinguished animate and inanimate inventions, neither would the court.[104]

Despite the court's exhortations, parliamentary intervention may not provide a better solution. Society's idea of morality changes over time and it is difficult to predict how long a particular moral stance will endure into the future, as Mills points out,[105] thereby suggesting that legislative enactments will fossilise rapidly. It is argued that policy should ebb and flow with the tide of informed public opinion and this book endeavours to construct a framework for how this may be actuated based on the political structures and underlying principles of participatory models, elaborated later in this book.

Even where detailed legislation is promulgated, Drahos claims that patent offices often alter the manner in which the system works by drawing up guidelines and through exercising a legislative function. This penchant stems from their constant interaction with patent applicants and the latter, many of which are large industries or public bodies, wield considerable influence in the patent process. Large patent offices employ thousands of officials who work much more closely with patent applicants than courts or legislatures.[106] Whilst patent examiners apply the law rather than making it, they are, nonetheless, the *de facto* gate keepers of the patent system. Even though courts may be the final arbiters of patent disputes, as the majority of patent grants are not challenged, the culture of the patent office in terms of how it interprets the statutes by which it is bound is significant. Large patent portfolios controlled by multinationals are accumulated through positive decisions taken by patent examiners. Moreover, dubious patents can be obtained easily but revoked with effort[107] and this tends to stack the system in favour of patent applicants, although it is also true that in Europe NGOs, such as Greenpeace are prominent actors. Specialised courts are likely to intensify any pro-patent disposition if, for instance, the CJEU does not retain its status as the court of final jurisdiction in patent matters. Pila and Wadlow speculate that it may not.[108]

Legislation may not be an appropriate means of reform for a variety of reasons, including the fact that morality may change and should, it is argued, be reflected in the law. Where a new technology is not well understood, laws could fossilise misunderstandings until they are repealed. Moreover, in a fast-moving area of technology, different moral concerns will surface regularly and legislation can ossify parameters that may later need to be altered. An absence of legislative clarity also causes problems because it then falls on patent officials to arbitrate what has not been defined. The legislative process itself can be fraught where different bodies representing various areas of expertise such as the European Commission,

104 Paragraph 93.
105 Mills, *op cit* 6.
106 Drahos, *The Global Governance of Knowledge*, 16.
107 Ibid 215.
108 Pila and Wadlow, *op cit* 23.

Parliament and Council are engaged in drafting: ethical issues may not receive equal consideration across the board. Courts often are desirous of a more active legislature but when legislation is passed, patent officials may negotiate around its parameters if their main contacts are patent applicants. As can be seen, more laws are not necessarily a good thing. Another avenue for reform is though the patent office which will now be examined.

2.5 Reform through the patent/intellectual property office

There is an inherent balance between public and private interests in patent law and the first place where this balance is tested is at intellectual property/patent offices. According to several writers, explored hereunder, this equilibrium is out of kilter for reasons which include lack of transparency, bias, funding, collaboration among different patent offices, lobbying, internationalisation of patent law, a failure to properly understand the technology and a discomfort in applying the morality provisions. This may lead to the granting of overly broad patents and consequently, the morality bar may not be given its due weight.

According to Drahos, patent offices have three main functions. The first is that they are obliged to make sure that a socially useful invention is produced; second, that information about the invention in the application is diffused, and; finally, ensuring that the patent system is entirely transparent to those likely to be affected by it.[109] He is sceptical whether this latter condition is widely observed and he denies that patents indicate clearly what is and what is not protected. In fact, he claims that the patent system may do just the opposite, given that intangible matter or information cannot easily be identified, regardless of the fact that patent drafting has become a highly skilled profession.[110] Warren-Jones also observes that the European patent system is susceptible to criticism that it is biased, given that the submissions of the patent holder are normally preferred to anyone or any group opposing the patent.[111] Patent offices tend to be pro-patent and are not likely to receive critical scrutiny favourably.[112] Yet they do owe duties to the public but in Drahos' view, these are not currently being honoured vigilantly.[113] Some of the reasons for this behaviour are now elaborated.

The manner in which patent offices are funded provides one of the principal incentives for cooperation with clients. When the examination process does not yield a patent, this signifies a monetary loss for the office in question as most patent offices are funded both through the application process and subsequent patent renewal fees. Organisations that get paid for services provided may often come to regard the one

109 *Op cit* 16.

110 Ibid.

111 Amanda Warren-Jones, 'Identifying European Moral Consensus: Why Are the Patent Courts Reticent to Accept Empirical Evidence in Resolving Biotechnological Cases?' (2006) 28 EIPR 26, 34.

112 Drahos, *The Global Governance of Knowledge: Patent Offices and Their Clients* (Cambridge University Press 2010) 142.

113 Ibid 289.

who pays as a client rather than an applicant whose rights must be balanced with potentially conflicting rights of the public. To view patent applicants as clients is a misconception on the part of patent offices which should not lose sight of their public service duty.[114] Collaboration among large businesses, patent attorneys and patent office officials may produce some insider governance of the patent system across a number of different bodies such as the Trilateral Offices club: an alliance between the USPTO, the EPO and the Japan Patent Office (JPO) and within World Intellectual Property Organization (WIPO) and the World Trade Organisation (WTO).[115] In Sell's account,[116] a lobby group known as the Intellectual Property Committee,[117] together with industry representatives in Europe and Japan devised a particular model of intellectual property rights to influence the Uruguay round of the TRIPS negotiations. Essentially, she says that the law in this domain was crafted by 12 corporations. Profit rather than morality is likely to be their motivator.

Kingston is critical of the extension of patent protection to biotechnological inventions, saying that before this action was taken, the matter should have been considered with more care. Patents may be unsuitable for biotechnology as given that the research is publicly funded, the public and private interest in the disclosure requirement in patent grants is difficult to calculate.[118] The slotting of biotechnological inventions into the patent provisions of Article 1.8.8 of the US Constitution has meant that a small number of private firms have managed to monopolise great swathes of development in the life sciences without ethical restrictions. The legislation has provided little restriction and courts have generally been favourable towards patent applicants. Kingston also observes that there is a striking contrast in the manner in which the Paris and Berne Conventions were formulated when compared with TRIPS. Whilst the former two Conventions featured the public good strongly in their drafting, TRIPS was the result of purely vested interests.[119] He also criticises the manner in which patents have been extended, noting that Article 118 of the Lisbon Treaty gives power to Brussels to create harmonised intellectual property rights within the EU.[120] The issue of the EU's reach in intellectual property law was challenged before the Lisbon Treaty's adoption, unsuccessfully, by the Netherlands[121] when the Biotech Directive was introduced and this judicial outcome has now been given legislative weight. How disputes may be resolved under the Lisbon Treaty is as yet unclear.

There is a perception among some academics that patents have been granted fairly easily and Waelde *et al* assert that broad patents are often granted on new

114 Ibid.
115 Ibid 177.
116 Sell, *op cit* 96.
117 This was a lobby group set up by 13 US corporations who lobbied for the introduction of a comprehensive agreement on intellectual property.
118 Kingston, *Beyond Intellectual Property* (Edward Elgar 2010) 132–133.
119 Ibid 111.
120 Ibid 160.
121 C-377/98 *Netherlands v Parliament and Council* [2001] ECR 1–070709 (at para 12).

technologies before they are properly understood.[122] Issues pertaining to morality may thus be swept aside in the drive to monopolise the development of new technologies. The significance of overly broad patents is described by Laurie who, in addition to identifying their injustice, explains that they may inhibit the development of drugs and therapeutic treatments or that said remedies may be too costly. This might have a negative effect on innovation.[123] The moral issue may not be entwined exclusively with the status of the embryo: some inventions are not deserving of patent protection as they do not fit within the relevant criteria, for other reasons. However, once patent grants proliferate, they can be difficult to rein in.[124] Patent applicants have incentives to make very broad claims and just because a given claim does not stand, the patent may still be granted in amended form at the very least, an example being *Harvard/Onco-Mouse* the patent on which was eventually granted after the breadth of the claim was reduced.[125]

The arbitration of morality may not be of prime concern where economic interests are so prominent yet it is a norm of higher ranking in the hierarchy of laws and thus its consideration is paramount and overarching. With the proposal for private arbitration in the Transatlatic Trade and Investment Partnership (TTIP), whether this agreement or other similar trade deals go ahead or not, consideration of the public interest was not at the forefront of negotiations. Yet despite an awareness in the academic literature of the need for institutional support,[126] commentary in relevant case law suggests that the publics' input is not of prime concern. In *Plant Genetic Systems*, the Technical Board of Appeal observed that it would not take into consideration the results of opinion polls or surveys any more than national laws which either sanctioned or failed to approve an invention's exploitation for the purposes of assessing ordre public or morality. It mattered not that a majority of people in all of the Contracting States opposed a patent grant on a specific subject matter.[127]

Enrobed in this dictum is the pervading notion that the views of Contracting States and their populations do not count, even if the views are in the majority across all states. It is as if the EPO's legitimacy does not emanate from its members so accountability and transparency do not trouble its judges unduly. Nor do they appreciate morality's hierarchical place in the administrative niceties of patenting. Patent offices are public bodies and as such are accountable ultimately to the publics. Whilst not downplaying the importance of other stakeholder interests and input, this book seeks to accommodate a plurality of views. Wheatley has observed that a deliberative model of governance confirms that the democratic legitimacy of laws is reliant on conversation between equal citizens within a

122 Waelde *et al*, *op cit* 507.
123 Laurie, *op cit* 64.
124 Bagley, *op cit*.
125 T0315/03 *Transgenic animals/HARVARD* of 6 July 2004.
126 Sheila Jasanoff, 'In the Democracies of DNA: Ontological Uncertainty and Political Order in Three States' (2005) 24 *New Genetics and Society* 139.
127 *Plant Genetic Systems v Greenpeace* [1995] EPOR 357.

voluntary constitutional order. However, this model does not provide a framework for where such a state sits within the international system.[128]

This statement indicates that decisions made on our behalf take place in a context that should represent a cross-section of interests. Arguably, the internationalisation of patenting morally controversial biotechnological inventions currently lacks structures to involve public voices. A challenge which will be faced by attempts to introduce significant deliberation into any system of law-making is the level at which it is proposed: whether national, regional or international. According to Cooke, where universal and binding legal, political and moral principles do not exist, such standards must be negotiated by the public through debate with the aim of providing the most convincing justification of particular laws or policies being proposed. Otherwise, citizens will not see themselves as the sources of such processes.[129] Where decisions on morality are likely to change in the future, it may be necessary to build structures into our systems of governance in order to ensure that as many viewpoints as possible get aired and that this happens at regular intervals. This book proposes to extend the reach of the public voice onto the international stage.

There is a strong presumption of patentability at the EPO which makes the morality bar's application unpredictable. Llewelyn and Adcock argue that morality only arises where the morality issue which the invention in question raises cannot be ignored or where a third party opposition is lodged.[130] It would seem from this that the threshold to the morality bar is set especially high, except perhaps where the human embryo is concerned. They also point out that the EPO seems to accept that a purported benefit outweighs any possible harm and the morality bar will only be applied where the only application of the invention is harmful.[131] Hence the exclusion will only operate in the rarest of circumstances. This implies that the balance between public or societal and private interests is not being maintained. Llewelyn observes that the presumption of patentability along with the patent holder's attendant rights permeate the process and she questions whether society's interests are being protected adequately by means of the exclusionary criteria in such a weighted system.[132]

There is often a strong presumption of patentability at patent offices due to issues of funding, industry lobbying, a failure to understand new technologies which leads to broad patents being granted and insider trading. The balance between private and public interests may be tipped unduly towards the former, leaving the issue of morality at the side-lines. Whilst there is an awareness of public voices, at present there is not a defined way for these to be expressed on a broad scale. Nonetheless, in many

128 Steven Wheatley, 'A Democratic Rule of International Law' (2011) 22 EJIL 525, 536.

129 Maeve Cooke, 'Five Arguments for Deliberative Democracy' in Maurizio Passerin D'Entrèves (ed) *Democracy as Public Deliberation* (Manchester University Press 2002) 65.

130 Llewelyn and Adcock, *op cit* 285.

131 Ibid.

132 Margaret Llewelyn, 'Schrodinger's Cat: An Observation on Modern Patent Law' in Drahos, *Death of Patents* 54.

jurisdictions, it is appreciated that morality has some role to play in aspects of biotechnological controversies. Having shown that judicial, legislative and remedies through the patent office are not appropriate frameworks for resolving morality, another option is to consider the establishment of various ethics committees. These could help to broaden the perspective of the gate keepers of the system to achieve a more rounded approach in accommodating a plurality of views. It is instructive to examine the actions of a range of such committees to assess whether they may promote some input into reform.

2.6 Ethics committees

Given that biotechnology spans a multidisciplinary field, it has become common in recent years to establish ethics committees in an advisory role across a range of public sector bodies and in legislation, although such developments are not universal. Several articles of the Universal Declaration on Bioethics and Human Rights mention the importance of ethics committees and public education.[133] UNESCO has approved of this development, providing procedural guides for their establishment and management.[134,135,136] The World Health Organisation is another such body,[137] along with the EU which established the European Group on Ethics in Science and New Technologies (EGE) in 1991.[138] The roles of such committees are largely evaluative, educative and consultative and mostly, engagement is optional. Moreover, the range of their deliberations tends to be narrow, depending, of course, on their brief. Nonetheless, their incarnations differ from place to place. Patents and related issues of morality are one of many matters they will debate, if requested. It is arguable that their role will need to be increased in line with the constitutionalisation of morality in patent law which is being observed in recent cases at the EPO[139] and the CJEU.[140] Ethics committees are also

133 Articles 19, 22 and 23.
134 UNESCO 'Establishing Bioethics Committees. Guide No 1' (2005) SHS?BIO-2005/01, http://unesdoc.unesco.org/images/0013/001393/139309e.pdf (accessed 5 March 2019).
135 UNESCO Bioethics Committees at Work: Procedures and Policies. Guide No 2 (2005), https://www.google.ie/search?q=UNESCO+%E2%80%9CEstablishing+Bioethics+Committees.+Guide+No+1%E2%80%9D+(2005)+SHS%3FBIO-2005/01&ie=utf-8&oe=utf-8&gws_rd=cr&ei=fmurVbWOH42u7AaTw4DIBg#q=UNESCO+%E2%80%9CBioethics+Committees+at+Work:+Procedures+and+Policies.+Guide+No+2%E2%80%9D+(2005)+SHS%2FBIO-2005%2F10 (accessed 5 March 2019).
136 Educating Bioethics Committees 2007, http://unesdoc.unesco.org/images/0015/001509/150970e.pdf (accessed 5 March 2019).
137 WHO Operational Guidelines for Ethics Committees That Review Biomedical Research, https://www.google.ie/search?q=UNESCO+%E2%80%9CEstablishing+Bioethics+Committees.+Guide+No+1%E2%80%9D+(2005)+SHS%3FBIO-2005/01&ie=utf-8&oe=utf-8&gws_rd=cr&ei=fmurVbWOH42u7AaTw4DIBg#q=WHO+%E2%80%9COperational+Guidelines+for+Ethics+Committees+That+Review+Biomedical+Research (accessed 5 March 2019).
138 https://ec.europa.eu/research/ege/index.cfm (accessed 5 March 2019).
139 G2/06 *WARF/Stem Cells* [2009] EPOR 15.
140 C-34/10 *Oliver Brüstle v Greenpeace eV* [2011] ECR I-9821.

involved in deliberating over ethical issues related to biotechnological inventions. Their role will now be described and assessed from the perspective of whether they can facilitate the inclusion of public voices in a pluralistic society.

An example of the use of ethics committees in the EU can be seen in Article 7 of the Biotech Directive which provides that the EGE evaluates all ethical aspects of biotechnology. The group is independent, pluralist and multidisciplinary and is composed of 15 experts appointed by the Commission both for expertise and personal qualities.[141] Ironically, however, Plomer notes that this is a committee of experts with no requirement for professional expertise in ethics.[142] The group is loosely linked to the legislative process but legislators are not bound by any of the information which it receives and therefore the nexus between the knowledge produced and its implementation or influence is, at best, tenuous.

However, some consultation with ethics committees could be facilitated. Warren-Jones states that currently consultation with the European Group on Ethics (EGE) in accordance with Recital 44 of the Biotech Directive in order to identify basic moral principles may occur. She does not believe, though, that this expert panel is perceived as being truly representative of the publics and, therefore, this voice is absent. She views this as an unjustified paternalism.[143] They could be called upon to help to identify patent applications which trigger the morality bar when it is unclear especially where no precedent has been established. Warren-Jones argues that the decision should ultimately be left to the publics but an ethics committee would be very valuable in identifying novel ethical issues that engage Article 53(a) EPC. Even where the group has been consulted – and such consultation is not mandated – its advice may not be followed. For instance, in the *Edinburgh* patent[144] the EPO followed a minority view of the EGE's Opinion No. 16, rather than that of the majority. This unpredictability and *ad hoc* approach does not encourage confidence in the role held and exercised by the committee.

The EGE produced an opinion in 2002 on the 'Ethical aspects of patenting inventions involving human stem cells', in which they postulated that ethical evaluations may need to be made where a patent application which raises specific ethical issues is being examined. Such evaluation should be routinised as part of review processes at national or European patent offices and should be conducted by panels of independent experts.[145]They also engaged with the question of what should be patented and what should be accessible through open access. In Recommendation 17, they urged the EPO and national patent offices to pay heed to Article 7 of the Biotech Directive and to engage with the committee when ethical issues arose. Without empirical research on this area it is difficult to know the extent of their influence or the outcome, if any, of their recommendations.

141 https://ec.europa.eu/research/ege/index.cfm (accessed 5 March 2019).

142 Aurora Plomer, 'The European Group on Ethics: Law, Politics and the Limits of Moral Integration in Europe' [2008] 14(6) ELR 843.

143 Warren-Jones, 'Identifying European Moral Consensus', *op cit* 27.

144 European Patent No. EP 0695351.

145 European Group on Ethics in Science and New Technologies, http://ec.europa.eu/european_group_ethics/docs/avis16_en.pdf (accessed 5 March 2019).

Such committees may have the potential to embed a multidisciplinary approach to ethically fraught issues. Busby *et al* opine that the EGE is very influential in the EU and often acts as a broker between various stakeholders in biotechnology.[146] Nonetheless, as already observed, consultation is optional and opinions are often sidelined or ignored. Some of their interpretations are not well regarded and it has been observed that where they have spoken about values such as respect for human life or dignity, they do not seek to ground their principles in a particular philosophy[147] or, indeed, legal text. This suggests that their opinions are unpredictable. Plomer has written critically about the infiltration of patent law by abstract concepts of human rights which does not help to address public concern about biotechnological inventions.[148] So ethics committees may not help to define morality any better than other bodies although better results could be yielded using different methodologies. Moreover, the membership seems to be *ad hoc*. Should there be representatives for people with specific genetic illnesses or based on ethnicity, age, gender, occupation, class and so on? All members must have a university degree. Does that mean that non-university educated people should not arbitrate on matters of morality in patent law?

Porter identifies another committee, albeit not in the field of ethics, with influence in Community decision-making: the Economic and Social Committee.[149] In contrast with the EGE, this committee purports to represent organised civil society, including interest groups such as farmers, trade-unionists, workers and members of the public in general. Its role is consultative and though members are appointed and consulted by the Council, the Commission may also seek its advice. The Committee criticised the first draft of the Biotech Directive, claiming that all issues had not been addressed, especially the implications for commodification of human beings,[150] albeit during a different context of the legislative process. This is an example of how opinions proffered by committees are often not taken into account by decision-making bodies. This is a form of deliberation in a vacuum as it does not appear to have much influence over patent law or practices. Moreover, I argue that deliberation should have a deeper reach than organised civil society. Disadvantage, disability and other factors can impede participation and endeavours to involve the public should, I shall argue, be more proactive and profound.

Petit cautions that national ethics committees can come to wield an unwarranted authoritative voice which can result in the institution acquiring a normative influence. This could be especially troubling if the basis of their opinions or advice is not clear. Ethics committees lack the democratic legitimacy[151] which vests in the legislative body

146 Helen Busby, Tamara Hervey and Alison Mohr, 'Ethical EU Law? The Influence of the European Group on Ethics in Science and New Technologies' [2008] 33(6) ELR 803, 835.

147 AM Viens, in Plomer and Torremans, *op cit* 90–91.

148 Aurora Plomer, 'Human Dignity and Patents' in Christophe Geiger (ed.) *Research Handbook of Human Rights and IP Rights* (Edward Elgar, 2014).

149 Gerard Porter, in Plomer and Torremans, *op cit* 18.

150 (1989) OJ C159/10.

151 The aim of this book is to devise a model which facilitates participation due to the perceived weaknesses of representation in the area of morality of biotechnological patent grants. Ethics committees as bodies set up to handle such decision-making would be even further removed from the democratic process. They are not elected, so

and the former's voice should not outweigh the democratic mandate of the latter. They may morph from a group offering general advice into one which issues decrees.[152] Such an evolution would go some way to eroding the boundary between church and state, albeit in a nominally secular environment. However, experience would tend to suggest that ethics committee voices are more likely to be ignored than to dominate.

In terms of establishing a pluralistic model in which morality can be arbitrated, the Universal Declaration on Bioethics and Human Rights 2005 mandates governments to educate their citizenry about bioethical issues and to set up ethics committees. Of course, it is only binding if ratified. The following articles are of relevance. Article 19 recommends the establishment of ethics committees which should assess and advise on a plurality of issues which arise from research involving human subjects. Moreover, they should encourage debate, public awareness, education and participation in matters concerning bioethics.

So this Declaration envisages a proactive approach from the government. It goes on to talk about the role states can play which is to facilitate the establishment of such ethics committees.

Ethics committees are consulted regularly on a variety of issues, according to Drahos who acknowledges that this often occurs whether they specialise in policy or adopt an advisory role.[153] However, he also says that such committees are often heavily influenced by big business and the patent attorney profession.[154] Ethics committees are not necessarily drawn from relevant university departments and other representation may be only token. As pointed out earlier, identification of appropriate membership is likely to be problematic.

The issue of delegation of decision-making powers to experts in this area is contentious. Snead claims that public officials have assigned important bioethical issues to be decided by a small group of experts and that this raises issues regarding accountability and legitimacy. This is due to the fact that science is perceived as an objective form of reasoning and its conclusions enjoy a standing in society which is lacking in other sources of knowledge. However, an ethical claim made by means of scientific reasoning, in his view, devalues the public sphere. When ethical concepts are sidelined in debates about biotechnology, values held dear by humankind may be diluted. This could include our conceptualisations of equality, justice, beneficence, autonomy, or even our definition of persons. In such an environment, he questions the roles of science, medicine, government and law and observes that as modern science provides no answers, it is tempting to ignore these questions altogether.[155]

Meaning can be reintroduced to such concepts through broadening the decision-making process across society. Ethics committees where they exist can, of course, discuss salient issues but the outcomes of their discussions tend not to feed

from a procedural perspective would not be satisfactory substitute. Their decisions may or may not fall foul of criteria of output legitimacy.

152 Eliode Petit, 'An Ethics Committee for Patent Offices' in Plomer and Torremans 313.

153 Drahos, *The Global Governance of Knowledge* 294.

154 Ibid.

155 Snead, *op cit* 1587–1591.

back into the legislative or judicial processes. Feyerabend observes that scientists have exerted a huge influence over Western Democracy. They reluctantly accept that competing ideas may be voiced but do not allow them any responsibility in the establishment of institutions such as law, education or economics.[156]

This section shows the difficulties which inhere in trying to accommodate a plurality of view on morality even where committees are set up to consider contentious issues. Unless opposing views are listened to and taken on board in a deliberative setting, consultation may prove to be a futile exercise or simply a tokenistic gesture.

2.6.1 National committees

At national level, ethics committees experience a similar status as described above. The Norwegian Patent Act[157] obliges the Norwegian Intellectual Property Office to consult with the ethics committee if there is uncertainty as to whether commercial exploitation would offend the morality and public ordre provisions of the Act. Nonetheless, Hellstadius claims that they declined to follow a recommendation of its ethics committee that a patent not be granted for genetically modified salmon some years ago.[158] In addition to ignoring the recommendations, the Office often does not refer applications to the Committee. Even where there is a referral, establishing which ethics model to follow is most difficult.[159]

Sweden has adopted an approach where the government has obliged courts and patent officials to seek out further particulars and reports on ethical matters. Legislation has been put in place to ethically review research on humans before examination[160] and this is carried out by ethics committees.[161] If it is decided that the research is ethically sound, the Swedish Patent Office does not engage in further deliberations as to morality and the patent will be granted. If, on the other hand, the research is not so deemed, then, in all likelihood, a patent will be denied.[162] Especially fraught ethical issues in European patent law tend to focus around inventions involving destruction of the human embryo[163] and EU

156 Paul Feyerabend, *Science in a Free Society* (NLB 1978) 144.

157 Section 15a, Cf Section 25, Third Paragraph of the Patents Act 1967, https://www.etikkom.no/en/library/topics/the-researchsocietal-relationship/research-ethics-and-patents/ (accessed March 2019).

158 Norwegian Patent No 321650, 19 June 2006.

159 Robert Brownsword, 'Ethics and Patenting: A Report for the Norwegian Advisory Board on Ethical Aspects of Patenting', in *Patentnemnd uten portefølje? En analyse av etiske utfordringer ved patentering* (Oslo 2008) 75, available at http://www.etikkom.no/HvaGjorVi/Publikasjoner/patent) in Åsa Hellstadius, 'A Comparative Analysis of the National Implementation of the Directive's Morality Clause' in Plomer and Torremans, 131, footnote 93.

160 The Act on Genetic Integrity (Lag om genetisk integritet m.m.2006:351), ibid, footnote 96.

161 Act on Ethics Review of Research Involving Humans, Lag om etikprövning som avser människor (2003: 460), ibid, footnote 98.

162 Åsa Hellstadius in Plomer and Torremans, 132.

163 Whereas animals and plants, whilst still causing some controversy, are patented more easily.

members are bound by the Biotech Directive which, as noted already, is becoming constitutionalised in its interpretation in that moral considerations are permeating the patent realm more frequently. The Swedish approach effectively signifies a shift in the moral decision-making from patent officials to an ethics committee. It could be argued that this is a positive step in that expertise in ethics is more abundant in such committees and this will depend on how they are set up. Training is available in ethical issues for some ethics committees[164] and ethics training is available across a multitude of sectors by organisations such as the Institute for Global Ethics.[165] Ethics and bioethics committees often produce detailed guidance themselves on composition and training.[166] More specifically, other resources include the Declaration of Helsinki 1964 which is a set of principles developed by the World Medical Association in relation to human experimentation and is directed towards the medical community. However, at times committees' membership can be random and may be hand-picked, depending on how they are constituted. This can create imbalances. MacDonald acknowledges that ethicists can become *de facto* secular priests in interpreting texts and can also come to work closely with corporations, which may be compromising.[167] The practice in Sweden appears to signify a shift in power and discipline from one elite groups of experts to another.

Other jurisdictions' approaches vary, many having also established ethics committees to adopt an advisory role in relation to biotechnology. In France, for example, the national ethics committee is called the Comite Consultatif National d'Ethique and its remit is to opine on both ethical and societal problems which science is raising. It is composed of 39 members, 5 of whom must represent the major philosophical and spiritual issues in French society. These areas are evolving especially quickly, however and members may have difficulty keeping up with such rapid change. The other members are chosen for their knowledge and skills in scientific, ethical, legal and social matters. Its influence was specifically recognised during the parliamentary debates on the first bioethics laws of 1994 when reference was made to the weight of the Committee's opinions in the formation of the legislative principles.[168] This is an example of a limited exercise in deliberative democracy's role in facilitating input into these decisions, because the deliberators come from multidisciplinary backgrounds, although it is somewhat technocratic. It is nonetheless fairly limited and the extent of its representation of the public in general is unclear. The knowledge being disseminated and decided upon is still

164 I sit on the Research Ethics Committee at the National University of Ireland, Galway and we have an optional yearly training.

165 Institute for Global Ethics, https://www.globalethics.org (accessed 5 March 2019).

166 Irish Council for Bioethics, *Operational Procedures for Research Ethics Committees: Guidance 2004* (2004), http://health.gov.ie/wp-content/uploads/2014/07/Operational_Procedures1.pdf (accessed 5 March 2019).

167 Chris MacDonald, 'Will The "Secular Priests" of Bioethics Work among the Sinners?' (2003) 3 *American Journal of Bioethics* 36.

168 Thérèse Callus, 'Patient Perception of the Human Fertilisation and Embryology Authority' (2007) 15 Med LR 62.

highly specialised – as are its experts. Moreover, in an increasingly diverse country and a rapidly changing ethical frontier, are national values set in stone, who gets to decide what constitute these values and how can these views be facilitated?

France has also appointed a species of legal decision-makers which have been designated as technocrats[169] and they play a role similar to that of expert witnesses in court rooms. They receive specialist training in an array of disciplines, including science, mathematics, economics, law, decision theory, and administration. They are especially well trained in science. With such a high level of expertise, their decisions may be very far removed from society's concerns and the group is also very small. In any case, Smith believes that the system does not differ greatly from the US where judges and juries would make decisions in the same terrain.[170] Moreover, the US patent appeals court is now widely acknowledged to have built up a body of precedent and of scientific knowledge and expertise, perhaps rendering such attempts at multi-disciplinarity redundant. In other jurisdictions there may be little state regulation, such as in Finland. Alternatively, nation states may set up committees such as the federal President's Bioethics Committee in the United States. All such endeavours operate only on a very small scale.

Engelbrekt[171] acknowledges the positive aspects of participation but a potential disadvantage of such inclusion is that decision-making processes may be affected. This could lead to judicial bodies becoming susceptible to political pressure. Nonetheless, it has been observed that the CAFC in the US, which handles all patent appeal cases, is decidedly pro-patent, meaning that judicial bodies' inclinations may need to be rebalanced.[172] Despite the presence of ethical advisory committees within the European Union, the EPO lacks such structures – a point noted in Opinion No. 16 of the EGE, above. *Amicus curiae* briefs are used instead.[173] Such a model of participation is limited and may not reflect public opinion accurately. Opposition and appeal procedures may assuage somewhat the apparent lack of legitimacy and accountability of the EPO's institutions but Engelbrekt distinguishes between influence which may be exerted on judicial decision-making and engagement in the legislative process, saying that the two do not equate.

Whereas European states may also adopt a model based on a national ethics advisory committee, which deliberates on broad ethical questions, these do not exist in all countries. Ireland, for instance, disbanded its Council for Bioethics in the wake of funding constraints in 2010.[174] The extent to which the establishment of an ethics committee would affect the current operation of patent systems may

169 Smith, *op cit* 106.
170 Ibid.
171 Antonina Bakardjieva Engelbrekt, 'Institutional and Jurisdictional Aspects of Stem Cell Patenting in Europe (EC and EPO): Tensions and Prospects' in Aurora Plomer and Paul Torremans (eds), *Embryonic Stem Cell Patents: European Patent Law and Ethics* (OUP 2009) 252.
172 Mills, *op cit* 45.
173 Engelbrekt, in Plomer and Torremans, *op cit* 253.
174 http://bioethics.academy.ac.il/english/links/ireland.html (accessed 5 March 2019).

be overstated. True engagement in matters of such importance may not be addressed adequately by tinkering along the fringes of the organs of government, whether it be by expert ethical input or *amicus curiae* briefs.

2.6.2 Other committees

The establishment and management of ethics committees is not without some detractors. Their existence manifests a possible interference in the smooth running of the separate branches of government. The selection of their members can be somewhat opaque, their expertise is highly specialised but they may lack expertise in law, science and economics.

Callus gives an example of where the public may not feel represented by an expert group set up to manage ethical concerns. The Human Fertilisation and Embryology Authority has 18 members, which include 7 clinicians, infertile patients, a religious representative, a philosopher, a lawyer, a broadcaster and financial consultants. In a MORI Report commissioned by the Office of Science and Technology in April 1999, entitled 'Public Consultation on Developments in the Biosciences', it was found that the public would trust an advisory body to a government made up of people representing different viewpoints and that such a body should be involved in decision-making.[175] In another poll conducted in 2005,[176] there was a desire to be included in decisions but a public perception that government neither engaged with nor informed the population about scientific developments. There is, therefore, a considerable disjuncture between a minimal, delegated deliberative engagement by the government and the kind of representation publics may desire in such situations, were they better informed. Moreover, such models are very small-scale and do not normally include representatives from all possible groups of citizens in their remit. Housewives, carers and the unemployed are often notable omissions. Whilst elite democrats would argue for their exclusion, this book seeks to establish a model whereby participation is open to all.

2.7 Conclusion

The judicial and legislative process, along with patent offices and ethics committees have been shown to be unsatisfactory to resolve the arbitration of morality for many reasons, elucidated above, especially if the critique is emanating from a failure to include meaningfully public voices. Judges have few tools in new technological realms, especially ones which are imbued with moral concerns. Legislative solutions can fossilise the law unduly and, in any case, legislatures tend to draft

175 Callus, *op cit* 62.

176 'Science in Society', Conducted for the Office of Science and Technology, Dept. of Trade and Industry, March 2005, 93–95, https://www.gov.uk/government/uploads/system/uploads/attachment_data/file/260670/bis-05-1038-science-in-society-research.pdf (accessed 5 March 2019).

scantily where new technologies are being regulated in the patent realm. Patent offices administer the law but where it is unclear, such as in the case of the definition of morality and ordre public in the EPC, they are hindered in their ability to carry out their task. Ethics committees, as elucidated above, would not facilitate widespread inclusion and would instead merely extend a little the ambit of who gets to decide. This chapter has shown that traditional seats of reform are inadequate to address issues of morality in patent law. The next chapter will explore the calls for inclusion of public voices through deliberative democracy and will examine this largely in a theoretical framework.

3 Decision-making in morally controversial biotechnological patent applications

3.1 Introduction

The first two substantive chapters of this study charted the growing role that morality plays in patent law and the unsatisfactory nature of the manner in which it is arbitrated. Legal devices such as legislative, judicial or patent office reform, as a means of resolution, were explored and found wanting. It was noted that there is some academic literature which alludes to a perceived need for more public involvement without specifying what form it could take. Such literature will be explored in this chapter in a theoretical context and in the next chapter in a practical manifestation. Models of popular input will be scrutinised to aid arbitration over questions of morality in patent applications as enshrined in Article 53(a) European Patent Convention (EPC) 1973 (as amended). These questions relate to the use of the patent system to incentivise or disincentivise various technological inventions.

The first part of this chapter will identify some academic recommendations for more public participation in biotechnological decision-making and patents and will show that such claims can be grounded in existing human rights instruments. The human right to participate, in particular, can be invoked to justify democratic exemplars such as initiatives, recalls and referendums. The reform envisaged in this book goes much further than simply affirmative or negative votes on a proposition and instead incorporates deliberation and public debate into the participatory decision-making process. Participation will not be limited to referendums. This will seek to ensure that patent officials become better educated about ethical matters; the publics about the patent system and its incentives, and; politicians about enshrining information and transparency into their practices and communication to the publics. The book will then define deliberative democracy, examine it in depth and deal with its critics before studying participation in practice in Chapter Four. This will lead into Chapter Five which draws participation and patents together into a blueprint for reform.

3.2 Academic calls for more public involvement in biotech patents

There is a small body of academic literature in law which recommends that there be more public involvement in decision-making on issues of morality when patenting biotechnological inventions.[1] It is sometimes argued that morality should not permeate patent law at all and that if we allow certain inventions to be created, then they should be patentable. However, some of the ethical qualms in the creation of the invention and in its subsequent patenting differ. We might wish to sanction research with public funds but reject incentivising the same research through the patent system which involves monopolies and property rights. Mills recommends more discussion and debate on both aspects and this should include social negotiation on the regulatory role the law can play in technological development and application if there are to be benefits for humankind.[2] He acknowledges that morality is enmeshed with the technological creation and is therefore problematic in the patent system, which concerns itself with protecting the technology once in existence. If patents are opposed on moral grounds, this research may be stymied due to a dearth of incentives. Nonetheless, the morality bar in Article 53(a) EPC is a higher ranking norm[3] and so an option to disapply it is not lawful.

In Crespi's view, in order for the discussion about the human embryo and patents to continue, we need to refer to a set of principles which enjoy widespread societal acceptance[4] and the examination of the case law in this book in Chapter One has shown that at present, such decisions are not based on such principles but instead are made on an *ad hoc* basis. There is no consistent reference point to define morality. Wells goes so far as to recommend that decisions regarding the use of genetic material and the ethics of patenting living organisms should be taken in a manner which encompasses the viewpoints of all interested people. He says that this can be achieved most effectively with a participatory decision-making process.[5] He also recommends that the government 'should restructure patent mechanisms so as to increase public participation in the decision-making process'.[6] No specific model is proposed, however and this gap is bridged later in this book.

There are, of course, rules which allow access to the patent decision-making process by non-governmental organisations (NGOs) and an array of political groupings and these are a conduit for different ethical views, already examined in Chapter Two. Moreover, the European Patent Office (EPO) acknowledges that it should enter into an enquiry as to whether patenting an invention is immoral or contrary to ordre public,[7] but they do not articulate how this can be achieved.

1 These include writings in this chapter by Bagley, Burk, Callus, Crespi, Derclaye, Darnovsky, Drahos, Harmon, Mills, Petit, Plomer, Ponet and Leib, Rogers, Smith, Torremans, Warren-Jones and Wells.
2 Oliver Mills, Biotechnological Inventions: Moral Restraints and Patent Law (Revised edn, Routledge 2010) 10.
3 As acknowledged by Sterckx and Cockbain and Treitel, p. 60.
4 R Stephen Crespi, 'The Human Embryo and Patent Law: A Major Challenge Ahead?' (2006) 28 EIPR, 575.
5 Angus J Wells, 'Patenting New Life Forms: An Ecological Perspective' (1994) 16 EIPR 111, 117.
6 Ibid 117–118.
7 Estelle Derclaye, 'Patent Law's Role in the Protection of the Environment: Re-Assessing Patent Law and Its Justifications in the 21st Century' [2009] 40(3) IIC 249, 260.

They are conscious of the existence of public voices but have no means of discovering where public opinion reaches an overwhelming consensus[8] for instance. Reliance on referendums to gauge public opinion is eschewed because it is believed that public opinion would inhibit inventive development. Mills urges the construction of an appropriate legal framework to accommodate and promote legitimate and accountable decision-making. In the absence of such parameters, patent attorneys cannot know clearly the legal and moral restraints.[9] Putting this matter to a mediated public debate and decision-making process will not lend predictability to the results but at least it will create a public space where a plurality of viewpoints can be advanced. Drahos[10] and Bagley[11] note that patent attorneys wield significant power in ensuring that patent grants are successful to the detriment of views that should be acknowledged. In addition to seeking internationally harmonized legislation, Mills sees it as the role of states to achieve consensus on the accommodation of morality within the patent system. This could be worked out through public deliberation. As its place is not currently clear, examiners' capacities to adjudicate on these matters are undermined.[12] If deliberation is to be included in the arbitration of morality in the patent sphere, different models will need to be explored and some will now be considered.

3.3 Different ways to facilitate public involvement

Some alternative approaches to the traditional ways of challenging decision-making which encourage inclusion will now be explored. Such devices can involve the provision of legal aid, or the creation of statutory bodies, ombudsmen, and commissions. These could oversee certain aspects of public policy and sponsor legal challenges in the public interest and this could further equality in this field.[13] It may also be worth exploring additional ways of institutionalising debate which may serve to improve the connections between the interested parties and legislative drafters by way of providing feedback for further legislation.[14]

Traditionally, contestation has taken place through the courts, but given the prohibitive costs, this hardly affords all citizens an equal opportunity to challenge public policy. When contemplating the introduction of deliberative devices, expense is a significant factor. The costs of mounting opposition proceedings at the EPO are also significant both in terms of economics and time. However, it could also be cost prohibitive to conduct polls on a case-by-case basis on issues of morality for each new

8 *In Re Howard Florey Institute-Relaxin*, [1995] EPOR 541.
9 Mills, *op cit* 2.
10 Peter Drahos, *The Global Governance of Knowledge: Patent Offices and Their Clients* (Cambridge University Press 2010) 215.
11 Margo A Bagley, 'Patent First, Ask Questions Later: Morality and Biotechnology in Patent Law' (2003) 45 WM & Mary L Rev 469.
12 Mills, *op cit* 81–82.
13 Cillian McBride, 'Reason, Representation and Participation' (2007) 13 *Res Publica* 171, 188.
14 Ibid.

invention, according to Warren-Jones. Nonetheless, she believes that there should at least be an endeavour to involve the publics in the decision-making process.[15] Some writers advocate the inclusion of empirical evidence to counter the perception that moral decision-making under the EPC is not objective[16] while others emphasise the importance of ensuring that citizens do not have to incur too much expense or expend too much time, as this can discourage voluntary participation.[17] Furthermore, cognitive access is equally important as physical access and the use of technical and professional terminology can be a deterrent, if such data is not explained adequately. This can be done by way of summaries which simplify the information[18] and the provisions on education in the Universal Declaration on Bioethics and Human Rights 2005 can also be employed as guiding principles, as explored later in this chapter. This legal instrument is used as an example as it encourages states to educate the population as well as facilitating deliberation and participation in the area of bioethics. Its ambit is also broad and encompasses morally controversial patents on biotechnological inventions.[19]

Citizens can also play their part and get motivated to become informed about matters that concern them, in McBride's view. The knowledge that they gain in such an exercise can be fed back into the public sphere to enhance deliberative content. He suggests that a device for triggering legislative review on any issue of concern could be established and this could involve formal, public, deliberative engagement between the publics and interest groups. Such processes could be initiated by way of popular petition and this would give publics the first step, rather than ceding this power to political elites. This could encourage legislators to ensure that their policies align with public views in order to ward off the triggering of such a process. This would go some way towards abating political dominance.[20]

In a strong judicial endorsement of citizen engagement, in 2015 the US Supreme Court in *Arizona State Legislature v Arizona Independent Redistricting Commission*,[21] ruled that direct legislation, embodied in democratic devices of the initiative and the referendum allows voters to engage in the legislative process as equal parties with their elected representatives. The initiative is a process whereby citizens can initiate legislation which is approved or rejected by a popular vote, and the court affirmed that this entitles citizens to initiate the proposal of statutes or amendments to the constitution which can then be voted on.[22] The court also

15 Amanda Warren-Jones, 'Identifying European Moral Consensus: Why Are the Patent Courts Reticent to Accept Empirical Evidence in Resolving Biotechnological Cases?' (2006) 28 EIPR 26, 28.

16 Drahos, 'Biotechnology Patents, Markets and Morality', *op cit* 444–446.

17 Yuhong Zhao, 'Public Participation in China's EIA Regime: Rhetoric or Reality?' (2010) 22(1) JEL 105.

18 Ibid.

19 I am involved in the UNESCO bioethics research group at NUG Galway.

20 McBride, *op cit* 188.

21 *Arizona State Legislature v Arizona Independent Redistricting Commission* 576 US, 135 S Ct 2652 (2015).

22 Quoting David B Magleby, *Direct Legislation: Voting on Ballot Propositions in the United States* (Johns Hopkins University Press 1984).

acknowledged that several states had incorporated direct law-making as well as retaining their representative legislative function.[23] The court also referred to the fact that the people are the source of all powers of government and the latter's authority derives from the people.[24] This might be indicative of a forthcoming trend in government and governance and this case signifies a top-down approval of the citizen's role in their own governance: a right to participate.

This chapter has sought, so far, to show that there is a quest among some academics to facilitate more public involvement in the biotechnological patenting process and that the current mechanisms are fairly limited. There are tentative suggestions as to which devices could be utilised and approval of the idea that the law-making function ultimately emanates from the people has been endorsed by the US Supreme Court. Deliberative participation may not just be desirable but is also feasible.

The next sections define participatory and deliberative practices showing that human rights instruments lend some weight to academic calls for more grassroots involvement in decisions of magnitude. It shows that deliberation can be slotted into a human rights framework of participation so that it becomes broad-based rather than narrow and elitist. This bridge forms part of the original contribution to knowledge of this book.

3.4 Participation defined

3.4.1 The human right to participate

Participation in democracy is a right which derives from human rights instruments such as the Universal Declaration of Human Rights. Article 21 enshrines the right to participate directly in government rather than solely through representatives. Participation gives citizens a chance to have an input into decisions which affect them and outcomes with which they do not agree become more palatable when they see that their contribution has been meaningful and not just cosmetic.[25] Participatory democracy rests on broad-based public education and knowledge. Education of a dedicated citizenry is one of a number of factors which is favourable to the success of democratic participation.[26] As we shall see, however, some models work better than others and this chapter will assess and critique different paradigms based on the extent to which they facilitate participation that actually feeds into policy-making and laws.

The impact of public participation varies greatly according to whether or not it is truly meant to affect policy. It has been divided into three categories by Arnstein. The first – non-participation – involves no more than a public relations

23 576 US, 135 S Ct 2652 (2015) 20.

24 576 US, 135 S Ct 2652 (2015) 24, 31.

25 Karl Rogers, *Participatory Democracy, Science and Technology* (Palgrave Macmillan 2008) 28–29.

26 Ibid 116.

exercise which is organised to garner support for a decision already taken and can involve changing public opinions through education or manipulation. The second category – tokenism – allows for a limited participation by the publics involving provision of information with an opportunity for the voicing of public opinions, which affects final decisions very little – if at all. The final category – citizen power – is the most influential and involves the capacity to negotiate and to veto government decisions.[27] It is this last model of citizen involvement that is a guiding principle in the context of deciding on patent grants on morally controversial biotechnological inventions because the participation translates into policy.

Nonetheless, there has been a common perception since Rousseau that democracy is either direct, where the publics vote directly on issues or representative, where politicians are elected and take decisions, ostensibly on behalf of the electorate, with nothing in between.[28] The latter has been described as a "pale imitation" of the former but reform of our institutions may be influenced by direct democracy. Representative democracy is likely to be here to stay but we can at least endeavour to adopt some features of direct democracy:[29] it does not have to be all or nothing. Rousseau's definition of direct democracy required citizens to assemble in a given venue to make decisions, whereas modern referendums can enable citizens to vote directly without having to converge in a specific place. Assembly would be challenging in modern democracies but referendums may co-exist with representative bodies[30] as is increasingly the practice. In any case, some countries are increasing the use of referendums on a broader range of issues than heretofore.

In general most people do not engage in participatory democracy as they do not have the chance to do so – representative democracy does not offer it to them. While thinkers such as Habermas encourage the creation of a vibrant public sphere for debate, he does not delineate in detail how this feeds into the decision-making process.[31] Rogers believes that until space has been created in which participation becomes viable, the current democratic deficit will not change. Society will not become more democratic and the technological imperative will continue to dominate societal evolution.[32] This may affect possibilities for involving the publics in decisions such as morally controversial patent grants. He says that democratic participation can only occur in the course of a struggle to democratise society in which the public take the initiative instead of waiting for politicians and technocrats handing it to them.[33]

27 Sherry R Arnstein, 'A Ladder of Citizen Participation' (1969) 35 *Journal of the American Institute of Planners* 216, 216.
28 McBride, *op cit* 171.
29 Ibid.
30 Ibid 172–173.
31 Habermas, *Between Facts and Norms* (W Rehg, Trans) (Polity Press 1996).
32 Rogers, *op cit* 105–106.
33 Ibid.

Rogers suggests that society will have to mobilise in order to achieve participation. Up until this point, most publics have been pointedly excluded. A potential space for discussion of biotechnological inventions sometimes arises where a controversial technology is developed and a period of reflection is sought. An example arose at the Asilomar Conference in California in 1974, in which scientists agreed a short voluntary moratorium on progressing with the technology but no public consultation was initiated.[34] Neither were public voices sought on whether these organisms could be patented or whether they should be labelled. It may have been wiser in light of the magnitude of the decisions to be taken to create a deliberative and participatory framework for discussion of the issues so that matters could be agreed rather than contested over such a long time. Moreover, a plurality of views was not accommodated. Without participation, decisions of significance have been and are being made, without general public awareness. The issues at stake are left to unelected experts whose specialities are in matters of great technical complexity but not, however, in matters of ethics or, indeed, social inclusion. Rogers asserts that democratic participation, in the absence of a single ethical and societal vision of the benefits which can be accrued from technological and scientific advances, is an imperative in order to encourage the publics to deliberate and reflect.[35]

When criteria for the evaluation of a technology are under consideration, and these are restricted to economic and technical aspects, and morality is not considered, consciousness of social exigencies may become subdued. Yet if the focus is changed to the broader perspective of societal aims, as Rogers suggests, everyone is potentially on a more equal footing.[36] Neither should pre-conditions such as rationality be placed on the right to participate, given that in a pluralistic world, such a standard is no longer uncontroversial. Rationality, like morality, does not have a universally and objectively defined profile by which matters can be assessed,[37] and participation in decisions relating to morality should be open to all, this book contends.

As Cooke has stated in the absence of a generally recognised moral standard, such standard must be arbitrated by the publics in a deliberative setting, failing which the link between the citizenry and representative will not be perceived.[38] It has been postulated by Philips that presence or representation in politics is necessary because otherwise marginalised social groups do not have their interests or experiences represented adequately. She says that exclusion from the political sphere can only be addressed by presence and

34 Paul Berg, 'Meetings that Changed the World: Asilomar 1975: DNA modification secured' (2008) 455 *Nature* 290.

35 Rogers, *op cit* 144.

36 Ibid 177.

37 Ibid 202.

38 Maeve Cooke, 'Five Arguments for Deliberative Democracy' in Maurizio Passerin D'Entrèves (ed) *Democracy as Public Deliberation* (Manchester University Press 2002) 65.

that we need to understand better the interconnection between experience and ideas.[39]

The right to participate in the Universal Declaration of Human Rights, Article 21 could be invoked to facilitate participation in such decision-making by a much wider sector. The UN has drafted other declarations that also advocate the right to participate.

3.4.2 A United Nations framework for participation

Soft law may have some overarching guidance on how participation can be approached in the area of biotechnology and patents. The Universal Declaration on Bioethics and Human Rights 2005 could provide legislative grounding and a vehicle for governments around the world to engage their citizenry, whether through law or policy. The following articles are of particular significance, in this regard, for the annotated reasons below as this instrument does contain a focus on education and training. In Article 3.1, the Declaration provides that human dignity, rights and freedoms should receive full respect. Article 3.2 elevates the individual's interests and welfare over societal or scientific benefits. This shows that individual rights do not cede to the "greater good" of groups which might have a lot of influence or, indeed, to the public interest. This can help make the case for individual participation in matters of concern.

Article 16 acknowledges the importance of the protection of future generations in the context of life sciences and genetic engineering. How this is to be assessed is unknown. We do not currently have a means of carrying out such evaluations. What impacts are envisaged? The promise of biotechnology for the treatment of disease and its eradication will be an important factor along with risk. Ethical issues will arise if human embryos are being used in research or if heritable genetic changes are being made. There will be calls, undoubtedly for public involvement in any such decisions and the ambit of such involvement and the identity of who makes the decisions will be significant. The declaration also advocates education. In Article 23. It emphasises the importance of informing and educating the publics and especially the young about bioethics. Article 23.2 opines that participation by international and regional intergovernmental organisations and international, regional and national NGOs should be encouraged by states in this objective.

Individuals at national level can also be included in any such participation. The model of participation envisaged in this book will go beyond the expectations of human rights instruments which tend to focus on engagement with groups which may belie their heterogeneity. Direct democracy can be accompanied by a certain baggage, including the fact that it can be very time consuming from the point of view both of preparation and meetings. Representation, on the other hand, frees

39 Ann Phillips, 'Dealing with Difference: A Politics of Ideas or a Politics of Presence?' in Seyla Benhabib, *Democracy and Difference: Contesting the Boundaries of the Political* (Princeton University Press 1996) 141–142.

up much of citizens' time to spend on other pursuits.[40] Deliberative processes involving delegates can also be very resource intensive in that large amounts of information may have to be digested and processed before one is enabled to instruct one's delegate.[41] However, participation is not mandatory and much time is also spent on opposition proceedings at the EPO, especially for those who do not live locally – which constitutes the vast majority of the EPO's "citizens".

3.4.3 Participation as a reform mechanism?

Participatory democracy does not aim to break radically from current democratic forms but instead seeks to enhance public participation in proportion to citizens' willingness to engage in their own governance, thus increasing their autonomy and liberty. The process itself is dynamic and needs to respond continually to changing events.[42] Just because flaws have emerged in the representative model does not mean that democracy itself should be abandoned.[43] Nylen and Dodd comment that the excluded should be included in the political process and observe that we need a democratisation of representative democracy[44] believing that the majority of people would prefer to improve democracy rather than abandon it as a mode of governance.

It is often forgotten that there is some mutual interdependence between representative democracy and its participatory counterpart. The processes of representation and of delegation are part of the manner in which participation comes to operate in practice.[45] Participatory democracy can be conceptualised as a complement to representation and it provides a mechanism whereby the social capital which is innate in civil society's political activity can be captured for democracy's betterment and renewal.[46]

Participatory democracy should be perceived as a means rather than an end in itself to reform and progress representative democracy where it is stagnant.[47] The context of government's role in facilitating deliberation in a pluralist society must occur within a constitutional setting of respect for established rights and freedoms. This will serve to protect minority rights and cultural diversity.[48] Barber's approach to integrating participatory practices into existing democratic models involves an incremental process of change from within where extant institutions

40 McBride, *op cit* 174.

41 Ibid.

42 Rogers, *op cit* 117.

43 Stephen Tierney, *Constitutional Referendums: The Theory and Practice of Republican Deliberation* (Oxford University Press 2012) 301–302.

44 William R Nylen and Lawrence C Dodd, *Participatory Democracy versus Elitist Democracy: Lessons from Brazil* (Palgrave Macmillan 2003) 11.

45 Boaventura de Sousa Santos, 'Participatory Budgeting in Porto Alegre' in Boaventura de Sousa Santos (ed) *Democratising Democracy: Beyond the Liberal Democratic Canon* (Verso 2005) 354.

46 Nylen and Dodd, *op cit* 12.

47 Ibid, 79.

48 Rogers, *op cit* 18–19.

become infiltrated by deliberation rather than being abandoned. This internal transformation ensures that the established values of reverence for the law and human rights together with an appreciation of pluralism and what it entails is not disturbed.[49] Participation can be seen in this context as enhancing and enriching existing good practice in governance and recognition of human rights, rather than being in any way disruptive. Tierney also acknowledges that direct democracy, which is very similar to its participatory form, is a seldom-used constitutional mechanism which arises within representative democracy. While it is often portrayed as a competing structure, in reality, the two systems usually operate in tandem.[50] He reminds the reader that participation by the citizenry and direct democracy takes place within a framework of representative democracy and that participants should have the ability to have their views represented if decisions are to reflect the views of those likely to be affected.[51]

Participatory democracy can emerge from within the representative system, but it tends to do so by making the representative system obsolete in parts rather than abolishing it or destroying it. In this respect, the democratic revolution would be synonymous with a social evolution.[52] Buhlungu states that it is not easy to praise participatory democracy due to prejudice that decision-making which is decentralised is not efficient and modern in the way in which the representative system is.[53] However, we shall see that much will depend on the way in which devices of deliberation and participation are established.

Santos challenges a prevailing misconception that the rise in participation diminishes the role of the state and infringes its sovereignty. Instead, in his study, it is experiencing a transformation in its dominion and is witnessing the genesis of a new model of regulatory activity.[54] Societal involvement in democratic processes can be perceived as an enriching and valuable practice. Such engagement seeks to redress the appearance that current models of democracy[55] have subdued participation and this means that decisions of great import are taken by a small number where public voices are not solicited. Participation in democratic processes can be focused on specific issues such as technology-related matters but consensus is not a prerequisite and public participation can involve interactions which include a plethora of institutions and organisation engaged in discussions relating to education, technological and scientific progress along with ethical issues.[56]

49 Benjamin Barber, *Strong Democracy: Participatory Politics for a New Age* (University of California Press 1984) Chapter 8, in particular.

50 Tierney, *op cit* 13–14.

51 Ibid 196.

52 Rogers, *op cit* 212.

53 Sakhela Buhlungu, 'Reinventing Participatory Democracy in South Africa' in Boaventura de Sousa Santos (ed) *Democratising Democracy: Beyond the Liberal Democratic Canon* (Verso 2005) 62.

54 Boaventura de Sousa Santos, *Toward a New Legal Common Sense: Law, Globalization, and Emancipation* (Cambridge University Press 2002) 489.

55 Rogers, *op cit* 28–29.

56 Ibid 170.

It may be argued that this is not a traditional interpretation of this right but the rights arena is fluid and every increment has a starting point. The main alternative to the state as a site for democratisation in general, and deliberative democracy in particular, is civil society, in Dryzek's view.[57] While civil society may be more independent, it is less likely to wield influence if it does not have a means of access to the corridors of decision-making. Tierney says that representative government can accommodate deliberative and direct democracy and where it does not, the publics may come to feel ignored if their interests are compromised in decisions where they have not had any input.[58]

This observation touches on two core issues of this book: the first which relates to the subject matter concerning the importance which many people give to the role of morality and their involvement in decisions of this nature. The second correctly asserts that deliberation and participation tend to occur within the context of a pre-established system of representative democracy.

Deliberation often complements participatory democracy as the state may facilitate both activities and they may act in tandem. Deliberation can be summed up as public discussion of issues which may go no further or may become the basis for decision-making. Mutz observes that some concepts of civil society mix participatory democracy and deliberative democracy and the latter represents merely a division of political participation.[59] The next section will define and examine deliberative devices to see how they fit within participatory practices.

3.5 Deliberative democracy and its rationale defined

While the term "deliberative democracy" was coined by Joseph Bessette[60] in 1980, it only made its way into the lexicon in force in the late 1990s and has come to represent a number of diverse models. Deliberative practices were evident in ancient Greece and Rome and also in the writings of philosophers such as Edmund Burke, John Stuart Mill and John Dewey. More recently, Rawls and Habermas have classified themselves as deliberative democrats.[61] Deliberation has not always meant inclusion for everyone in the debate. Its practice derived from debate about science, and discussion in parliaments and courts. The importance of these institutions grew steadily and reason has come to be defined through their oratorical styles and rules. Where deliberation is confined to courts and parliamentary debate, the discussion tends not to be so free. Reciprocity is not enshrined: on the contrary, many deliberative forms in practice may be

57 John S Dryzek, *Deliberative Democracy and Beyond: Liberals, Critics, Contestations* (Oxford University Press 2000) 99.

58 Tierney, *Constitutional Referendums: The Theory and Practice of Republican Deliberation*, 247.

59 Diana C Mutz, *Hearing the Other Side: Deliberative versus Participatory Democracy* (Cambridge University Press 2006) 2.

60 Joseph M Bessette, *The Mild Voice of Reason: Deliberative Democracy and American National Government* (University of Chicago Press 1997).

61 Dryzek, *op cit* 2.

antagonistic. The ultimate goal may be to win the argument rather than be persuaded to change or modify one's view.[62] However, the essence has been expressed by Tierney, who observes that deliberative democracy's core value is that public reason should shape decision-making which can take place after public reflection and debate. Such a model moves the political system from being built around voting to meaningful participation which involves compromise and possible consensus.[63]

In the absence of profound participation, public judgments may be impulsive rather than considered and weighted and in such cases, consent is not genuine but based on a whim.[64] This can be avoided by a comprehensive participatory educational programme beforehand so that decision-making is informed. Moreover, the legitimacy[65] of decisions taken after such a process is likely to be improved[66] and often all sides modify their views somewhat in order to reach agreement or consensus. Such decisions should be arrived at through a process of reasoned debate where the pros and cons of a particular proposal are discussed. The overarching goal is to achieve an outcome which is at least tolerable to everyone.[67] Public debate encourages transparency and openness and lessens the opportunities for secretive decision-making.[68] Ponet and Leib assert that deliberation is becoming a more important feature in assessing the legitimacy of political decision-making even if at present we lack agreement on the form it should take.[69]

Deliberative democracy is often understood as a principle whereby the concept of legitimacy[70] is dependent on the power of all citizens to take part in genuine deliberation about any decision by which they are affected.[71] Fishkin believes that the people are given a voice through democracy and everyone should be included.[72] People should also strive to be motivated to think about the issues in question. Political equality and deliberation can thus be

62 Iris Marion Young, 'Communication and the Other: Beyond Deliberative Democracy' in Benhabib (ed) 123.
63 Tierney, *op cit* 198.
64 James Fishkin, *Democracy and Deliberation: New Directions for Democratic Reform* (Cambridge University Press 1991) 195.
65 Legitimacy refers here principally to the input but also to the output in that at times these two aspects are conflated in our conception of legitimacy.
66 Amy Gutmann and Dennis Thompson, *Why Deliberative Democracy?* (Princeton University Press 2004) 179.
67 Ibid.
68 Matthew Festenstein, 'Deliberation, Citizenship and Identity' in Maurizio Passerin D'Entrèves (ed) *Democracy as Public Deliberation* (Manchester University Press 2002) 96–97.
69 David L Ponet and Ethan J Leib, 'Fiduciary Law's Lessons for Deliberative Democracy' (2011) 91 *Boston University Law Review* 1207, 1249.
70 This approach to legitimacy is mainly procedural in that it emphasises large-scale participation.
71 Dryzek, *op cit* 85.
72 Patent cases such as *OncoMouse* affect a broad variety of interests and spectrum of views, ranging from the deontological to utilitarian.

accomplished.[73] Deliberation should have as its goal an on-going search for democratic legitimacy[74] rather than accommodating the existing regime.[75] In addition to achieving a greater understanding of the outcome of debate, deliberation implies that decisions can be justified to the people from whom political authority is derived. After all, those bound by laws ought to have such laws explained to them, where they have chosen their representatives.[76] Where decision-makers are obliged to justify their policies to those affected by them, including an educated populace, they are more likely to be accepted.[77]

Such deliberation should not be confined to an elite group. Furthermore, deliberation should not just take place for its own sake but should lead to a decision and result in a vote of some sort. The making and taking of a decision is essential,[78] otherwise deliberation just becomes a forum in which a lot of talk, and little else, takes place. Deliberation and decision must go hand in hand and when they do so, their amalgamation produces a potent vindication of political decision-making to those bound by such decisions. Majority vote by itself is often not enough to avoid the subjugation of a sector of the populace but deliberation must also culminate in action. The resolution in question may not be correct but at least competing rationales will have been discussed and a greater understanding of varying positions achieved.

This book holds that publics should make decisions on Article 53(a) EPC applications because morality is a matter of deep disagreement. It changes from generation to generation and should not be dominated by educational privilege or be side-lined by technocratic imperatives. Nor should it be overtaken by populism or ideology. Deciding on the scope and depth of penetration is a concern for deliberators and the physical location of the activity is also an important matter for consideration. The question has been raised as to whether the institutions of representative democracy are sufficient or whether deliberation's domain should be much broader in a societal context.[79] Deliberation is generally regarded as valuable because better decisions result and citizens become more independent and equal in their governance. It has educational and societal benefits and even where matters are contested, it fosters societal solidarity.[80]

Deliberative democracy can provide a platform from which to initiate dialogue. A central tenet is to promote the legitimacy of decisions arrived at collectively, and by increasingly using deliberative democracy mechanisms, citizens will have more opportunities to engage in debate. This will ideally result in decision-making

73 James Fishkin, *Democracy and Deliberation: New Directions for Democratic Reform* (Cambridge University Press 1991) 1.
74 Legitimacy is used in a broader sense than just input in this instance: process and outcome are both considered important in the quest for legitimacy.
75 Dryzek, *op cit* 8.
76 Gutmann and Thompson, *op cit* 49.
77 Ibid 102.
78 Tierney, *op cit* 54.
79 Ibid 7.
80 Ponet and Leib, *op cit* 1250.

which exhibits mutual respect[81] in spite of moral disagreements. Deliberative democracy's role is acknowledged by Smith as facilitating a forum for the commencement of a dialogue on biotechnological matters and he recognises its purpose in promoting the legitimacy of collective decisions.[82] In Smith's version of this procedure, the legislator will commence the process, await citizens' responses and amend proposals accordingly once these views have been received.

He gives an example of how this occurred in Oregon in the early 1990s. The state was trying to establish priorities for publicly funded health care under Medicaid and initially employed a utilitarian cost-benefit plan. However, much public criticism was encountered and thereafter a process of consultation was undertaken through open meetings.[83] The legislators could have gone a stage further and invited constituents to set the budgetary priorities themselves as it is now becoming common wherever participatory budgeting is practised. The consultation exercise was a step along this road. When public involvement of this nature becomes routine, the quality of the interaction between legislators and constituents changes and the latter become more involved in setting the agenda as the relationships evolve. In the case of science and technology and the patent system which incentivises innovation in this realm, greater input can be made into educating the publics and also into weaving transparency into the decision-making process of politicians. If the publics do not have access to this knowledge, deciding whether research should be encouraged or curtailed cannot be made in an informed manner.[84] This also presupposes that there is widespread public knowledge about morally controversial biotechnological patented inventions, which is not currently the case.

3.5.1 The nature of deliberation: confrontation or comprehending?

Deliberation has many hues and it ranges from what Fishkin describes as "refined" and "raw" public opinion:[85] the latter tends to emerge from democratic initiatives of a partial participatory nature such as referendums, polls and focus groups, in his view. Public opinion in referendums and recalls may be unrefined or "raw".[86] This has been bolstered by polling which tends to anticipate and predict results sometimes more accurately than others. However, bringing government closer to the citizenry through such processes diminishes the role of deliberation.[87] The former constitutes views which have been tested publicly, challenged, reflected on and hence refined somewhat. Public institutions can be distinguished in this area as between those which seek to refine public opinion and those which allow its

81 George P Smith, 'Judicial Decisionmaking in the Age of Biotechnology' (1999) 13 Notre Dame JL Ethics & Pub Pol'y 93, 102.
82 Ibid.
83 Ibid 103.
84 Rogers, *op cit* 5.
85 Fishkin, *op cit* 14.
86 Ibid 48.
87 Ibid.

unfettered expression.[88] These different forms of public outlook can also be contrasted as being considered or merely reflected.[89] Most institutions provide a mix of these forms but in recent years, the "raw" has been favoured over the refined.[90] Deliberative approaches tend to be associated with elitism while mass opinion is seen as impulsive and not necessarily based on fact.[91] Both approaches often yield different results.[92] This may explain in part the EPO's dislike of taking seriously the result of polls as they are not considered to reflect public opinions accurately. However, a third way, between elitism and raw opinion may be possible.

Gutmann and Thompson advocate that where deliberation reveals disagreement, especially on moral issues, participants should seek to minimise their points of divergence and disagreement.[93] When everyone softens their position somewhat, mutual respect among deliberators becomes enshrined. Where opinions on moral matters are held deeply, some citizens oppose policies based on reasons that will not be accepted across the board. Nonetheless, citizens who deliberate are disposed to changing their views in the aftermath of such activity. This tendency has been noted across the spectrum of social, educational and economic class and appears to be universal in its application.[94] Gutmann and Thompson cite examples of deliberations over research using foetal tissue by the Warnock Commission and the Fetal Tissue Research Commission in the United States in which there was a search for points of convergence rather than divergence.[95] Both these bodies were highly specialised. They also considered single issues and, while complex, they could focus intensely. Values such as reciprocity become embedded in this practice so that individual citizens come to a heightened respect for each other in that differing positions are heard and understood.[96]

When appropriate procedures are put in place to facilitate discussion about moral issues and to assist in the resolution of discord, there is no need to favour a particular outcome or theoretical approach.[97] This can facilitate fairness and, indeed, a perception of equal treatment. It will be easier to morally justify decisions if decision-makers seek to defend their policies to others, whether they be informed citizens or the representatives of those affected by the same decisions.[98] Reasoned arguments are used to persuade people to change their views or, indeed, to accommodate those of others in deliberative and participatory regimes. Confidence in the ability of people to respect very different viewpoints even where their own are held passionately is a core value of deliberation. This will be assisted

88 Ibid 14.
89 Ibid 15.
90 Ibid 20.
91 Ibid.
92 Ibid 26.
93 Gutmann and Thompson, *op cit* 153.
94 Fishkin, *op cit* 52.
95 Gutmann and Thompson, *op cit.*
96 Ibid 101–102.
97 Ibid 130.
98 Ibid 102.

greatly by effective mediation of public debate. Peaceful pluralism may be achieved when discussions and explanations are held and it is more likely that each person will accommodate the views of the next. Communication is deemed to be key.[99] Fishkin observes that seeing others' points of view in discussions about moral issues is essential in order to comprehend different standpoints.[100]

Deliberation enshrines mutual respect into verbal disagreements where discordant views may be held very deeply. It requires more than tolerance,[101] which may be seen as a passive rather than active state. Mutual respect requires a dynamic approach to those who hold opposing views. The manner in which the debate is managed will be important and as can be seen below, there is an array of models of deliberation.

3.5.2 Classes of deliberative democracy: elitist or populist?

The literature on deliberative democratic practices has tended not to feed into the decision-making process on any significant scale and deliberative groups rarely are made up of more than a handful of people. Often, when not focused on including the citizenry broadly, they are composed of small, interdisciplinary groups of experts whose decisions are speculative or advisory rather than determinative. Examples have already been given in Chapter Two in discussions of ethics committees and other deliberative groups such as consensus conferences which advise or render their opinion but heed need not be paid to their recommendations. The closest that the EPO has come to dealing with alternative views is a robust engagement with NGOs, such as Greenpeace, which often successfully challenge the granting of patents, either before or after the grant.[102] Certainly, all sides that want to be heard have a chance to do so but the current manner in which this operates is that the information dealt with is highly specialised and there are outright winners and losers in the grant and appeal process. Moreover, the publics are hardly aware of the issues at stake.

In deliberative democratic settings, listening is as important as speaking and those who partake in deliberation should be open to modifying their stances on the issues in question.[103] Deliberation and participation may be combined[104] as is, in fact, the case in the participatory practices examined in Chapter Four. However, deliberative democracy has a number of different incarnations, and both elitism and populism can be a feature of deliberation that is not entwined with participation. This will now be explored.

99 Frank Vibert, *The Rise of the Unelected: Democracy and the New Separation of Powers* (Cambridge University Press 2007) 65.
100 Fishkin, *op cit* 125.
101 Ibid 79–80.
102 *Harvard/Onco-Mouse; Plant Genetic Systems v Greenpeace; Edinburgh Patent Application* No 949131742 and *Brüstle v Greenpeace eV.*
103 Tierney, *op cit* 4.
104 Fishkin, *op cit* 53.

Two types of democrats are distinguished by Ponet and Leib: the elitist and the populist. The former focus on deliberation among the expert class, those being members of the judiciary, the legislature and possibly some interest groups, whereas the latter concentration is on deliberation among the citizenry. They identify theorists, such as Ackerman and Habermas who have endeavoured to disrupt this dualist aspect of deliberative democracy by deepening democratic discourse in both spheres.[105] However, an aspect of this dualism that has not been addressed adequately is that both systems still operate in parallel spheres rather than intersecting with each other. The question as to how citizen discourse is to influence formal politics has not been worked out because points of contact are absent. They claim that Habermas believes that a state's legitimacy in part depends on the ability of civil society to centralise concerns which arise at the fringes of public discourse[106] and is critical of any failure on the part of the state to give expression to these deliberative impulses of civil society.[107] Habermas is depicted as being overly sanguine about the extent of civil society's influence and his description of this influence is largely indirect and oblique.[108] They perceive that many deliberative democrats bifurcate the levels at which deliberation and decision-making occur. One takes place among the citizenry and the other level of deliberation happens among the representative branches of government: the legislators and other government officials.[109] The forum for debate between legislator and citizen is insufficiently explored and the reason is that it is normally a prerequisite of deliberative democracy that discussions only take place among equals. Legislators debate with the citizenry from a privileged position, both from the vantage point of their political standing and also their expertise or access to expert advice, reserving to themselves the privilege of vetoing any unwelcome proposals. Ponet and Leib believe that this unexplored space should be addressed by drawing on aspects of fiduciary law in order to highlight the fact that legislators hold their political power on trust for their constituents. If we conceptualise this relationship in this manner, it is possible to see that this dialogue is important and necessary. They opine that our elected public representatives have a duty to facilitate public discourse and that they should enable deliberation among unequals: the holder of political office and the legitimate beneficiary of that power.[110]

Legislators, in this paradigm, have duties towards their constituents and hold their interests on trust. They should strive to deliberate with the publics and neither maintain a secrecy over matters of public concern nor conduct a one-way conversation in which publics do not have the opportunity to have an input.

One of the most frequently cited advocates of deliberative communication is John Stuart Mill[111] who claimed that where there is little contact with opposing

105 Ponet and Leib, *op cit* 1249.
106 Habermas, *Between Facts and Norms, op cit* 330.
107 Ibid 335.
108 Ibid 330.
109 Ponet and Leib, *op cit* 1249.
110 Ibid 1249–1250.
111 Mutz, *op cit* 8.

viewpoints, the chances of developing a public sphere is diminished. He believed that exposure to different points of view meant that one's own opinions might be erroneous and that where public discourse is scarce, one loses the opportunity to be exposed to the truth.[112] In this debate, however, I am not seeking to achieve an evaluation of right and wrong positions but, rather, a process whereby the morality bar is decided by publics on a case-by-case basis. Mutz concludes that exposure to opposing positions broadens people's comprehension of the views of others even where they do not come to agree[113] although she also observes that those with similar views communicate with greater ease and more readily than those with oppositional viewpoints.[114]

While homogeneous groups may effectuate positive political change, they can often foster extreme views and thus fail to represent a wider sector of the population. By way of contrast, when the political network is heterogeneous, many benefits accrue but levels of participation tend to be lower.[115] Adjudicators may have to confront difficult choices: where they take a positivist stance, they may be perceived as defending their position. However, should they attempt to accommodate radical views, it may be challenging to arrive at an agreement which is perceived to be legitimate.[116] While outcomes resulting from exposure to cross-cutting views are regarded highly in democratic systems, they are not always positive.[117] Bitter discussions can also ensue, at times ending in violent exchanges or hostile silences.[118] However, deliberative democracy, if well-organised can minimise such conflict as much as possible.

In addition to being feasible and desirable, politicians may also be *required* to engage in deliberation with the governed.[119] While much of deliberative democrats' focus is on finding ways to facilitate deliberation among citizens themselves, more focus will be placed in this book on how citizens can debate with their representatives[120] and ultimately be the law-makers in this area.

Proponents of both popular and elite deliberative democracy emphasise the importance of deliberation in decision-making if it is to be deemed democratic. Such processes are enhanced by this interchange. This also tallies with civic republican ambitions regarding the involvement of the publics in general in deliberation and the legitimacy of such decisions is heightened.[121] Citizens become empowered and the extent of their participation becomes more profound.

112 John Stuart Mill, *On Liberty* (Longmans, Green, Reader, and Dyer 1869) 21.
113 Mutz, *op cit* 66.
114 Ibid.
115 Ibid.
116 Brownsword, *op cit* 30.
117 Input legitimacy alone may foster a legality which does not necessarily deliver justice and therefore the outcome may have to be factored into reform as it evolves.
118 Jason A Scorza, 'Uncivil Friendship: Emersonian Lessons for Democratic Disagreement' Paper presented at the annual meeting of the American Political Science Association, Boston, quoted in Mutz, *op cit* 62.
119 Ponet and Leib, *op cit* 1255–1256.
120 Ibid 1261.
121 Tierney, *op cit* 185.

This enhances pluralism as the formerly excluded seek and obtain inclusion. Participation also enhances the representative aspects of democracy rather than destabilising them and corruption and clientelistic politicking decrease.[122] It is not enough, however, to approve of participation without ensuring that it is also meaningful.[123] This means that decisions must emerge after the deliberative process has taken place.

The idea of exclusion in liberal philosophies may be ingrained in definitions of personhood so that those on the margins of society may not be deemed fit to participate due to prejudices about their capacity for reasonable communication.[124] Where elites dominate, the very best that can be achieved is a democracy for the people rather than by them.[125] This negates general involvement and smacks of paternalism. While liberal thought may encourage the belief that people do not change their views during the participatory process, this viewpoint is not universal and critical theorists postulate that the process is transformative.[126]

The mistrust of elites does not, however, require everyone to acquire expertise in order to counterbalance their power, although a minimum level of knowledge is necessary for meaningful participation and some studies would suggest that the more ignorant people are, the less they want to be informed.[127] Much will depend, however, on the sources of information and the means of imparting it, which will be explored in the next chapter. A healthy dose of scepticism around advice meted out by experts along with inquiries into their qualifications, seeking second opinions about contested matters and ensuring that research has not been financed by vested interests should offer protection against domination by elites.[128] Rogers observes that dismantling hierarchical structures will result from citizens learning skills which will enable them to disband privilege and strengthen democracy.[129]

Having established that democratic engagement between the governors and the governed is a creditable aspiration, the extent of information which representatives should impart forms the focus of some debate. When consultations with the publics are initiated by the government but the information provided is paltry, this form of politics is thin. When only elites are consulted, as is the case in some deliberative models, this is hardly representative.[130] And if the elites are not within the democratic framework and are unelected, they themselves may be very cloistered from public perspectives.[131]

122 Nylen and Dodd, *op cit* 28.
123 Tierney, *op cit* 47.
124 Dryzek, *op cit* 19.
125 Fishkin, *op cit* 7.
126 Dryzek, *op cit* 21.
127 American Psychological Association, 'Ignorance Is Bliss When It Comes to Social Issues' in Science Daily, https://www.sciencedaily.com/releases/2011/11/111121142446.htm (accessed 5 March 2019).
128 Dryzek, *op cit* 165.
129 Rogers, *op cit* 211.
130 Fishkin, *op cit* 176.
131 Vibert, *op cit* 32.

In the context of patents and the relevance of the foregoing discussion to the controversies enshrined by competing interests, at present in the area of morally controversial biotechnological patents, NGOs, particularly Greenpeace, play an important role in Europe as they have succeeded in defeating or at least challenging a number of patent applications, as follows. They are active in mounting challenges throughout the various processes of patent applications both at national and supranational level. Such cases include *Brüstle*,[132] *Plant Genetic Systems*[133] and *Harvard/Oncomouse*.[134] In some respects, they have become a substantial moral torch-bearer in the absence of a consistent approach from various judicial bodies involved in patent grants in European organisations and countries. While they represent a very different moral standpoint from that of the EPO, they are not universally representative and decisions, therefore, often are played out between patent advocates, on the one hand and powerful NGOs on the other. This book seeks to broaden the access to the decision-making process so that societal-wide discussion and decisions take place. Given that morality has many hues, there may be groups of citizens who would favour patents on inventions involving destruction of the human embryo if, for example, this held promise for cures for genetic diseases. Currently such arguments are not being made publicly. It may be that such debates could get hijacked by vocal minorities but effective deliberation is carried out in an environment where unbridled views will be curtailed. Deliberative democracy does not take place in a vacuum but, rather, within a human rights framework.

The discussion above shows that the human right to participate can be used as a basis to involve the publics in the decision-making process in a deliberative setting so that the represented viewpoints are broader in scope and not confined to experts alone. This theme is explored further in the next section.

3.5.3 Early and meaningful input

When public engagement is meaningful, according to Harmon, genuine debates take place and these have the benefit of highlighting different viewpoints. Total consensus is all but impossible to achieve but where the debate takes place upstream, policy decisions and laws may be more versatile.[135] "Upstream" in the domain of patents would be at a phase before the grant, the difference to present practice being that there would be debate and participatory public education followed by a plebiscite. While it could be argued that this would disfavour industrial interests, the reality is that it might make it easier for patents to be granted in cases such as *WARF*,[136] where the definition of morality was broad, if the publics were

132 C-34/10 *Oliver Brüstle v Greenpeace eV* [2011] ECR I-9821.

133 *Plant Genetic Systems v Greenpeace* [1995] EPOR 357.

134 T 315/03 *Transgenic Animals/HARVARD* 6 July 2004.

135 SHE Harmon, 'The Rules Re-Engagement: The Use of Patent Proceedings to Influence the Regulation of Science (What the Salmon Does When It Comes Back Downstream)', 2006 IPQ 403.

136 G2/06 *WARF/Stem Cells* [2009] EPOR 15.

given a say. Harmon criticises an important aspect of the processes of engagement in bioethical debates which relates to their timing and the way in which questions are posed. Only particular questions tend to be asked and while queries such as those pertaining to risk may be examined and debated at length, other matters such as values and vested interests underlying scientific endeavour are frequently neither asked nor answered.[137] By the time the publics know about the issues, it may already be too late to have influence over the direction of a particular technological development. The scope for potential public engagement may have already been circumscribed by stronger vested interests. Any meaningful debate must take place at the right time when all questions are still open to influence.[138] Examples of where such openness has not prevailed can be seen in the next sections.

In an exercise of public participation in a Chinese example relating to environmental issues, Zhao writes that under the current Environmental Impact Assessment (EIA)[139] regime, public input happens too late, lasts too briefly and does not extend to the post-EIA approval stage. Public engagement usually occurs in a window of time only after EIA reports are drafted and before they are submitted to environmental authorities for approval. There is only minimal public input before the drafting of EIA reports and there is no further public engagement after submission. When the reports are ready for submission, all the key decisions have already been taken. Moreover, the consultation time lasts only for ten days.[140] While public input is not stifled, it takes place downstream and, in the biotechnology arena, this has tended to be exemplified by oppositions based on grounds of morality, given that this is an aspect which has not been teased out or clarified in a satisfactory way to date at the grant stage.[141]

An example of tardy downstream input was seen in the announcement in July 2006 by the Human Fertilisation and Embryology Authority (HFEA) that it would hold a consultative process on egg-sharing and donation in September 2006. However, it had already granted a licence to one clinic to allow egg-sharing but emphasised that the experience from the licensed clinic would feed into the consultation. The consultation, in that case, was going to have a limited, if any effect, on its subject.[142] Harmon also asserts that there are recurring demands for publics to be involved more in policy-making in the area of biotechnology and that our model of legislation needs to move from government to

137 Harmon, 'The Rules Re-Engagement', *op cit* 403.

138 Human Fertilisation and Embryology Authority press release, 'Should Women be Able to Donate their Eggs for Scientific Research?' 27 July 2006, available at www.hfea.gov.uk, in Callus, *op cit* 62.

139 Zhao, *op cit* 89.

140 Ibid.

141 Shawn HE Harmon, 'From Engagement to Re-Engagement: The Expression of Moral Values in European Patent Proceedings, Past and Future' [2006] ELR 642, 642.

142 Human Fertilisation and Embryology Authority press release, 'Should Women be Able to Donate their Eggs for Scientific Research?', 27 July 2006, available at www.hfea.gov.uk, in Callus, *op cit* 62.

governance.[143] In debates where questions were being posed too late to influence matters, the stage of interaction was adjusted and this engagement occurred earlier. Such questions included addressing reasons why particular inventions were being developed, how ownership responsibility and control were allocated and who its beneficiaries should be. The mechanisms included a number of deliberative devices such as polling, consensus conferences, citizens' juries, mapping and stakeholder study circles.[144] All of these devices are small-scale and this book argues for a society-wide model which will afford all citizens the right to express their views on morality through this medium, should they so choose.

What would be the consequences of not giving the publics an appreciable input into the direction of patenting practice in this area? Burk indicates that if public unease in this area is addressed inadequately, through either belittling or dismissal of oppositional views, as was the case with regard to the handling of concerns about nuclear power, civil society could mobilise to resist further development of the technology in question.[145] This also occurred during plans by the European Commission and some national governments within the EU to authorise the planting and putting on the market of genetically modified organisms.[146] NGOs such as Greenpeace and Friends of the Earth resisted this activity and activists regularly uprooted these crops due to a number of reasons including disquiet about safety, environmental impact and the perception that the authorisation processes had not been sufficiently transparent.[147] If the rationales for decisions are not made public, those who lose the argument in a given controversy will not know why matters were decided as they were and what influenced the judgment of the merits of the case. This approach would therefore eschew private deliberation in favour of public discussion of how we use the patent system to incentivise biotechnological research.[148]

Dewey believed that intelligent inquiry could be used to endeavour to resolve moral matters at the institutional level, given that it had already been so successful in the field of natural science.[149] Patents and the moral issues raised can also be deliberated publicly.[150] Some of the literature on deliberative democracy does seek to address the dilemma about how to discuss public concerns regarding

143 Shawn HE Harmon, in James Wilsdon and Rebecca Willis, *See-through Science: Why Public Engagement Needs to Move Upstream* (Demos 2004) 18, https://www.demos.co.uk/files/Seethroughsciencefinal.pdf?1240939425 (accessed 5 March 2019).

144 Ibid.

145 Dan L Burk, 'Patenting Transgenic Human Embryos: A Nonuse Cost Perspective' (1993) 30 *Hous. L. Rev.* 1597.

146 The Commission ended up declaring a moratorium in 1998 prior to introducing a new, more restrictive directive in 2001 – Directive 2001/18/EC.

147 Maureen O'Sullivan, *op cit.*

148 James D Fearon, 'Deliberation as Discussion' in Jon Elster (ed) *Deliberative Democracy* (Cambridge University Press 1988) 62.

149 Kory Spencer Sorrell, 'Principled Legal Pragmatism: Reconciling Posner and Dewey on Law and Democracy' (2010) 23 Thomas L Rev 245, 291.

150 Lisa C Ikemoto, 'Disentangling Fact from Fiction: The Realities of Unequal Healthcare Treatment' (2005) 9 DePaul J Health Care L 1101, 1101.

biotechnology without leading to a manipulation of this discursive space by narrow-mindedness. At present, the tendency is to pursue scientific inventions without paying very much attention either to risk or impact on other aspects of humanity's welfare and to side-line discussion of moral controversies, especially when concerns are driven by religious conviction.[151] Where there is little education, discussion or engagement, publics can demonstrate a lot of ignorance about technologies in question. For instance, in the US, a national survey of views on genetically modified foods showed that Americans were opinionated about this technology but not knowledgeable.[152] On the other hand, a Eurobarometer survey conducted in 2010 shows that support in Europe for genetically modified foods had declined, and this was in the context of a population who were quite well informed about the technology.[153] However, much transparent debate before decision-making may soften hard-line views. The legitimacy inherent in this sort of process trumps a model of democracy in which private interests are prioritised over those of the citizenry in general. Public debate encourages transparency and openness and lessens the opportunities for secretive decision-making.[154]

While deliberation can enhance the decision-making process, it is the argument of this book that in order for it to be meaningful, it should be as inclusive as possible. There are a large number of ways in which deliberation can be included in policy considerations and these vary greatly in terms of size and scale. The next section will examine this issue.

3.5.4 Deliberative devices and scale

There are, for the deliberative democrat, an array of mechanisms from which to choose in order to engage the publics on political issues, such as morality. These include deliberative polls, in which a statistically representative section of the population is surveyed, following which the group may take part in a weekend discussion. This involves small-group discussions, plenary sessions, expert opinion and a final survey of participants. McBride regards these polls as a significant endeavour to engage citizens in the discussion of questions of policy.[155] However, how such weekend sessions could intersect with high-level political decisions is not teased out. An important feature to maximise the success of deliberative polls is that relevant reading material should be made available several weeks in advance of the subsequent discussion. This allows participants to contemplate the material in a reflective manner and also to discuss the issues with friends and colleagues.

151 Marcy Darnovsky, 'Moral Questions of an Altogether Different Kind: Progressive Politics in the Biotech Age' (2010) 4 Harv L & Pol'y Rev 99, 101.

152 The State of New Jersey Rutgers, 'National survey shows Americans are in the dark regarding genetically modified foods' (2005) https://www.sciencedaily.com/releases/2005/01/050131224504.htm (accessed 5 March 2019).

153 European Commission, 'Eurobarometer Biotechnology' (2010) 13–33, http://ec.europa.eu/public_opinion/archives/ebs/ebs_341_en.pdf (accessed 5 March 2019).

154 Fenstenstein, in D'Entrèves, *op cit* 88.

155 McBride, *op cit.*

Additionally, information can be gleaned through the media, depending on the issue. Such preparatory work will enhance the weekend debate. Plenary sessions including experts and small group discussions appear to achieve exposure to cross-cutting discourse with individuals who hold very different viewpoints to one's own. Callus acknowledges that difficulties inhere in the organisation of deliberate forms of participation, but suggests that the Internet, e-mail and the establishment of a People's Panel can facilitate public engagement.[156] Other devices include citizen juries and consensus conferences which are popular in Denmark. The kinds of meaningful opportunities often suggested by leading advocates include more direct referendums at the national level and greater citizen involvement in community-level political institutions.[157]

There is some disagreement in the literature about whether participation should operate on a small or a large scale. Fishkin believes that the size of the participatory groups must be restricted arguing that what should be aimed for is a diversity of viewpoints rather than societal-wide participation. This can be achieved, in his view, through equal representation. This suggests a choice between the participation of the masses and random sampling. Deliberating groups cannot really exceed 18 in number, he argues, as once this number is surpassed individuals cannot interact meaningfully as their input is too miniscule to be significant.[158] His conceptualisation of participatory democracy is that not all decisions need to be made directly, believing that at national level, it is impractical. Instead, consultation with the publics should happen often and be meaningful. A way of addressing this is to establish small groups of limited size to which participants can be randomly assigned,[159] he argues. A democracy in which we all had substantive opinions would also seem to take too many meetings and this speculation will be explored in the context of practical examples of participatory budgeting in the next chapter which robustly refute this supposition. While he believes that consultation should extend beyond elections, participation is not extended to all and sundry on the basis that the masses are just too substantial. Yet he still claims that participation facilitates public opinion by allowing it to be voiced.[160] His view of what constitutes the publics, however, does not appear to be particularly clear-cut.

The deficiency which Fishkin identifies of small voices being drowned out can be addressed in another way and that would be to allow for the creation of power structures so that all voices can feed into the decision-making process. Parallels to the structures of representative democracy can be constructed so that participation is more nuanced and more connected at grassroots level. This shall be explored in Chapter Four.

Structural features of deliberative democracy which seek to broaden the ambit of discussion of important societal and political matters include citizen juries,

156 Callus, *op cit* 62.
157 Mutz, *op cit* 135.
158 Fishkin, *op cit* 38.
159 Ibid.
160 Ibid 76.

consensus conferences and tele-voting, among others. Each model seeks to reflect deliberation of a tiny percentage of the publics.[161] At very least, deliberative paradigms such as citizen juries are intended to enhance representative institutions. This can be achieved through integrating educated citizens' points of view into political decision-making.[162] These examples are best understood as enshrining practices of small-scale deliberation rather than being a form of participatory democracy as such, although wide-scale participatory democracy tends to enshrine deliberative features as part of the processes of negotiation and voting.

3.5.4.1 Small scale

In Denmark, as aforementioned the use of consensus conferences is popular especially where decisions have to be taken about technology-related ethical issues. Recruitment is through newspaper advertisements and diversity is sought in the selection of participants. Participants do self-select, however, meaning that the ambit of recruits is not likely to be especially wide.[163] Moreover, it assumes literacy and, indeed, literacy in the dominant language or languages of a given country. Given the large number of recent immigrants and refugees in Europe this point merits consideration. The illiterate are tacitly excluded and are thus rendered invisible in such decisions as are those who lack access to ICTs if such methods are used. Would-be participants who do not hold strong views are unlikely to seek to participate and, therefore, this model attracts an arguably unrepresentative subsection of the population. A further difficulty with this model, which also pertains to citizen juries, is that it does not have a secret ballot as consensus must be achieved. Alternatively, deliberative polls do use secret ballots but these also only represent a microcosm of the publics.[164] There are also many critics of such small-scale schemes and claims have been made that they are something of a sham. Decision-makers can select or ignore resolutions at will, although in the case of citizen juries, contracts can be drawn up beforehand which might mitigate such behaviour.[165]

However, an advantage of small-scale deliberation is that it is manageable and not inordinately costly. Moreover, participants are likely to be genuinely interested in the issues to be discussed. Undertaking deliberation on a larger scale is a much more complex logistical task.

3.5.4.2 Large scale

Citizens will also need to be more knowledgeable in matters of science and technology, in addition to receiving training in political participation. The techno-

161 Ibid 55.

162 Graham Smith and Corinne Wales, 'Citizens' juries and deliberative democracy' in Maurizio Passerin D'Entrèves (ed) *Democracy as Public Deliberation* (Manchester University Press 2002) 172.

163 Fishkin, *op cit* 57.

164 Ibid.

165 Smith and Wales, in D'Entrèves, *op cit* 172.

sciences will also need devolved, decentralised democratic governance which will involve the elimination of technological and political hindrances to democracy.[166] This vision, of course, would extend beyond the realm of patent reform but it may be that participation would spread to different areas over time. Rogers, in contrast to Fishkin, believes that participation cannot be achieved on a small scale, so deliberative models such as random sampling are not recommended by him. Instead, deliberation should include the entire population,[167] although he does not advance a model of how this might be achieved. This entwines both deliberation and participation in its practices. He also advocates public funding for furthering the education of second- and third-level teachers in matters of the interconnections among science, technology and democracy.[168] Patents, ethics policy and public interests could potentially be added to that list and governments will play an important role in such developments.

3.5.5 Government oversight

The context of government's role in facilitating deliberation in a pluralist society must occur within a constitutional setting of respect for established rights and freedoms. This will serve to protect minority rights and cultural diversity[169] and the sensibilities of various groups as there are many different conceptualisations of morality. Satisfactory resolutions will not be achieved by one group's dominance, by a ballotocracy in which people vote without deliberation once every five years or so, nor will any good ultimately come out of secretive and hidden agendas. Benhabib describes pluralism as modern democracy's demarcation and as such consideration will have to be given as to how to address this in an inclusive fashion.[170] This should not be avoided, as moral difference will often be reflected in political discord. One of the main challenges is to find the best possible ways of reaching binding decisions when disagreement continues.[171] Of course, pluralists aim to ensure that deliberation achieves agreement wherever feasible but where disagreement persists they also strive to maintain a harmonious co-existence where such disparities cannot be resolved. Some acknowledge pluralism as intrinsic to humanity but others differ in perceiving it as a problem which needs resolution through deliberative means.[172]

Governments can involve citizens by allowing them to assist in defining the issues or in setting the questions. Information may be circulated to foster discussion and rules regarding fair financing may be implemented.[173] These measures will not always meet with success where parts of the electorate are disinterested.

166 Rogers, *op cit* 145–146.
167 Ibid 168.
168 Ibid 164.
169 Ibid 18–19.
170 Chantal Mouffe, 'Democracy, Power and the "Political"' in Benhabib (ed), *op cit* 246.
171 Gutmann and Thompson, *op cit* 125.
172 Ibid 28.
173 Tierney, *op cit* 261.

However, such concerns are not confined to referendums and the malaise of disaffection among voters affects democracy on a much wider scale. Voter nonchalance or ignorance, however, is never cited as a ground for restricting the franchise and, arguably, neither should disengagement, for whatever reason, be used to exclude people from meaningful participation. Moreover, the town of Ovar in Portugal has achieved a participation rate of 25% in their participatory budget by using gamification, or the use of game design elements in non-game contexts.[174] Of note is that gamification has been found to have positive effects on voter engagement[175] and the use of certain technologies may, therefore, incentivise participation.

Where participation is not mandatory, often better educated, wealthier citizens are more active. Those at the lower echelons of society are less likely to participate as often their struggle is not for an improvement in resource allocation but simply to survive. Much will depend, therefore, on the subject matter of the participatory practice. Their mobilisation may be patchy. Compulsory voting will not necessarily have a positive effect on outcome as much voting will have been impulsive and ill-prepared.[176] Dryzek believes that not everyone will seek to participate in deliberative processes and that there should be a right, and not an obligation to do so.[177] Indeed, obliging participation among the disadvantaged could be unduly burdensome. Participation should be encouraged, but not forced.

It is incumbent on politicians to facilitate this process and not to adopt an inactive approach. However, citizens too should be proactive about their participation in establishing their rights to information and to question innovation relating to technological development and also the role that morality plays in patent grants. This will most likely further citizen interest in technology and will undoubtedly increase public awareness of its potential.[178] Far from freezing technological advancement, the incorporation of citizen voices may have the opposite effect and could soften the battle lines currently drawn between private commercial interests and some specialised NGOs. Our pluralistic society is a pre-condition to decisions about the direction of our development and where participation is not allowed and public information and discussion discouraged – or not encouraged – we risk creating a totalitarian technocracy. Moreover, a broad-ranging input will greatly enhance the collective font of knowledge, along with experience and perspective that will help pre-empt the unforeseen. Such governance cannot be established in a hierarchical and centralised mode and in any case, genuine democracies incorporate pluralism. Participation on a broad scale should augment the ability to think laterally about objectives as well as means.[179]

174 http://www.shareable.net/blog/portuguese-town-uses-gamification-to-get-an-amazing-25-turnout-for-participatory-budgeting (accessed 5 March 2019).
175 https://www.huffpost.com/entry/improve-voter-turn-out_b_2127459 (accessed 5 March 2019).
176 Fishkin, *op cit* 80.
177 Dryzek, *op cit* 172–173.
178 Rogers, *op cit* 96.
179 Ibid 164–165.

A twofold task presents itself to those who would lay down ground rules for deliberation where there is moral disagreement. The varying stances require attention but so too does the manner in which these are maintained or articulated and viewpoints which are morally worthy can be defended in dishonourable ways. Ultimately, even though the losing side may disagree with the outcome, they should still treat the victors in a respectful manner.[180] This will help establish ground rules for future disputes about moral matters. When mutual respect is practised, a more widespread political consensus may emerge as to how moral disagreements should be conducted, regardless of people's private moral beliefs.[181]

Some deficiencies in the interrelatedness of deliberative democracy with actual representation have been posed by Squires who asks whether public spheres which are both pluralistic and informal can permeate more formal political arenas. While the literature addresses some of the challenges involved in establishing diverse public spheres, it is relatively silent when it comes to the mechanics of how public deliberation, if located outside of formal politics, can influence the decision-making process.[182] A vibrant public sphere or civil society is the other principal site in which deliberation can take place and democracy will flourish in its presence as it provides scrutiny of the state and ensures that its obligations to the citizenry are fulfilled. Dryzek also argues that public opinions can be converted into political power through a variety of mechanisms which include, but are not confined to, discursive devices and elections.[183]

In addition to facilitating participatory involvement, governments should ensure that citizens are sufficiently informed about the issues at stake so that their input is valuable and meaningful.

3.5.6 Education of the citizenry and inclusion

The citizenry must be well educated in order for democracy to flourish. This has been recognised for a long time by democratic theorists. The ability to deliberate on a prolonged basis – for sufficient time to ensure the accountability of elected representatives – is an intrinsic part of this education. A civil society which affords space to practise political deliberation will help this endeavour.[184] Such processes should be facilitated by governments committed to enhancing the role of deliberation and participatory activity. Santos indicates that the government in Porto Alegre arranges training sessions for councillors and delegates every time a new budgetary committee is set up,[185] so the commitment to and awareness of the

180 Ibid 79.
181 Ibid 90.
182 Judith Squires, 'Deliberation and Decision making: Discontinuity in the Two-track Model', in D'Entrèves, *op cit* 149.
183 Dryzek, *op cit* 171.
184 Gutmann and Thompson, *op cit* 35.
185 Santos, 'Participatory Budgeting in Porto Alegre: Toward a Redistributive Democracy' in Santos (ed) *op cit* 341.

empowerment and necessity of education is deeply appreciated among certain sectors of the political class in Brazil.

Rogers argues in favour of the extension of literacy in science across society and believes that this will enable citizens to communicate their doubts about scientific development to each other. Such dialogue will also heighten public comprehension of technological advancement. This will serve to contextualise science more broadly and site it in a more interdisciplinary and multidisciplinary setting. A more expansive perspective will thus be brought to bear on considerations of civil society. Instead of excluding citizens from such debates, the intricacies of science justify a more inclusive approach to the weighing of the implications of the direction of technological development.[186] Any such debates should also extend to the patent system in that it is deeply enmeshed in incentivising such progress.

The importance of education should not be underestimated as it plays a significant role in citizens' ability to change their position. Tierney advises, however, that public education campaigns, if dominated by elites with vested interests may not present an entirely balanced viewpoint and, moreover, they may seek to embed further established opinions.[187] While meaningful participation is a commitment of republicanism, the matter under discussion must be comprehended. Dismissing the publics as unqualified indicates an elitist approach but it is also vital that publics understand the issue which they are being asked to consider.[188] Public involvement brings more transparency to the scientific process and makes it more accountable.[189] This can be elucidating in the context of morally controversial biotechnological inventions. It will be difficult to educate and engage citizens. This is not a search for an ideal but seeks a process of improvement of democratic legitimacy in the decision-making process.[190]

Deliberative discussion by itself does not herald the existence of democracy and where disputes are dominated by spin doctors or manipulative orators they suffer from a deficit of democracy. Deliberation can be conceptualised as democratic where participants hail from a plurality of backgrounds and are able to debate in an environment free from intimidation and exploitation.[191] For instance, where specialists highlight their expertise so as to quieten contested points, this can constitute a form of verbal pressure.[192] Of course, it may also be a reasonable and helpful interjection, depending on the context. In any case, it has been noted that the majority of moderators of deliberative forums are aware that discussions, if not well managed can be controlled by assertive individuals. For a substantial percentage of the population, public speaking is a daunting prospect.[193] There are examples, of course, where public groups debate and articulate well with experts –

186 Rogers, *op cit* 145–146.
187 Tierney, *op cit* 52.
188 Ibid 239.
189 Rogers, *op cit* 171.
190 Tierney, *op cit* 241.
191 Dryzek, *op cit* 77.
192 Ibid 70.
193 Smith and Wales, in D'Entrèves, *op cit* 169.

examples being radio shows such as those hosted by Professor Michael Sandel on BBC Radio 4 – but these groups are self-selecting and therefore are likely to be in the minority who enjoy such public discussions.[194]

The majority of people are not confident public speakers and this leads to a significant criticism of Habermas' concept of the public sphere. While he claims that this space is potentially open to all, many voices cannot find a means of expression through fear, being oppressed or lack of articulateness, for instance.[195] There is also the relatively narrow conception of the exclusively discursive rationality that is operative in this sphere and the delimitation of communication to rational verbal discourse. In short, this universal arena, even within the confines of a nation or a political unit, is less than universal in its constitution.[196] The design of such deliberative sessions requires adequate planning and care should be exercised in ensuring that cogs to the flow of free and fair deliberation be anticipated.

A common objection to participatory democracy and deliberation among the masses is that the public are insufficiently educated to make such debate meaningful. For instance, Judge Richard Posner is an ardent opponent of deliberative democracy for a number of reasons, not least of which is his scathing conclusion that the vast majority of people are ignorant about almost everything.[197] Posner also asserts that as half of the population's IQ is below 100, he is an advocate of an elitist form of democracy[198] – quite the antithesis of deliberative and participatory democracy. He defines it in disparaging language, saying that it epitomises an elite group of self-interested politicians who seek votes from a disinterested but also self-interested electorate.[199]

It very much depends on how publics are treated and Posner does not appear well versed in the nuances of deliberation and participation. In somewhat less harsh terms, Smith reiterates Posner's concerns about the knowledge gap between the representatives and the represented. He agrees that while it may be an attractive idea to consider deliberative democracy's role as a complement to the legislative process, the main disadvantage is that the majority of people do not have enough information to deliberate meaningfully on any ramifications of biotechnology. Such debate can get swamped with emotion which determines the outcome. Scientific language is out of reach for the average citizen[200] and this is a gap into which government can step, providing education and facilitating debate. The government can be constrained from using public money to favour a particular outlook and models exist where education is not just a series of

194 Prof. Michael Sandel, 'Why Democracy Matters?' BBC Radio 4, 14 March 2015, http://www.bbc.co.uk/programmes/b01nmlh2/episodes/downloads (accessed 5 March 2019).

195 Carol C Gould, 'Diversity and Democracy: Representing Differences' in Benhabib (ed) *op cit* 175.

196 Ibid.

197 Richard A Posner, *The Problems of Jurisprudence* (Harvard University Press 1993) 112.

198 Richard A Posner, *Law, Pragmatism, and Democracy* (Harvard University Press 2003) 107.

199 Ibid.

200 Smith, *op cit* 103–104.

lectures in which the masses are passive. Neither Posner nor Smith appear to have any plan to deal with an educated citizenry whose views contradict those of their rulers and their default view is patronising. Nor do they suggest how morality is to be arbitrated where it is enshrined in law, as is the case of the EPC.

There may be drawbacks to deliberative democracy, however but these revolve around the fact that debate among average, reasonable citizens is meaningless if they are insufficiently educated about biotechnology. Debates, therefore may become overly emotional.[201] Resistance to citizen participation goes back to the times of Plato and Aristotle, according to Fischer.[202] It was feared that democracy could lead to the less intelligent ruling over their more brainy counterparts, hence Plato argued that an elite group of philosophers should rule.[203] Yet some of these reservations could be addressed by Fishkin's advocacy of refined debate – which involves some education – and such engagement with the publics may lead to a governance which involves educational programmes so that they come to citizen engagement with a knowledgeable background. The language of experts can be inaccessible so the courts and legislature have stepped into this breach to date. However, we have seen that neither the legislative nor judicial branches of government are operating in a predictable manner in this realm. A change from one expert body to another may not improve matters. In any case, how, in a pluralistic world can we talk about "expertise" in moral issues? This would suggest that an objective truth is knowable and in reality all we have is a plurality of viewpoints. Petit comments that the award of property rights over living organisms is a matter of societal-wide concern and should be debated in a forum which supports public debate.[204] Institutions may not have the capacity to provide such an environment.

Why is it important to re-engage the citizenry? Arguably, if they choose to absent themselves, then that is their prerogative. However, there are views that liberty is threatened more by disengaged citizens than by those who are active in society. Putnam claims that the least tolerant people and communities in the US are also the most disconnected.[205] If they are not accessing others' views on moral issues, for example, their minds will not be changed easily and this may be important as public views are being sought on biotechnological patents. In examples from China, when citizens congregated to deliberate about infrastructure options, they were inclined to act expansively and choose projects that would benefit a larger number of people rather than individual villages.[206] This may be due to the fact that discussion broadens perspective.

201 Ibid.

202 Frank Fischer, *Democracy and Expertise: Reorienting Policy Inquiry* (Oxford University Press 2009) 53.

203 Ibid 137.

204 Elodie Petit, 'An Ethics Committee for Patent Offices?' in Aurora Plomer and Paul Torremans (eds), *Embryonic Stem Cell Patents: European Patent Law and Ethics* (OUP 2009) 319.

205 Robert Putnam, *Bowling Alone: The Collapse and Revival of American Community* (Simon and Schuster 2000) 358.

206 Fishkin, *op cit* 142.

Arguments are often made that the most deprived are the least likely to participate. However, if given the chance, the marginalised most often succeed in sourcing delegates from among themselves who advance their interests effectively. This contradicts what critics of participation tend to believe. Such representatives are often very dedicated. It has been said that groups which have been side-lined suffer from a lack of power rather than an inability to argue effectively. Disadvantaged groups often utilise passionate debate in order to progress their claims and relying on emotional and heated appeals may be an effective mobilising strategy. Critics may assert that passion has no place in the rational basis of deliberation but this dichotomy is a false one, according to Gutmann and Thompson. The truth is that privileged groups equally resort to passionate debate when their own interests are threatened.[207] It has also been postulated that deliberation may discriminate against disadvantaged groups, especially if their oratorical skills have not been honed. However, many opponents of deliberation may gain from its quieting and where decisions do not have to be subjected to public scrutiny, they may be inordinately beneficial to such opponents or, indeed, indefensible.[208]

Even where education is provided, access to the locus of decision-making is changing in a globalised world, as explored in the next section.

3.5.7 Location of debate and expert bodies

Deliberative democracy also necessitates a public sphere where discussion and debate can take place among citizens and various civil society organisations. This facilitates a focus on the constraints that can be placed on discussion in some detail. It also serves to highlight some of the opposition between liberalism and deliberative democracy. The former model of governance does not favour the input of the masses and tends to foment institutions in which particular modes of communication are enshrined, which may serve as an exclusionary force for the majority of the public.[209]

Squires identifies the diversity of views within the literature on deliberative democracy relating to where such deliberation should take place. Among the different examples cited are formal or informal spaces among representative or unrepresentative bodies. She also mentions deliberative forums, town meetings and designated deliberation times, among others, as considered models, adding that parliaments, executives and judiciaries should also be examined. She advocates for a nexus between formal and informal deliberative spaces where the latter feeds meaningfully into the former in order to ensure the legitimacy of its processes.[210]

Meaningful deliberation occurs where there is a nexus between deliberating and decision-making. Civil society frequently provides a more favourable location than

207 Gutmann and Thompson, *op cit* 50–51.

208 Ibid 55.

209 Selya Benhabib, 'Toward a Deliberative Model of Democratic Legitimacy' in Benhabib (ed) *op cit* 80.

210 Judith Squires, 'Deliberation and decision making: discontinuity in the two-track model' in D'Entrèves (ed) *op cit* 149–150.

formal political structures for deliberative practices which involve democratisation, due to the different functions provided outside of rigid political formats, according to Dryzek.[211] Civil society discourse involves contestation rather than voting and, therefore, strategic behaviour is less likely to be problematic due to the more transparent nature of discussions.[212] However, at the level of discourse, as opposed to decision, it is improbable that any important determinations are imminent so its ambit will most likely be broader and, indeed, freer. The gap between civil society and government bodies has become greater in recent times as the latter have come under the influence of unelected bodies, which will be explored in the next section.

A significant challenge to modern democracy is the rise of national and international unelected entities which operate in the interstices of law and politics.[213] The role and influence of technical experts in policy-making has been identified by Jasanoff as the fifth branch of government.[214] The nature of the unelected bodies may vary greatly: some having a human rights focus while others are commercially orientated. Whether their influence is positive or negative will depend on their enterprise and will also determine whether they can serve to enhance transparency. Elsewhere Vibert acknowledges that these entities' powers may be abused if interests other than the publics' are prioritised. Relationships which do not rank citizen interests highly may develop at an insufficient distance to ensure objectivity and fairness.[215] Rogers defends the public's right to make laws and administer public goods and this includes the extension of knowledge.[216] Technological innovation would thereby be scrutinised by the publics, by other scientists and democratic assemblies,[217] some of which, of course, may not be elected but could contribute positively in terms of facilitating knowledge. He speculates how such public participation would take shape saying that it would halt unelected officials and vested interests who may think that they have a better right to govern from making decisions out of public view.[218] It would also be important to consider such innovation in decision-making at the international level, and not just domestically, as follows.

At present, even if deliberative processes were established nationally, we are still left with the problem in the patent sphere that important bodies involved in decision-making such as the EPO would not be subject to such processes. Participation that gets encouraged at national level might find itself being stymied at its physical boundary.[219] The relevance of this commentary is that patents on morally controversial biotechnological inventions are decided often at a regional rather

211 Dryzek, *op cit* 103.
212 Ibid.
213 Vibert, *op cit* 75.
214 Sheila Jasanoff, *The Fifth Branch* (Harvard University Press 1998).
215 Vibert, *op cit* 172.
216 Rogers, *op cit* 162–163.
217 Ibid.
218 Ibid 145.
219 Gutmann and Thompson, *op cit* 39.

than national level and so the political structures are less amenable to deliberation and participation. These bodies in political science circles are defined as institutions or entities of the government to which some form of specialised public authority has been delegated. They are not elected as such and neither are they directly answerable to any elected officials.[220] The EPO would conform to this description. They do not fit neatly within traditional models of either participatory or deliberative democracy which centralise the role of the vote and the act of bargaining, or discussion respectively, nor do they adhere to precepts of the rule of law.[221] Where these novel bodies misuse their powers and perform under par, there needs to be a mechanism through which this can be improved. Otherwise, they will lose the publics' confidence.[222] If the lack of deliberation in a trans-boundary context is not redressed, democracy will be absent from important scientific issues in today's world.[223] That is likely to fuel both discontent and apathy.

Political engagement by the citizenry has declined and growing globalisation may deplete public faith in the representative aspect of democracy as the migration of power to either supranational, *quasi*-constitutional realms or to private multinational corporations and entities means that citizens' concerns are not centre stage. The rising interest in direct democracy may be as a result of the emasculation of democratic governance during these changes.[224] The move by technocratic government away from the scrutiny of public oversight in the context of a heightened vigilance on the part of the media and civil society activists, along with countervailing tendencies of private interests all impinge on the development of a healthy domain for deliberation.[225] While global governance is permeating the discourse on democracy, a blueprint for the democratisation of institutions that would arise in such political internationalisation has not been conceptualised as public involvement persists in being perceived in a domestic context. This makes it easy for international entities to operate relatively free from concerns about accountability or representation of external interests.[226] However, if an effort is made to encourage international bodies to become more deliberative they, in turn, may gain greater respect.[227]

While some theorists such as Held[228] believe that new global institutions can effectuate an international integrative approach to deliberative practices, Gutmann and Thompson advocate a nuanced method. Their rationale is that in some cases, new institutions may be necessary but increasing the number of entities which

220 Vibert, citing Mark Thatcher and Alec Stone Sweet (2002) 'Theory and Practice of Non-Majoritarian Institutions' *West European Politics* 25 (1): 1–22, 5.
221 Ibid 16.
222 Ibid 114.
223 Dryzek, *op cit* 175.
224 Tierney, *op cit* 9.
225 Ibid 26–27.
226 DL Sheth, 'Micro-Movements in India: Toward a new Politics of Participatory Democracy' in Boaventura de Sousa Santos (ed) *Democratising Democracy: Beyond the Liberal Democratic Canon* (Verso 2005) 3, 13.
227 Gutmann and Thompson, *op cit* 39.
228 David Held, *Democracy and the Global Order* (Polity Press 1995).

have a role in decision-making might have the opposite effect. The fact that many international institutions are fundamentally undemocratic would have to be addressed[229] as their influence has outweighed what was expected of them. Consideration would also have to be given to the breadth of the extension of deliberation. While some matters are appropriate for national negotiation only, arguably, such as taxation and education, where the effects will be felt more widely such as in cases of trade and economic development, there will be a greater need to deliberate across national boundaries, at an international or supranational level.[230] Patents on morally controversial biotechnological inventions in my hypothesis fit in the latter category.

There is a demand that international organisations be amenable to public scrutiny in order to establish democratic accountability by NGOs, which have sought to influence policies on a plethora of issues on the grounds that civil society's perspectives may otherwise be side-lined.[231] Greenpeace, for example, is one of the principal opposing forces to patent applications before the EPO and the Court of Justice of the European Union (CJEU) (in cases such as *Brüstle*,[232] *Plant Genetic Systems*[233] and *Oncomouse*[234]). Nonetheless, where moral issues are played out between hierarchical international organisations and NGOs which may also be internationalised and administratively tiered, deliberation might not receive much public attention.[235]

When publics are invited to get involved in public consultations on environmental matters or health care expenditure, for example, they can display an early mastery of complex events.[236] If a patent application involved a technological cure for genetic diseases, public views may differ greatly from NGOs which often mount challenges to such patents on environmental or other grounds. Publics may not always arrive at the same decision that competing vested interests have in a particular outcome of a given debate. Moreover, the use of the patent system to incentivise this type of research is not simply a matter of economics or scientific development: ethical concerns also figure in the equation and cannot be brushed aside lightly. Those with technical expertise are experts in one area only of a multidisciplinary arena.

The various developments in modern governance, including government's expansion, and the increasing globalisation of political decisions where external bodies hold more and more sway, contribute to the perception that citizens' influence over policy-making is decreasing. This has augmented apathy when it

229 Gutmann and Thompson, *op cit* 62.
230 Ibid 37.
231 Robert O. Keohane, 'Governance in a Partially Globalised World' in David Held and Anthony Grew (eds) *Governing Globalization: Power, Authority and Global Governance* (Polity Press 2002) 325–347.
232 C-34/10 *Oliver Brüstle v Greenpeace eV* [2011] ECR I-9821.
233 *Plant Genetic Systems v Greenpeace* [1995] EPOR 357.
234 T315/03 *Transgenic animals/HARVARD* 6 July 2004.
235 Dryzek, *op cit* 100.
236 Vibert, *op cit* 93.

comes to participation in traditional politics although involvement in protest and mobilisation via the Internet has not abated. The desire to participate has not disappeared but conventional means are being resorted to less and less.[237]

It has been argued that democracy is not necessarily incompatible with technology and science but the discordance lies in the way in which society is currently organised. If society is reorganised to become more democratic, it should follow that science and technology will similarly become more democratic.[238] The patent system can then be restructured to follow suit, although democratisation does not have to progress in this order as this book does not advocate societal reform on a broad scale: it focuses specifically on the application of some deliberative and participatory democracy principles and actualities to the decision-making process on morally controversial biotechnological patent grants at the EPO. The environmental movement has pioneered the establishment of more transparency through a number of means, including public inquiries, freedom of information legislation, public input and mediation, as examples. Rogers argues for the democratisation of technological and economic development by wresting it out of the exclusive domain of experts. This will enable the citizenry to choose its future rather than feeling that matters have been pre-decided.[239]

3.6 Conclusion

This chapter has shown that deliberation is cited in some of the literature on morally controversial biotechnological patents as a desirable feature of the decision-making process. It has examined several devices and has concluded that they are small-scale and would be unlikely to bring about significant change. However, when coupled with participation and appropriate structures, deliberation can be meaningful if it feeds into policy-making. There is a human right to participate within whose framework deliberation can be housed. If combined with education, public input into complex decisions can be made in a constructive way. It can avoid both elitism, which excludes many potential participants and populism which can lead to rash, ill-informed decisions. This chapter has looked at this matter largely in a theoretical context and the next chapter will explore participation and deliberation in action where it exists in Brazil in the structure of the participatory budget. It will then seek to glean principles which can be applied to the decision-making process on morally controversial biotechnological patent applications for the reform model in Chapter Five.

237 Tierney, *op cit* 32.
238 Rogers, *op cit* 103–104.
239 Dryzek, *op cit* 164.

4 The participatory budget in Brazil

4.1 Introduction

As seen already in this book, although moral criteria are taken into consideration in patent grants by the European Patent Office (EPO) and national patent offices, a number of difficulties arise from the design and functioning of the current system. There is no consensus on what morality actually is, nor is agreement ever likely to be achieved. It is also debatable whether a universal standard of morality can be defined in the context of the scope of this book, which comprises morally controversial biotechnological patents in Article 53(a) European Patent Convention (EPC) 1973 (as amended). When regulated too tightly, laws may become formalistic and not allow for flexibility. A popular alternative is for judges to exercise their common law jurisdiction in the absence of legislative guidance. However, the judiciary tend not to favour shouldering this burden[1] and often comment on and even protest at glaring lacunas in the law.[2] This raises a question as to who gets to decide on such issues when decisions have to be taken, and which means are optimal (or at least legitimate and effective) in doing so.

One of the primary arguments of this book is that judiciaries, legislatures and executive bodies, such as patent or intellectual property offices are not appropriate forums because they have difficulty arbitrating such issues for the population at large. Morality is not easily defined but is even less so in fast-moving technological realms and the responsibility for adjudicating morality for such a large jurisdiction as the EPO is a considerable burden. Nor do I favour the shifting of decision-making in this matter to ethics committees as the proposal of this book is to decentralise these decisions to the grassroots. Moreover, it is not sought to achieve an objective moral good but, rather, to maximise the number of voices who can have their meaningful say, in the context of a deliberative arena. The quest is to find practices and principles for reform which can guide the EPO in its future activities so that the heavy burden on administrators of arbitrating what constitutes morality is divested to the publics.

1 *Diamond v Chakrabarty* (1980) 447 US 303, 318.
2 *Moore v Regents of University of California* (1990) 51 Cal.3d 120, 138.

The purpose of this chapter is to set out a model of participatory democracy which involves deliberation, epitomised by the participatory budget in Porto Alegre, Brazil. I have selected this particular case study as its structures and principles can be adapted as a model for wide-scale deliberative participation. It does not exist just as a theoretical construct but has had several readjustments over the years to maximise inclusivity. No such paradigm exists in patent practice, yet in the controversial realm of morally controversial biotechnological patents, some academics argue that deliberation and participation should be a feature of the decision-making process. The budgetary model will serve as a blueprint for a radical reimagination of the manner in which the patent system, at the decision-making stage as it relates to morally controversial biotechnological patents, currently operates in Europe.

This chapter will address issues such as the involvement of the population, how information and education are dealt with and it will chart this evolution. The purpose is to show that there are principles of democracy – both participatory and deliberative – that are operating in a long established regime and these provide a model of public involvement in decisions of magnitude. This chapter links theories of deliberative democracy with their practice in this participatory regime in Brazil where they have been in use for nearly 30 years. This chapter will identify a set of principles extracted from the participatory budget for the proposed reform of the decision-making process under Article 53(a) EPC 1973 (as amended).

4.2 Participatory and representative democracy: some general points

It is important to be cognisant of the different climate in which participatory democracy has developed in Brazil when compared to older democracies. Its current Constitution dates from 1988 and was drafted in the era of international human rights law where pluralism and the notion of citizen autonomy were becoming enshrined. The citizenry has pushed back against repressive regimes – even as they pervade – and a significant emphasis has been put on endeavouring to ensure that the state transforms itself into an agent in making democracy function more effectively where structures are built to move the state closer to rather than further away from the public at large.

The Brazilian incarnation of participatory democracy is in the form of the participatory budget which allows the citizens to determine how a portion of public funds are spent. The principles and the evolution of citizen involvement have some lessons for the patent granting process on morally controversial biotechnological inventions. While involving the publics can be time-consuming and it can require a significant adjustment in the manner in which decisions are taken, if executive bodies reconceptualise their relationship with the publics, the manner in which information is imparted can change. Education, deliberation and discussion become part of the interchange between patent office and citizen. Participatory democracy goes far beyond the remit of representative democracy by holding that citizens can be involved in decision-making and not just wait passively for representatives to make decisions for them. Participation in decisions, and not just in choosing those who make the decisions, is vital to this process. This evolves into a kind of power-sharing model between civil society and elected politicians which Santos describes as co-government.[3] The state becomes more accountable to the society which it governs and, in fact, ultimately becomes more susceptible to control by that very society.[4]

The endeavour shall be to glean from the budgetary process an adaptable structure that can be used to put to a mediated vote the morality issues which arise in Art 53(a) EPC. This would involve an opportunity for individuals, as well as civil society groups to vote on patent grants where the morality bar is triggered. The participatory budget has not been confined solely to interest groups as ideological, inclusion is maximised. Such structures also tend to invigorate civil society – sometimes to the consternation of non-governmental organisations (NGOs) which may lose out, as civil society engagement with government inevitably spurs an evolution and transformation of civil society itself and, indeed, in the mode of governance. The participatory budgeting model is especially useful given its longevity as many of the potential objections to such political change, such as low participation or an ignorant public have already been encountered and the success, or otherwise, of attempts made to resolve such issues has been documented. An account of the participatory budget shall be set out below, describing the changes this has brought about to governance and the growing pains of the structure will also be analysed. Its potential relevance to patent law reform in the aforementioned area will also be discussed. I will demonstrate how the seemingly unrelated model of budgets and patent grants is, in fact, highly relevant to the core problems of the democratic deficit within the European patent system and morality.

The participatory budget provides a blueprint which can be used to explain the complexities of the interaction between representative and participatory democracy models. Participatory democracy interacts with representative democracy at a number of levels. One is where it meets municipal institutions which are a manifestation of representative democracy. The other is its evolutionary creation of ground-up representative institutions as its own practices become more sophisticated and some representative structures emerge at community level. It creates an intermediate political layer between governors and the governed. It is at this level of abstraction and operation that the model offers lessons for European patent reform.

4.2.1 Background to the participatory budget

The Brazilian Constitution 1988 provides that power derives from the people and they can exercise this power through their representatives or directly, under the Constitution.[5] There is also a right of assembly, a right to petition public

3 Boaventura de Sousa Santos, 'Two Democracies, Two Legalities: Participatory Budgeting in Porto Alegre, Brazil' in Boaventura de Sousa Santos and César A Rodríguez-Garavito (eds) *Law and Globalization from Below* (Cambridge University Press 2005) 331.

4 Ibid.

5 Article 1.

authorities and the Law on Fiscal Responsibility provides for transparency. This will be guaranteed through the involvement of the publics in meetings in which budgetary plans and guidelines are designed and discussed.[6] There is therefore an intention to embed deeply the notion of participation within political decisions. Of note is that this participatory space has been created within a constitutional framework and in the context of a human rights climate. Direct democracy in this manifestation does not seek to exclude representative democracy but endeavours to improve it from within. A new conceptualisation of rights emerged during this time which involved new relationships between civil society and the state and new forms of social relationships mediated by the state[7] which went beyond the simple acquisition of pre-existing rights. It extended to the citizenry who were enabled to redefine the rights that they desired. This has enshrined the principle of participatory democracy in civil society and also in broadening the ambit of human rights attainable.[8]

Seeking to merge class struggle with citizenship, and so bring civil society activism together with the mechanics of the political system, the Workers' Party evolved a concept of good governance, based around citizenship and embodied in participatory democracy. It was known as a party which gave a voice to social movements and it broke with tradition in that it sought to move away from the clientelism which had dominated Brazilian political life up to that point.[9] Citizenship was promoted through participatory institutions.[10] In contrast to the Eastern European form of socialism, it sought to encourage popular participation, expanding the ambit of its programmes beyond organised social movements, unions and neighbourhood associations to reach the poverty stricken. Sectors of the working and middle classes which did not traditionally participate in organisations were also sought out.[11] During the 1990s, there was a move to decentralise governance which spurred the drive to experiment with new institutional forms.[12]

Some aspects of democracy in Brazil have become transformed.[13] Such changes have been founded on grassroots political activity, especially in the global South where democracy reputedly was not deeply embedded. These practices have rejected the idea that representation is the only form of democracy available and, instead, have come to rely upon other forms such as participatory or deliberative

6 Ubiratan de Souza, 'Basic Principles' in Iain Bruce (ed) *The Porto Alegre Alternative: Direct Democracy in Action* (Pluto Press 2004) 60.

7 Gianpaolo Baiocchi, *Militants and Citizens: The Politics of Participatory Democracy in Porto Alegre* (Stanford University Press 2005) 10–11.

8 Evelina Dagnino, 'Dimensions of Citizenship in Contemporary Brazil' (2006) 75 Fordham L. Rev. 2469.

9 Baiocchi, *op cit* 11.

10 Boaventura de Sousa Santos (ed), *Democratising Democracy: Beyond the Liberal Democratic Canon* (Verso 2005) Preface x.

11 Ibid 12.

12 Ibid 8.

13 Ibid Preface xiii.

democracy. The interaction between representative and participatory democracy can be both confrontational and harmonious.[14]

Theories of participatory democracy have been translated into practice in Brazil and other jurisdictions which have adopted participatory budgeting. This has been achieved by adapting existing and creating new power structures which permeate formal decision-making – a question raised earlier by Squires who wondered how and whether this could be achieved.[15] This also occurred both at local government and state level where the Workers' Party had political influence. As Nylen and Dodd have indicated, participation had allowed the process of democracy to be reformed by the addition of a citizen-led tier of checks and balances to the representative system in Brazil.[16]

Where participation is widespread, the political process is legitimated by the consent of the people and outcomes are approved, giving government a mandate for the policy in question. However, three factors are enmeshed in assuring a more democratic approach, in Fishkin's view. These are deliberative practices, equality in the political sphere and wide-scale participation. Fishkin believes that the realisation of any two of these milestones inhibits the attainment of the third[17] but this observation may not resonate too strongly in some Latin American democracies which have enshrined participatory mechanisms in their constitutions, thereby diluting the danger of descents in the perceived anarchy of citizen participation on a grand scale. Porto Alegre's participatory budget has developed peacefully within the structures of the state.[18] The establishment of the participatory budget epitomises a model of co-government or of sharing political power through a system which links democratic institutions which have been set up to utilise deliberative decision-making mechanisms.[19] This is true involvement and interaction between the governed and the governors where the latter become scrutinised by the former but where both ultimately work together to achieve common, rather than opposing, goals.

4.2.2 The participatory budget and how it operates

Prior to the introduction of the participatory budget, Porto Alegre already had a rich tapestry of community groups, organised through neighbourhood associations, which were referred to as popular councils. These had been involved in the

14 Santos, 'Two Democracies, Two Legalities: Participatory Budgeting in Porto Alegre' in Santos and Rodríguez-Garavito (eds) *op cit* 312.
15 Judith Squires, 'Deliberation and Decision Making: Discontinuity in the Two-track Model' in Maurizio Passerin D'Entrèves (ed) *Democracy as Public Deliberation* (Manchester University Press 2002) 150.
16 William R Nylen and Lawrence C Dodd, *Participatory Democracy versus Elitist Democracy: Lessons from Brazil* (Palgrave Macmillan 2003) 146.
17 James Fishkin, *Democracy and Deliberation: New Directions for Democratic Reform* (Cambridge University Press 1991) 46.
18 Iain Bruce, 'Participatory Democracy – The Debate' in Bruce (ed) *op cit* 23.
19 Santos, 'Two Democracies, Two Legalities: Participatory Budgeting in Porto Alegre' in Santos and Rodríguez-Garavito (eds) *op cit* 325.

political struggle against the military dictatorship[20] and most of these organisations were brought together in the mid-1980s by the creation of the Union of Neighbourhood Associations of Porto Alegre (UAMPA).[21] UAMPA has come to play a significant role in the administration of the participatory budget, examined below.

Municipal power in Brazil is divided between the mayor's office, which hosts the executive power and the Chamber of Deputies, which is the legislature. The Constitution provides for legislative approval of the budget.[22] In theory, the legislative branch of the municipal government is vested with the power to approve the budget under the Constitution of 1988 and they have a significant degree of autonomy to decide on the allocation of funding in relation to works and equipment.[23] From 1989, the Workers' Party controlled the Executive but not the legislature in Porto Alegre[24] and they used the Executive to involve the public in the administration of the budget.

The participatory budget, known in Portuguese as "Orçamento Participativo", was introduced in 1989[25] and its genesis was not entirely smooth. The budget is founded on three major principles and a set of institutions serve to maintain participation in the municipal government's decision-making process. The principles comprise the right of everyone to participate; the rules of participation include a mixture of representative and direct democracy which are conducted through institutions whose rules are determined by the participants, and; investment is decided based on an objective method which comprises general and technical criteria.[26] Nonetheless, most public monies are spent on paying the wages of the city's workforce and cities are also obliged to spend over 40 per cent on education and on health,[27] not leaving very much for participatory budgeting works. In the first decade of the Workers' Party governance, locally raised taxation increased almost 200 per cent.[28] Although it is the best known example of the participatory programmes which had become commonplace in the Workers' Party dominated municipalities by the mid-1990s, it is also now prevalent in municipalities dominated by other political parties,[29] either because they have inherited it or have sought to introduce it themselves.

As part of the evolution of the budgetary process, as of 1990, two plenary meetings were held in each district. Additionally, civil society groups could assist in

20 From 1964 to 1985.
21 Iain Bruce, 'From First Steps to Final Strategies' in Bruce (ed) *op cit* 39.
22 Santos, 'Participatory Budgeting in Porto Alegre: Toward a Redistributive Democracy' in Santos (ed) *op cit* 313.
23 Santos, 'Two Democracies, Two Legalities: Participatory Budgeting in Porto Alegre' in Santos and Rodríguez-Garavito (eds) *op cit* 315.
24 Santos, 'Participatory Budgeting in Porto Alegre: Toward a Redistributive Democracy' in Santos (ed) *op cit* 312.
25 Baiocchi, *op cit* 14.
26 Santos, 'Two Democracies, Two Legalities: Participatory Budgeting in Porto Alegre' in Santos and Rodríguez-Garavito (eds) *op cit* 316–317.
27 Iain Bruce, 'From first steps to final strategies' in Bruce (ed) *op cit* 49.
28 Ibid 50.
29 Baiocchi, *op cit* 11–12.

the coordination of intermediary meetings for delegates heightening involvement, thus creating a kind of parallel democratic structure. The municipal government assisted in the organisation of all these meetings, ensuring that participation was widened beyond such movements. This involvement could be a source of controversy in that government may be accused of trying to micromanage what is, essentially, an independent and autonomous structure. However, their involvement surmounts Squire's doubt as to how formal political structures can be made permeable to civil society's input.[30] This is not deliberation in parallel spheres where the people talk but do not have any realisation of their views in policy. The creation of a parallel sphere of democratic structures, however, where civil society mobilises and gets involved in seeking election to the decision-making bodies does have the effect of influencing policy and decision-making.

Any participant can attend the plenary meetings and delegates are chosen from among these to deliberate in the districts. Councillors are chosen from among the delegates to participate at the Budget Council. Every year there is a fresh intake of participants, which number between 15 and 20 per cent, who lack previous experience of the Budget and who are without ties to neighbourhood associations. Many progress to become delegates and councillors.[31]

In relation to its structures, the participatory budget may manifest itself in a variety of forms. It can be revolutionary but it need not be so and reform is another of its incarnations. This is relevant in the sense of principles which may be extracted in order to construct a particular model of patenting approval in the realm of morally controversial biotechnological inventions. It has been observed that where deliberative devices such as consultative assemblies are used, indirect representation is optimised and this does mobilise the population but this does not build a power structure.[32] However, participatory devices can be revolutionary and transformative and they can change the operation of the state from within. Close relationships between the private sector and public representatives can be disturbed where civil society is more involved with the running of the state. It brings the management of the budget down to grassroots level, comprehensible to the common person. It also comes within public control.[33]

The participatory budgeting structure has evolved over its lifespan and priorities are not set solely by the government. In this way, new forms of citizen power have been created. The relevance for patent law reform on morally controversial biotechnological inventions is that if publics are more involved in the process of incentivising technological developments, biotechnology and its promises may advance much more speedily. More voices will also be heard on the varying moralities and a greater understanding of different viewpoints may be achieved.

30 Judith Squires, in D'Entreves (ed) *op cit* 150.
31 Baiocchi, *op cit* 43.
32 Iain Bruce, 'The Participatory Budget in Two Other Cities (interview with Edinho Silva)' in Bruce (ed) *op cit* 85.
33 Ibid.

4.2.3 Increase in scope of issues and political organisation

In Brazil, during the development of the participatory budgeting process, more and more issues came under the collective decision-making umbrella. In 1991, the administration created a Budget Council, which had two representatives from each district, along with one each from UAMPA and the municipal employees' union.[34] Participants came to be involved in all stages of the budgetary process from making demands, to assessing overall priorities and monitoring outcomes.[35] Administrators eschewed organising participation around pre-existing neighbourhood associations in order to facilitate the participation of all citizens. This was inclusive beyond what is normally seen in participatory politics where citizens may be given a chance to vote in a referendum or else attend consultation sessions but not actually delineate the content of what is to be decided.

The administration became more involved in mediating societal needs and in coordinating participation. This broke with previous political practice in which civil society operated under a system of tutelage.[36] This favoured politically partial sectors but also created resentment and protest among associations not so favoured.[37] Massive participation from poor districts was encouraged and relied upon. The administration no longer privileged certain groups or political allies but, rather, facilitated citizens in formulating their own demands.[38] It also sought to include the middle classes, many of whom supported the Workers' Party but who did not participate in forums which focused on urban infrastructure needs. This outreach extended to NGOs, unions and social movements and this was done by setting up new thematic meetings on issues such as transport, health, education and culture, economic development and urban planning. Community members now are able to deliberate, propose, decide and vote on how a portion of the city's budget is spent. In subsequent years, these same participants can monitor the progress of works they have chosen to see implemented. Such organisation took some years to consolidate.[39] District level meetings were not appropriate forums for matters such as education and culture, for instance, because they deal with local issues. Thematic meetings were set up for this purpose to impact on daily running of these departments rather than focusing solely on investment in the area.[40] This shows that the budgetary process is an evolutionary one which has adapted to tackle new challenges and has not become fossilised.

There was also a greater willingness on the part of the administration in Porto Alegre to adapt when certain complaints were made about the small

34 Baiocchi, *op cit* 37–38.
35 Ibid 37.
36 Ibid 39.
37 Ibid 41–42.
38 Ibid 39.
39 Catalina Pérez Correa, 'Managing Violence: Law as Fetish, Alibi or Deceit, Distrust and Disobedience: Discourse and Practice of Law in Mexico' (2008) 77 *Rev Jur UPR* 345, 363.
40 Baiocchi, *op cit* 40–41.

number of meetings held at the outset. It responded to criticisms by increasing the number of district meetings to 16 and a representative was elected for each district. They participated in a committee set up to select the actual projects for 1990.[41] Other changes wrought in response to criticisms included the fact that originally, a single meeting was held in each district without any preparatory meetings. This meant that participation equated to merely articulating demands – and no more. Participants were not satisfied with this model of participation and they requested that the process be commenced earlier in the year, that the yearly budgeting cycle be explained and that a yearly meeting be held to update those present on the progress of continuing projects. The municipal administration responded positively and a day of accounting also became a regular feature of the budgetary cycle.[42] Decisions are not just taken, therefore but results are expected to be shown so there is a sense that the budget is seen through to its outputs. This demonstrates that the Brazilian model of participatory budgeting is a continuing process of engagement between politicians and civil society, along with activists who have become involved in the budgetary process. Communication occurs in both directions, debate is mediated and potential weaknesses in such a system are minimised by the mutuality that exists between governors and citizens.

The principles of participation which can be extracted for the reform of Article 53(a) EPC decisions will similarly require some adjustments over time and it is to be expected that much interaction would occur over issues such as whether Article 53(a) EPC had been triggered along with information campaigns, location and voting procedures. In principle, the executive body in the form of the EPO could use its skills to administer debate once an ethical issue is identified. An ethics committee would need to be established for this purpose. This will be elaborated further in the next chapter.

4.2.4 Obligatory participation or encouragement to participate?

Whether participation should be encouraged or made obligatory is sometimes raised. In a comparative sphere, in Brazil, voting is mandatory, and a poll carried out in 1998 showed that 75 per cent of respondents could not recall whom they had voted for in the previous elections.[43] Whereas statistics for participation remain relatively low in that often below 1 per cent of the population will participate regularly in budgetary decisions,[44] arguably, an essential component of democracy is that the option to participate is open. When voter turnout is low, it does not mean that the right to vote will be taken away and the same applies to the rationale of allowing and encouraging participation. While only about 20 per cent of delegates in the participatory budget were inactive in civil society before

41 Ibid 34.
42 Ibid 36.
43 Nylen and Dodd, *op cit* 14.
44 Ibid 95.

taking part in this process,[45] almost half of those who were previously disinterested became involved subsequently.[46]

The participation rate at the first round of participatory meetings, held in five different venues in the city, was under 1,000 people in total. These meetings were somewhat chaotic as the organisers were not well prepared. Moreover, given that the city has a population of over one million, transport for some community members proved to be cost prohibitive and time-consuming.[47] These issues are pertinent to the prospect of the creation of a patent suffrage as the logistics of accessibility will have to be considered, for example. Advance planning on locations, transport and accessibility along with times of any meetings will be important. Fishkin opines that turnout is imperative[48] but the only way that this could be assured in participatory politics would be to mandate participation or the vote and this option tends not to be popular.

In terms of citizen involvement, the numbers have increased progressively over the years, rising from 3,000 in 1991 to 6,000 in 1992, 7,600 by 1996,[49] and by 2000, more than 14,000 participants attended the first yearly participatory budget assembly.[50] Some biographers point out that normally between 2 and 7 per cent of the population participate.[51] The profile of the average participant is someone who is less well-off and less well educated than the citywide average. This shows that common myths about disadvantaged people not participating in schemes to address their own inequalities can be inaccurate. Significant improvements have been made to the city's poorer areas in particular. Between 9 and 21 per cent of the total municipal budget[52] is ring fenced for participatory budgetary investments and poorer areas get the largest share of investments. Numerous projects, such as improvements in infrastructure, education and health have been approved and completed. The participation of the poor has been secured by connecting their participation to redistributive outcomes.[53] When the poor see that their participation yields results, they are incentivised to participate. Without a similar connection to patents on biotechnological inventions, it is unlikely that participation rates around moral issues would be high. However, with more public discussion on the promises for disease prevention, especially given a rapidly ageing population and diminishing resources along with an understanding of the costs involved for the biotech companies, participation could be incentivised. Publics may also decide to look more favourably on technological development than do many NGOs which often challenge patents successfully. Involvement of the citizenry in decisions

45 Ibid 70.
46 Ibid 71.
47 Pérez Correa, *op cit* 364.
48 Fishkin, *op cit* 179.
49 Baiocchi, *op cit* 40.
50 Ibid 14.
51 Yves Cabannes, 'Participatory Budgeting: A Significant Contribution to Participatory Democracy' (2004) 16 *Environment and Urbanization* 27.
52 This Stood at US $610 Million in 2000.
53 Baiocchi, *op cit* 14.

relating to morally controversial biotechnological patent applications could similarly encourage more participants in the shaping of genetic research upstream which attracts this intellectual property protection.

The participatory budget is not a panacea for the ills of citizens' perception of a democratic deficit in their dealings with the political class. Most of those who do get involved have already been activists in civil society[54] and tend to continue their participation beyond the first year, which is when many people get exhausted. Furthermore, the most deprived were among the least likely to engage with the participatory budget.[55] Yet, the activists are not members of the elite but space has been created for their participation in municipal administration and when the participatory budget was rolled out at state level in Rio Grande do Sul for a few years at the beginning of the twenty-first century, non-elites were empowered at that level too. The participatory budget process provides a means of empowering non-elites and providing space for their political activity. This has the effect of bringing diversity and it pluralises political structures somewhat, which helps to ensure that there are checks and balances to political power at society's upper echelons. In Brazil it has been found that allowing decision-making through a direct vote has attracted ordinary, non-activist citizens to the process and civil society organisations can also mobilise participants to engage and vote.[56] It has been reported that regular participation took off when individual citizens with a particular concern started attending meetings.[57] The vote is direct but community groups are also represented and alliances can be formed because it is appreciated that there is strength in numbers.[58] Over time, participants mobilise neighbours who share their concerns and this often eventually matures into an association. This ignites activity in civil society and foments the growth of new organisations.[59]

In the realm of morally controversial biotechnological patents, citizens may engage more if they are aware of the issues and it concerns them in some way such as in the case where there is a patent application for a morally controversial invention which promises to treat disease. Genetic diseases such as cystic fibrosis are becoming increasingly difficult to manage given growing resistance to antibiotics and a genetic fix paid for by a patent monopoly may well encourage advocacy groups to decide that morality is on the side of the patent applicant. Biotech firms could also benefit from the opportunity to counter negative publicity from the press and fringe groups by the holding of public debates. Moreover, at present, there is not a lot of public awareness of biotechnology and its associated patents, either from the perspective of pertinent moral issues or possibilities for improving human health. It may be that this will not change significantly as patents do not affect as many people daily as do municipal budgets but principles of

54 Nylen and Dodd, *op cit* 70.
55 Ibid 71.
56 Iain Bruce, 'From First Steps to Final Strategies' in Bruce (ed) *op cit* 45.
57 Baiocchi, *op cit* 43.
58 Cabannes, *op cit* 27.
59 Baiocchi, *op cit* 43.

the right to participate in debate still apply. Moreover, more public debate may lead to a greater awareness of the technologies, the moralities and the interests at stake.

4.2.5 Education and educating the educators

There are a number of erroneous assumptions in the academic literature about the identity of participants in participatory democracy in general – for instance, that they are educated and rich which is challenged by empirical work on the participatory budget. In studies of two cities in Brazil, Nylen and Dodd found that most of the participatory budgeting delegates did not have a high school education. They were drawn mainly from the working class or were housewives, had retired or were unemployed.[60] Many participants have also emerged from living under a long period of dictatorship. They thus differ significantly from traditional, archetypal public sphere participants in much Western literature.[61] While taken in the context of Brazil's hierarchical political structure which does not engage the citizenry very much, the disadvantaged tend to be prepared to engage in substantial numbers in local administration, given the chance. This leads to a broadening of engagement in democracy and hence a transformation.[62]

Those at the very bottom echelons of society can be difficult to reach (and certainly very easy to ignore) although the problem of their disengagement is likely to have very deep roots.[63] What has tended to tilt the balance towards engagement somewhat is when those persuaded to get involved see results: that promised works are actually carried out and that voices have been heard. When people have access to details of the budget, they come to understand the interrelation between society and the state and the limits on funding, due to the public debt and the influence of the International Monetary Fund on budgetary matters.[64]

Steps have been taken in Brazil to educate where needed, recognising that participatory institutions and processes enable the placement of decision-making in the public sphere.[65] Education and capacity-building is essential and this facilitates a greater understanding among delegates of the limited choices that sometimes face politicians. For instance, delegates come to comprehend that public funds are significantly limited. During negotiations in relation to the budget, being able to access and understand pertinent information is, in all probability, the most basic prerequisite for effective communication. Much of the information is technical and, so, local government has made an effort to render it more comprehensible whereas before, this was monopolised by staff

60 Nylen and Dodd, *op cit* 90.
61 Baiocchi, *op cit* 3–4.
62 Nylen and Dodd, *op cit* 90.
63 Ibid 79.
64 Ubiratan de Souza, 'On a Bigger Scale: Rio Grande do Sul and Nationwide' in Bruce (ed) 107.
65 Nylen and Dodd, *op cit* 121.

with technical know-how.[66] The transfer of this practice of educating both technical staff and the populace in, respectively, effective communication and response and comprehension of the subject matter can be modelled closely on what has proved effective in terms of citizen knowledge and participation. Issues surrounding morality under Article 53(a) EPC are complex and, therefore, an educational process is likely to be required on matters relating to science and economics as well as ethical foundations such as deontological and utilitarian approaches. Before engaging with the public, anyone imparting knowledge in their discipline would have to make sure that the language that they use is accessible. An educational process would involve training citizens in matters such as relevant aspects of biotechnology, ethical issues, what the patent system seeks to achieve, business interests, animal experimentation and matters relating to the status of the human embryo, along with other ethical issues which could arise. The recent cases at the EPO and the Court of Justice of the European Union (CJEU) of *WARF*[67] *and Brüstle*[68] respectively could be used to explain some of the issues with which Boards of the EPO and courts within the EU are faced. Given that both these cases were not expansive when it came to patent law, they would be a good place to start the debate.

The participatory budget involves a society-wide negotiation of access to public resources through deliberative means, in Avritzer's account. This model replaces elitist customs and approaches the issue of technical control over decision-making in an alternative manner to that of our established concept of democracy.[69] The educative process is as important for the communicators as for those to whom communication is made. Santos observes of participatory budgeting that staff have undergone a learning process in terms of their engagement with the publics. They have to adapt the language they use in order to communicate more clearly and effectively. They must persuade rather than mandate and there has been a shift from a very bureaucratic to a more democratic approach.[70]

In other words, the technical staff must learn to communicate in layman's terms. Continual engagement between elite holders of knowledge and their electors will facilitate such mutual understanding. This book recommends that such techno-democracy be extended to the area of morally controversial biotechnological patent grants. This can be achieved by an educational process, to inform the publics about such technologies which potentially attract intellectual property protection. The publics will then deliberate and decide on whether these be granted or otherwise. In two Brazilian cities where the participatory budget has been adopted – Belo Horizonte and Betim – the executive has provided courses at

66 Santos, 'Participatory Budgeting in Porto Alegre: Toward a Redistributive Democracy' in Santos (ed) *op cit* 340.
67 G2/06 *WARF/Stem Cells* [2009] EPOR 15.
68 C-34/10 *Oliver Brüstle v Greenpeace eV* [2011] ECR I-9821.
69 Leonardo Avritzer, 'Modes of Democratic Deliberation: Participatory Budgeting in Brazil' in Santos (ed) *op cit* 399.
70 Santos, 'Participatory Budgeting in Porto Alegre: Toward a Redistributive Democracy' in Santos (ed) *op cit* 352.

a highly regarded school of public administration,[71] signifying that participation is taken seriously and delegates' competence is valued and cultivated. Moreover, the simplification and distribution of complex information by way of pamphlets and hand-outs, sometimes in comic format, is routine.[72]

It would be within the capabilities of the EPO to deal with issues relating to morally controversial biotechnological patents in a similar manner. Adapting the presentation of information is essential, not only for people from different disciplines, languages and educational backgrounds but also for different types of learners. For instance, the use of diagrams and entertaining presentations could be used to explain biotechnological inventions as a supplement to dense text. Broader discussions about morality and how to navigate controversial issues could also be held. The establishment of an ethics committee to oversee the morality provision in Article 53(a) EPC could be considered and it could contribute to and manage these debates without offering an opinion.

Informed negotiations over limited budgets often encourage compassionate approaches – exemplified where disadvantaged neighbourhoods vote for projects in worse off areas. Much of this change of perspective is achieved through informed deliberation: where delegates and participants have had a chance to see for themselves the needs of particular areas. When they also deliberate, they may increase their comprehension of what will benefit them both individually and collectively.[73] Moreover, the participatory budget can be seen to be effective so that citizens do have a genuine perception of goals being set – and met. Santos gives an example of how redistribution has been effected. While in 1989 only 49 per cent of Porto Alegre's population had water and sewerage services, by 1996, 98 per cent were connected to the water supply and 85 per cent had secured access to sewage facilities.[74] The increased transparency over the way in which budgetary resources were allocated is believed by a former mayor of Porto Alegre, Tarso Genro, to have increased the motivation to pay taxes. When tax revenues increased, more funding became available for participatory budgeting projects.[75]

The participatory budget in Brazil has addressed the issue of the need to educate public contributors to budget negotiations by providing training for delegates. The EPO can pro-actively pursue a strategy of a more educated citizenry in terms of technology and morality, so that awareness of the manifold moral issues which arise in biotechnological inventions is increased and this may foster participation. Indeed, the politicians who do not have a good grasp of the issues which they are delegating to unelected experts may choose badly and may be no more suited to assessing the competence of said experts than the uneducated public at large. This stark polarisation has been alleviated in Brazil by the training of delegates and, although arguably this

71 The Fundação João Pinheiro in Minas Gerais, in Nylen and Dodd, *op cit* 122.

72 Ibid.

73 Amy Gutmann and Dennis Thompson, *Why Deliberative Democracy?* (Princeton University Press 2004) 12.

74 Santos, 'Participatory Budgeting in Porto Alegre: Toward a Redistributive Democracy' in Santos (ed) *op cit* 336.

75 Ibid 337.

creates a specialised class of grassroots participators, their states can be understood as intermediate to the elite class and the masses in general. This intermediate class may help bridge the current divide between the educated and educators.

Rogers discusses the introduction of deliberation whereby the populace could question scientists about their work, however, such communication would be in one direction only, involving the imparting of information to the citizen without a concomitant right of the citizen to reply. A more appropriate approach could be to educate the scientist simultaneously about the publics' trepidation regarding the research being conducted and this could foster greater cooperation in a cross-sectorial fashion.[76] This could also be stressful for scientists but were this to become routine, people from different backgrounds may find a common language. Principles for such an approach can be gleaned from the participatory budget where a bridge has been built between administrative expertise and participatory citizens. NGOs could benefit from learning how to communicate better and everyone could also receive instruction on ethical issues in a deliberative and participatory environment.

4.2.6 Quasi-legality or legislation?

According to Santos, the participatory budget lacks formal legal recognition and is a political amalgam approved by the executive branch of local government. It is, however, illegal from the viewpoint of the legislative branch of local government.[77] Once the budget has been deliberated, the mayor's office is supposed to submit the proposal to the legislature. From a legal perspective, the legislature has the options of approving the proposal unconditionally, seeking some changes or rejecting it outright. However, given that the budgetary proposal has already been negotiated through the mechanisms of the participatory process and, therefore, has been approved by the citizenry, in political terms, it would be highly risky to raise objections and be seen to vote against the popular will. This subversion of the legislature's function is a cause for ongoing conflict between the executive and legislative branches of government in Porto Alegre.[78] The Mayor's Office actively helped to bring about the legislature's exclusion. In terms of principles applicable to Article 53(a) EPC, officials at the EPO currently responsible for deciding issues of morality could instead be charged with the task of facilitating civil society deliberation and voting rather than making these fraught decisions themselves. The costs could be absorbed by the patent grants, thus increasing these somewhat but this process may also result in more patents being granted as currently there is a bar on patenting inventions involving the destruction of the human embryo. *WARF*[79] would have an opportunity to put

76 Rogers, *op cit* 145.
77 Santos, 'Two Democracies, Two Legalities: Participatory Budgeting in Porto Alegre' in Santos and Rodríguez-Garavito (eds) *op cit* 316.
78 Ibid.
79 G2/06 *WARF/Stem Cells* [2009] EPOR 15.

its case to the public in a mediated debate where participators are already well versed in the issues. The EPO should also have an ethical committee to advise on which applications engage Article 53(a). These changes in responsibilities would require a revision of the EPC and the Biotech Directive.

Some Brazilians would like to see the budgetary process codified.[80] As matters stand, the budget is part of a political contract between the Executive and the citizenry. An ongoing debate revolves around whether it should be enshrined in law in order to preserve its existence. To do so, however, would bring it under the control of the legislature and such codification could threaten the manner in which it has been able to evolve.[81] While legislative protection could buffer it from future political interference or change, codification would serve to subordinate the participatory process to representative democracy. This debate is likely to continue, especially as in the newly demarcated political spaces of the participatory budget, the legislature will continue to try to carve out a niche for itself.[82]

In terms of the relevance of this debate to any change in the decision-making process at the EPO, codification can be quite final and it would also take some time to achieve, given that reform of an international convention is an onerous process. It may be possible to let public involvement to develop as a practice before legal reform is considered and to allow for the establishment of an ethics committee that would be charged with identifying patent applications that engaged the morality bar in Article 53(a) EPC. From the point of view of proponents of the participatory budget that favour legislation, participation could be disempowered by a hostile executive and therefore there is an argument in favour of legalising and clarifying its status. It would be best to legislate for public involvement after a period of trial and error in which unexpected issues can arise and the legislation can then be based on experience rather than exclusively on theory. In any case, the participatory budget does exist in a legislative framework, in some places, as will be shown.

Peru is the first country in the world in which municipal authorities are now legally required to devise participatory development plans and budgets as the participatory budget has been put on a legislative footing. Co-governance has developed through this practice and Hordijk observes that participation by citizens must be mirrored by institutional reform by governments to create space for their activity. This entwines participation with representation.[83]

She claims that the Peruvian law emerged from discussions between government and civil society and incorporated suggestions from both.[84] This raises the issue as to when it may be necessary to formalise the participatory process.

80 Santos, 'Participatory Budgeting in Porto Alegre: Toward a Redistributive Democracy' in Santos (ed) *op cit* 355.

81 Santos, 'Two Democracies, Two Legalities: Participatory Budgeting in Porto Alegre' in Santos and Rodríguez-Garavito (eds) *op cit* 333–334.

82 Ibid 335.

83 Michaela Hordijk, 'Participatory Governance in Peru: Exercising Citizenship' (2005) 17 *Environment and Urbanization* 219.

84 Ibid 222.

Without an adequate legal structure, there is a danger that it will not survive. On the other hand, if it is formalised, it might be sabotaged or heavily bureaucratised. What is important for its continuity is that it becomes institutionalised so that there is a point of no return.[85] In that way it survives changes in government.

Santos opines that its force lies in its potential for destabilising existing practices and that its survival will depend not on any consolidation of its legal status but, rather, in the extent to which it becomes an entrenched practice and the breadth of its penetration in other areas, not currently within its domain. It may well succeed in permanently ending the former political practices which its establishment sought to address. Its principal positive influence to date has been the promotion of the involvement of the citizenry in the actualisation of greater distributive justice, with all that this implies in terms of accountability and political transparency. As it matures as a political project, participants continue their involvement but the community representatives will steadily become more specialised. Over time, a balance will have to be achieved between its subversive traits and the limits of such insubordination.[86]

Political scientists and constitutional theorists have been accredited by Tierney with identifying several conundrums with the modern incarnation of representative democracy. These can be categorised as a lack of balance among institutions, one-sidedness and influence from outside.[87] The doctrine of the separation of the powers is not fully operational in that the Executive, in many cases, dominates inordinately the legislature and this allows the former to monopolise the latter's agenda.[88] Such controversies have caused ongoing political disagreement in Brazil but before the establishment of the participatory budget, it was the legislative wing of government – certainly at municipal level, if not at state and federal levels – which dominated the Executive. Its clientelistic version of politics saw the legislature often undermine Executive plans and the latter therefore in turn subverted the function of the former by opening the vote on how some of the budget was to be spent to the people in general.[89] By not putting these practices on a formal footing, the participatory budget retains an almost anarchic character which seems to disturb a common trend in which the institutions of representative democracy become fossilised and far removed from the electorate after a time. Again, any grafting of this scheme onto patent matters will require a significant degree of oversight and fine tuning and a legislative framework rather than an *ad hoc* process would be necessary to achieve this. It is unlikely that any such modification of the role of officials at the EPO would be subversive in the manner described of the Brazilian participatory budgetary process where there was political struggle over

85 Cabannes, *op cit* 27.

86 Santos, 'Participatory Budgeting in Porto Alegre: Toward a Redistributive Democracy' in Stephen Tierney, *Constitutional Referendums: The Theory and Practice of Republican Deliberation* (Oxford University Press 2012) 357.

87 Tierney, *op cit* 25.

88 Ibid.

89 Santos, 'Participatory Budgeting in Porto Alegre: Toward a Redistributive Democracy' in Santos (ed) *op cit* 354–355.

limited resources. The change in focus of the activities of the EPO would be delineated clearly and carried out.

4.2.7 Effect on civic life of participation

Brazil's transition to democracy witnessed the emergence of an active civil society against a backdrop of a corrupt political system dominated by patronage.[90] Civic engagement is often assumed by scholars of social capital and the public sphere, according to Baiocchi to take place entirely outside of the realm of the state.[91] In Brazil, while it is true that the popular council meetings are autonomous and voluntary, nonetheless they are encouraged and supported by government. Their activities are also integrated with the municipal administration.

Many citizens who began taking part in the participatory budget because of a particular issue got involved in popular councils and neighbourhood associations.[92] These latter associations at times engaged with politicians in order to facilitate communication between the state and citizens. There were, therefore, strong bonds between these groups and municipal administrations.[93] Popular councils at times serve as intermediaries between these associations and the municipal government but this is not always the case.[94] Some popular councils oppose the participatory budget, especially where neighbourhood associations may have felt wronged by an adverse decision in the budgetary process.[95] For the most part, however, the budget has become central to life in the community. Participation in civil society is affected by participation in the budgetary process: surveys reveal that 10 per cent participate less in civil society, 27 per cent report no change but an equal number claim that their involvement has increased. Some start their civic life through the participatory budget while others do the opposite.[96]

The routinisation of the participatory budget has brought about an evolution in civic life. Access to governmental decision-making has been democratised and new community figures have emerged.[97] Moreover, the institutionalisation of the participatory budget has changed the relationship between community leaders and the people that they represent. There is now a new political tier through which negotiation must occur. Clashes are frequent but are also often resolved through the intervention of experienced activists.[98] Those experienced at deliberation in a participatory setting will be aware that individual preferences are likely to be transformed in order that collective decisions may be taken. Moreover, these will generally be regarded as fair.[99] Baiocchi

90 Baiocchi, *op cit* 9.
91 Ibid 132.
92 Ibid 3–4.
93 Ibid, 27.
94 Ibid 3–4.
95 Ibid 122.
96 Ibid 43.
97 Ibid 134.
98 Ibid 133.
99 Ibid 73.

speaks of Robert Putnam's investigations of what makes democracy work. Civic networks are deemed to be important in promoting and facilitating cooperative behaviour in order to reach the point of a shift from individual to collective concerns.[100]

Many societal activists became part of the Workers' Party which sought to democratise society further. Formal political institutions have thus been connected with informal ones involving political activism. This has dynamised the political system which appears to be addressing to some degree the above-mentioned stagnation associated with representative democracy.[101] Baiocchi notes the positive effect that facilitated participation has had on access to services and resources.[102]

In the case of the budget, processes tend to be ongoing because many meetings are needed to become informed, to elect delegates, to monitor the processes and also, of course, to vote on issues eventually. Fishkin believes that participation does not privilege prior deliberation[103] but this is not true in the Brazilian example expounded in this book and much will depend on the manner in which any reforming or revolutionising system is designed. The patent reform envisaged in this book requires deliberation because of the complexity of the issues at stake and the fact that education and debate would need to take place before decisions could be made. Participation without deliberation and education would be meaningless and, indeed, could be very counter-productive.

4.2.8 The role of the state in approximating representation to participation

Supporters of the participatory budget argue that a new concept of democratic efficiency is nigh, believing that the optimal way of reforming the state is not to take it apart but to transform and democratise it from within by establishing participatory institutions to ensure accountability.[104] A gentle internal revolution can be achieved by refocusing the functions of some of the bodies of the state. Tierney notes the interconnectedness between representation and popular sovereignty. Participation should be interlinked to representation and the former will be constrained somewhat within a constitutional framework but can also flourish in this environment.[105]

The upsurge in participatory democracy has been detailed by Santos who describes it as a mechanism for resistance against exclusion that has been used by disadvantaged communities and civil society groups. Many of these initiatives arise both in rural and urban settings and are beginning to interconnect at national levels so the scope is expanding. He says that a point of conflict between the North and South emanates from a confrontation between representative and participatory democracy. These are not always seen as complementary forces or

100 Ibid 96.
101 Nylen and Dodd, *op cit* 20.
102 Baiocchi, *op cit* 152.
103 Fishkin, *op cit* 179.
104 Nylen and Dodd, *op cit* 120.
105 Tierney, *op cit* 136–137.

practices and the polarity derives from efforts by democracy's representative face to suppress its participatory facets. This can only be addressed and remedied if both forms of democracy are made to work together in a complementary fashion.[106] Participatory practices undermine elitism in that they demonstrate that change can be effectuated simultaneously with administrative competence. It appears that the complexities of modern democracies are no bar to the infusion of participation in practice. In fact, greater justice can become enshrined in the manner in which public resources are shared out.[107]

Some experts on the operation of the participatory budget in Brazil, while acknowledging its ideological roots in the popular councils of the Russian revolution, distinguish it sharply from power structures in Eastern Europe. The participatory budget's function is not to legitimate the state: instead, it must be autonomous. However, this does not mean that its operation is anarchic. Instead, the participatory budget structures require organisation and encouragement while still maintaining independence from the state.

Porto Alegre's participatory budget is based on three main tenets – two of which are relevant to this discussion: that all citizens can participate equally – local associations are not favoured. Representative and direct democracy rules apply in combination and participants decide on the rules which govern the channelling institutions.[108] The budgetary model shows that wide-scale participation of individuals is possible over a long period of time. Much depends on structure, communication and that participation is conceptualised in a deliberative climate where matters get discussed.

4.2.9 Global recognition and transplantability

Porto Alegre has achieved international recognition for its participatory budgetary scheme by activists, international organisations and from policy makers from all over the world.[109] In the last 20 years, different varieties of the participatory budget have been adopted by over 200 cities in Brazil.[110] Countries including Peru, the Philippines, and the State of Kerala in India have legislated in order to mandate that citizens have an opportunity to express directly their budgetary priorities at local government annually.[111] International organisations include the United Nations Development Programme (UNDP)-funded International Observatory of Participatory Democracy (also the International Budget Network, the

106 Santos, 'Participatory Budgeting in Porto Alegre: Toward a Redistributive Democracy' in Santos (ed) *op cit* Preface x.

107 Ibid Preface xiii.

108 Ibid 314.

109 Baiocchi, *op cit* 15.

110 Scott Burris, Michael Kempa and Clifford Shearing, 'Changes in Governance: A Cross-Disciplinary Review of Current Scholarship' (2008) 41 Akron L. Rev 49.

111 See World Bank, 'The Social Accountability Sourcebook' (Social Development Paper No. 76, 2004) http://www-esd.worldbank.org/sac/essd9.swf (accessed 5 March 2019).

European-based Budget Participatif network, International Forum of Local Authorities). The charter of the 'Radically Democratize Democracy Network', a group based in Europe with members in over 20 countries, eulogises the participatory budget and acknowledges the novel relationship between civil society and elected politicians that this practice has established.[112]

At the United Nation's Habitat II Conference in 1996, the participatory budgets of the Brazilian cities of Porto Alegre and Betim were chosen as being among the world's most exemplary models of public administration.[113] Santos believes that the participatory budget could be employed at regional and national level[114] and Portugal has become the first country in the world to introduce the participatory budget nationwide in 2017.[115] Bruce argues that the federal budget should also be debated and notes that the participatory budget has had a presence at state level in Rio Grande do Sul.[116] The population of Portugal and Rio Grande do Sul, at approximately ten million each, are similar in terms of scale. This book advances the hypothesis, that it could be extended to international level, specifically to Article 53 (a) EPC decisions and it also advocates that it should be, given the fact that many international institutions could adopt more robust democratic structures.

There is a need to search for and demand a more inclusive mode of governance, given that so much of the world's population has little or no input into policies which affect us, in Crawford's view. He advocates the adoption of a model which utilises participatory and representative democratic mechanisms in the context of climate change governance[117] and, of course, other areas could also be decided in this fashion. Participatory governance is believed to be adaptable to a number of different areas in addition to budgets. It has been described broadly as a system whose discourse is not necessarily confined to specific areas of spending such as health or education and its remit can be extended.[118]

This would not, however, involve substituting representative democracy by participatory but, rather, would introduce a participatory element to representative democracy, involving the adaptation to a new form of governance: co-governance.[119]

Proponents of representative democracy sometimes argue that Grecian models of direct democracy cannot work in the modern world as size is a constraint along with the complication of more diversity. Absent in this mindset is public discussion of notions of the common good and in its place resides a liberal adherence to

112 Baiocchi, *op cit* 154–155.

113 Nylen and Dodd, *op cit* 89.

114 Boaventura de Sousa Santos, *Toward a New Legal Common Sense* (2nd edn, Butterworths 2002) 491.

115 Portugal has announced the world's first nationwide participatory budget, https://apolitical.co/portugal-world-first-participatory-budget/ (accessed 5 March 2019).

116 Ubiratan de Souza, 'On a Bigger Scale: Rio Grande do Sul and Nationwide' in Bruce (ed) *op cit* 100.

117 Colin Crawford, 'Our Bandit Future? Cities, Shantytowns and Climate Change Governance' (2009) 36 Fordham Urb. L.J. 222.

118 Baiocchi, *op cit* 102.

119 Crawford, *op cit* 251.

diverse viewpoints which render common goals unattainable. This consideration tends to encourage the idea that the champions of rights do not need to be beneficiaries and that effectively anyone can act as a representative of any viewpoint or circumstance and this book rejects this proposition.

The questions of how deliberation influences policy and whether it needs enabling mechanisms are interrelated and tested in Brazil but the Workers' Party agenda was to encourage civil and political society to connect. Societal mobilisation is channelled through structures, which reverses traditional hierarchies, culminating in a situation where civil society starts to control the state. The intermediate layer of parallel democracy which has emerged as a unifying feature in the twilight between civil society and the political class has survived for over two decades and continues to evolve and may help to inform reform of the current decision-making processes at the EPO when Article 53(a) EPC is triggered.

The deployment of participatory democracy mechanisms could change the nature of political practices, encouraging organisations to educate and engage citizens and to become involved in the development and implementation of plans and ventures. Society would, in this system, become more decentralised and citizens would wield more power over decisions which affect them and their communities directly. Rogers envisages that the decision-making process could be carried out through decentralised, outward looking participant networks rather than a more hierarchical structure.[120]

4.3 Principles of participation for patent reform

There are elements of the participatory budget's structure which, when abstracted from the subject matter can be applied as a means to reform the decision-making process of the patent system at the EPO when the matter of morality arises. In brief, these are as follows:

1 Participation is a human right which is open to all – individual input is welcome as group membership is not prerequisite. This would constitute a right to be heard or the right to have a voice.
2 Where there is an information gap, efforts to educate can be made in a deliberative setting where those imparting information can be questioned. Their language must be pitched at the appropriate level. In this way, there will not be a need to glean one's information from various state bodies and NGOs which tend to use highly specialised language. Communication would comprise the essence of this principle.
3 Those imparting information will learn to listen as well as to speak and hierarchical structures are not favoured, facilitating a two-way interactive audience.
4 Participation and deliberation go hand in hand and these democratic processes culminate in societal-wide decisions. This has the effect of reforming the

120 Rogers, *op cit* 112.

structures of representative democracy from within and can be epitomised by the concept of influence.

5 There should also be feedback loops along the lines of the day of accounting[121] in Porto Alegre's participatory budget to ensure that deliberation and participation are not purely tokenistic. This would ensure that accountability is in-built into participatory practices.

These principles can be mapped onto the system of arbitrating morality in controversial patent applications and will involve the Executive body – the EPO and national patent or intellectual property offices in managing the debate. An ethics committee will need to be appointed to identify patent applications which raise ethical concerns. Every Member State could appoint or elect a well-renowned ethicist so that each country would have a voice. An educational programme can also be devised whereby the nuances of the patent application and its underlying invention can be studied. Public programmes and debates can then be held in which all concerned parties can give their views and a public vote subsequently can be taken to decide whether the patent should be granted or not. Portugal's recent decision to introduce a national participatory budget has raised the issue of how best to facilitate the vote. They have decided to make it possible through ATM machines, thus minimising risks of votes being traded or going astray, which can be a problem with postal votes. Moreover, people will tend to be quite careful about guarding the secrecy of their ATM cards. They also hope to increase participation significantly using this method of voting.[122] As one of Portugal's cities has achieved a participation rate of 25 per cent using gamification, participation could become a mainstream practice with proper management.

4.4 Conclusion

This chapter has drawn together deliberative and participatory democracy practices in a case study of the participatory budget in Brazil. The purpose of this is to show that some of the ills of various forms of democracy such as elitism or populism can be avoided if the democratic structure's design is adaptable and well planned. Roles of public and government bodies can be adjusted and this chapter has also demonstrated that participation can be facilitated on a large scale. The final chapter of this book will propose a model for how a patent suffrage can be constructed, based on principles and power structures adapted from the participatory budget and deliberative practices.

121 Baiocchi, *op cit* 36.

122 Portugal has announced the world's first nationwide participatory budget, https://apolitical.co/portugal-world-first-participatory-budget/ (accessed 5 March 2019).

5 Recommendations for reform and conclusion

5.1 Introduction

The last chapter showed that participation incorporating deliberation can engage the publics in complex matters such as budgets. The study of the participatory budget in this book has aimed to show that morally controversial biotechnological patent applications could similarly be put to a public vote in a participatory and deliberative setting which would address the issue of deliberation and participation in a non-elitist and non-populist way. My reliance on participatory budgeting as a model for reform was not done on the basis of the subject matter of the budget but, rather, on the principles of public education, deliberation and participation embedded in participatory budgeting practices. These are of relevance when decisions are made on matters of public importance. I believe that patents on morally controversial biotechnological inventions are of general concern given the promise such inventions hold for human advancement coupled with the moral issues that these present.

This book thus fills several gaps in the knowledge. It analyses deliberative democracy with a focus on patents utilising a practical example to propose reform of the decision-making process at the European Patent Office (EPO) when these patent applications arise. Furthermore, it designs a loose model of how such a scheme could work, detailed below, with tentative answers to some anticipated difficulties. It is not the only possible model of reform to change controversial decision-making practices, of course, but I believe that if the aim is to seek a more inclusive, deliberative and democratic way then this can address many, if not all of the concerns raised in the legal literature about elitism and lack of transparency. It is a model worthy of consideration if carried out in accordance with principles of mutual respect in debate and deliberation. It should also involve the education of delegates so that they become equipped to debate more meaningfully. Thus society in general can acquire a greater understanding of the importance of the patent system in biotechnological inventions along with moral issues which may arise.

This chapter will now offer a blueprint as to how the manner of decision-making and who gets to vote in the proposed inclusive regime can be addressed.

5.2 Proposed structure of a universal patent suffrage at the EPO

This section sketches a paradigm of how a public vote on morally controversial biotechnological patent applications could be managed. When a patent application is made that potentially invokes the morality bar, most of these being for biotechnological inventions, we do not currently have much guidance on whether morality even needs to be considered and as the case law shows, new areas not alluded to in the legislation or case law sometimes arise. I would propose the following structure could be utilised and it would be held in three phases.

5.2.1 Phase one

1 First of all, the EPO should establish a permanent patent ethics committee to manage the process involved in deciding whether the morality bar is engaged and also to identify all the relevant ethical issues which a particular invention raises. Each EPO Member State should select a national representative with expertise in ethics who would sit on this committee. International courts could provide an example of how nation states can address national representation. Vibert believes that unelected bodies have a role to play in the development of democracy in which they can increase the amount of information available.[1] However, such national representatives could either be selected or elected: a public consultation could be held in order to engage public opinions on this process.

2 When the EPO receives a patent application for a biotech invention, they should be obliged to vet this with the patents ethics committee. The committee would decide whether the application raised any significant ethical issues of public importance. This would be useful as committee members would be trained in what sorts of questions to ask. Their role would not be to make any decisions or offer any opinion on the outcome of the patent application but that they advise on whether Article 53(a) European Patent Convention (EPC) has been triggered. Tierney has observed in the context of agenda setting for referendums that this tends to be managed by executives and that this stymies citizen involvement and the availability of deliberation.[2] The EPO's role would be administrative only and would oblige their involvement with other bodies and, of course, with the publics. Thus they would not monopolise either the process or the outcome.

3 The patent officials at the EPO would then be charged with administering a public education campaign to inform the publics about the patent application, what it promised, who was making it and why. Some details on how this educational process can be approached will be explored further after detailing the design of the voting process. This would be the first phase of public engagement.

1 Frank Vibert, *The Rise of the Unelected: Democracy and the New Separation of Powers* (Cambridge University Press 2007) 65–66.

2 Stephen Tierney, *Constitutional Referendums: The Theory and Practice of Republican Deliberation* (Oxford University Press 2012) 188.

The committee would give a grounding on ethical issues relating to the patent application and contribute to this aspect of the public education campaign. Publicity for public information sessions would be made through traditional and digital media with ample notice. National patent or intellectual property offices would assist in the organisation of national venues and logistics. The education could be carried out by video and also live media and with televised sessions available to view after the event. Phase one would comply with the second, third and fifth principles, of communication, audience and accountability set out in the framework developed at the end of Chapter Four. This public education would be a prelude to the second phase of the process, as follows.

5.2.2 Phase two

This second phase which would involve public deliberation and debate would give an opportunity for interested parties such as civil society groups, non-governmental organisations (NGOs), charities, individuals, industry, researchers, the health service and special interest groups to organise participation in a deliberative setting in public debate. These debates would be arranged by national patent offices and synchronised centrally with the EPO so that they would be held on a designated day or days. In order to avoid a descent into partisan, rabble rousing, it would be very important to design these sessions well and to follow principles identified in this book of mutual respect and refined debate. The sessions should have a goal in mind and that is to inform and prepare people to reach a decision about whether a given patent application merits a grant, when all factors are weighed up. There are plenty of examples in the literature of where deliberation is not successful, where opinions are raw and possibly ill-informed and this is not envisaged in the model proposed. Instead, the debate should be mediated, rules about how long people's contributions can be should be put in place and these can be revisited if they are not found to be appropriate. If managed well, the ultimate outcome should be more palatable to those who disagree because they will have had an opportunity to hear the other side and also to question it. This process may result in the eventual need to revise parts of the EPC and the Biotech Directive as they relate to morality and ordre public. However, it would be recommended that this process proceeds slowly in order to avoid rash decisions being taken.

I would not expect the process to run smoothly at first. Where officials are obliged to engage in this manner with the public for the first time, they often communicate poorly in inaccessible language and may not be receptive to concerns. Rogers believes that it is the elites' privilege rather than citizen incompetence that poses the most significant impediment to the establishment of participatory democracy.[3] The reciprocal process developed in participatory budgeting can assist in helping to train officials in the need to listen and adapt as well

3 Karl Rogers, *Participatory Democracy, Science and Technology* (Palgrave Macmillan 2008) 203.

as to inform. A period of education would require significant input initially but as societal understanding is increased, each new application would possibly not require similar effort as a store of knowledge would have been built up. There may be some concern that patent or intellectual property offices would not manage the debate fairly, given that they have a vested interest in granting patents. However, rules can be put in place that would oblige them to act in a non-partisan way and just to administer the process rather than direct the outcome. For instance, in Ireland, the government cannot use public money to encourage a "yes" or "no" vote on a referendum which they have proposed and if they do, the outcome can and has been challenged in the courts, sometimes successfully.[4] The publics can be informed, educated in a deliberative environment and decisions regarding incentivisation can be taken together in the form of a mediated vote, based on an adaptation of the participatory budget in Brazil. This novel form of governance is referred to by Santos as co-government[5] and reforms existing structures from the inside.

Where no effort is made to enshrine mutual respect, emergent policies will be disputed by a significant number of people, therefore it is very important to establish a robust framework for deliberation and participation. The procedure to be followed can be focused on to ensure a result which can be tolerated. This will involve a learning curve both for citizen and official where both come to regard each other as moral agents. Instead of bargaining solely for self-interested gains, weight can be given to moral reasoning. New rules for the conduct of such debate can be drawn up[6] and institutional design is vital if the public sphere is to be opened up to more dialogue and participation. In addition to being able to talk, one must also have the leisure to listen. It is much less likely that a respectful zone for deliberation will occur organically or without a framework.[7] And Tierney observes that deliberation often changes participants' views of particular matters.[8] The resolution in question may be controversial but at least competing rationales will have been discussed and a greater understanding of varying positions achieved. Moreover, the legitimacy[9] of decisions taken after such a process is likely to be improved[10] and often all sides modify their views somewhat in order to reach agreement or consensus. The deliberative process itself incorporating an acceptance of having to defend one's views within a forum where others are doing likewise with potentially polarised opinions signifies a willingness to debate in this

4 *McKenna v An Taoiseach* [1995] Ir Rep 10.
5 Santos, 'Two Democracies, Two Legalities: Participatory Budgeting in Porto Alegre' in Boaventura de Sousa Santos and César A Rodríguez-Garavito (eds) Law and Globalization from Below (Cambridge University Press 2005) 331.
6 Amy Gutmann and Dennis Thompson, *Why Deliberative Democracy?* (Princeton University Press 2004) 79–80.
7 James Fishkin, *Democracy and Deliberation: New Directions for Democratic Reform* (Cambridge University Press 1991) 51.
8 Tierney, *op cit* 209–210.
9 At times the process and outcome are inextricably entwined.
10 Gutmann and Thompson, *op cit* 179.

manner. While seeking to bring others around to their view, they similarly accept that their own minds may be changed.[11] While consensus may often be attainable locally, within relatively homogeneous communities, at societal level this participation inevitably becomes pluralistic.[12] Phase two corresponds to the principles of participation, communication and audience (one, two and three) in particular of the framework set out at the end of Chapter Four.

After a period of deliberation and debate, the next phase would invite a universal vote on the patent application. Voting would be open to everyone, even if they have not taken part in deliberation because they may not have been able to access the information sessions first hand. This obviously raises some danger that large swathes of ill- or uninformed citizens could sabotage the vote and it is a matter which would need to be borne in mind. Participation tends to start off in quite low percentages so such a risk would be difficult to predict but registration and attendance requirements could be introduced at a later point.

5.2.3 Phase three

Several methods of voting could be considered. Electronic voting without a paper record has been unpopular in some jurisdictions due to fears about transparency and traditional methods with a paper trail could be used alongside if this were chosen. Public buildings used in local elections such as town halls, schools and libraries could be employed and a postal vote would also be possible. In Portugal, where a national participatory budget has just been announced, it has been decided to facilitate the vote through the use of ATMs which is likely to enhance the integrity of the vote and diminish the risk of votes being traded. People are reluctant to share their PIN numbers. There are members of society who do not possess bank accounts but skeleton accounts with cards could be offered to address any such impediment to voting. A threshold number of votes would not be a prerequisite for the validity of the vote because participation would be optional.

The opposition proceedings at the EPO would be undisturbed. When citizens engage in deliberation about moral issues and reach agreement, there should be a possibility of revisiting such decisions at a later stage by way of appeal. It is important to be able to reopen resolutions[13] because opinions and standards can change over time as can information, as seen in the partial backtrack on the judgment in the *Brüstle*[14] case in *International Stem Cell Corporation*[15] where new information about the viability of parthenotes came to light. The route of taking part in deliberation involves recognition by citizens that their opinions may alter and that their current demands may not remain the same in the future.

11 Ibid 20–21.
12 Rogers, *op cit* 170.
13 Gutmann and Thompson, *op cit* 157.
14 C-34/10 *Oliver Brüstle v Greenpeace eV* [2011] ECR I-9821.
15 C-364/13 *International Stem Cell Corporation v Comptroller General of Patents* (Grand Chamber) 18 December 2014.

Moreover, opposition may be less likely to occur if voices that have wanted to be heard had an opportunity to do so during, rather than after, the application process. During participatory budgetary negotiations, for instance, even though the legislature can override the Executive's budgeting, once the public voice has been expressed, decisions are largely respected. This would offset some of the costs involved in setting up a system of public voting at first instance.

Phase three would reflect the principles of influence and accountability (four and five) especially which were developed in the framework at the end of Chapter Four.

Of crucial importance in any such reform is that if the aim is to maximise societal engagement, education must be provided. Such programmes could be modelled on experimental paradigms which exist, especially in the area of disseminating knowledge on Information Communication Technologies (ICTs). Having laid out the three phases of engagement, above, the next section considers one such example which could provide a useful educational structure for the EPO to consider.

5.3 A model for public education on technology-related issues

Conducting public education campaigns is not an easy task and if elitism or attempts to influence outcomes are to be avoided, careful design will be necessary. I give an account here of a large-scale public education project in a region in Western Spain called Extremadura of one million people which was put in place some years ago. It answers some logistical questions which are likely to arise where such education is being rolled out. Important questions include how to achieve outreach and genuine engagement.

In 1999, the regional government or Junta of Extremadura introduced a Digital or Technological Literacy Plan of which the aim was to introduce the entire population to (ICTs). It sought to ensure that everyone had access to the Internet and knowledge of how to use it. Stimulating interest among the population so that they would engage was also deemed to be important. The Junta considered technological illiteracy to be harmful. It was decided to carry out this digitisation plan by setting up a type of Internet cafe throughout the region which were called New Knowledge Centres and their number peaked at 45. Each centre employed two people comprising a technical expert and an outreach person, each of whom designed software programs and other programmes for the local community. The outreach person did not have a set profile. This was because it was appreciated that skills would be dictated by local conditions, depending on whether they were situated in cities or small, rural areas. Programmes were designed not only *for* the populations but *in conjunction* with them because it was the understanding of the Junta that the Information Society was a two-way street and not one where unilateral decisions should be taken. In order to ensure that older people engaged with the centres, the outreach person would liaise with other points of contact in a given region such as churches, bridge clubs, active ageing groups and other similar organisations. It was found to be more effective to attract local populations on a peer-to-peer basis and through friends and so a devolved approach was taken. This management style could also be used to encourage participation in voting on morally controversial biotechnological patent applications.[16]

In addition to these centres, 1,500 Internet points were set up in the region and all secondary schools were equipped with one computer per every two students and the ratio was five per pupil at primary level. This had a transformative effect in the classroom as students were often able to help out the teacher and keyboards were shared between two, ensuring collaboration among classmates. Although a total cost of ownership (TCO) was never carried out, the Junta estimated a saving of 18 million euros on licensing fees as a version of Linux rather than proprietary software was used. This wide-scale deployment of ICTs created many job opportunities, spurred an interest in computer science at university and had the unexpected effect of aiding the market for proprietary software too as some programs such as games may be developed more effectively with private funding. General knowledge of ICTs was heightened in the region during this period. This case study demonstrates that knowledge of technologies can be deployed widely, although the initial set up would require an investment of both monetary and temporal resources.

The relevance of this model to the topic of education is that there will need to be a receptive approach on the part of officials engaged in public education on technology and debate facilitation. Initial structures and arrangements will have to be flexible and amenable to change. Effective outreach can be a useful way of reaching a widespread number of citizens. It may be argued, however, that science is too complex to be decided on in this way and this issue will now be addressed.

5.3.1 Does education about science present specific challenges?

Literature on the issue of how best to educate the general public about science so that decisions can be taken indicate a number of difficulties with its delivery. De Bruin and Bostrom observe a dichotomy between the information that experts tend to convey as contrasted with what people actually need to know. This can arise because scientists are accustomed to converse mainly with others in their field.[17] They recommend that surveys should be composed at an appropriate level for the target audience and cognitive pilot interviews, in which it can be ascertained whether questions have been understood as intended, should be conducted.[18] There may be a financial incentive to do so: it is claimed that intangibles including goodwill and reputation constitute up to 70

16 I was invited to write a case study on this programme in 2013 for JoinUp, a publication of the European Commission. Maureen O'Sullivan, 'Extremadura's Free and Open Source Policy amid Storms of Political Change', https://joinup.ec.europa.eu/community/osor/case/extremaduras-free-and-open-source-software-policy-amid-storms-political-change (accessed 5 March 2019).

17 Bruin de Bruin, Wändi and Bostrom Ann, 'Assessing What to Address in Science Communication' *PNAS* 20 August 2013 vol. 110, suppl. 3, 14062.

18 Ibid, 14065.

per cent of private firms' assets and that these can be depleted where communication is inadequate.[19]

Some theories of decision-making hypothesise that decisions are based both on beliefs and values. Beliefs include facts, which should be informed by science and when science informs decision-making, facts and values ought to be separated.[20] However, it has been found that science communication often comprises only facts and it will need to address values too. This can be achieved by including public participation which can help to integrate facts and values in the decision-making process.[21] Good practice in public participation includes iteration in which public concerns are integrated into the issues which science addresses. It has been shown that public participation can have a positive effect on foreseeing policy effects that science's exclusive lens would have missed. A multi-faceted approach together with two-way communication is effective and Dietz notes that the literature demonstrates a greater likelihood of success when there is genuine rather than unilateral interaction.[22]

Any public education scheme in the area of morally controversial patent grants should include the following principles:

1. The facts relating to the technology should be ascertained in an exercise conducted by scientists and put into language which can be understood by the publics.
2. Patent officials should then put together a brief on controversies which arise through the use of the patent system to encourage such research and the development of the inventions.
3. Members of ethics committees could contribute to highlighting the advantages and disadvantages of the technologies.
4. The language could be refined in conjunction with representatives from NGOs and civil society groups through a consultation process.
5. Pilot interviews could be carried out with a small cross-section of the population chosen through random sampling to ascertain whether the language is comprehensible.
6. Adaptations would most likely have to be made.
7. Public discussion and debate could then take place and the information available would also, in all likelihood, change once more, given a multi-faceted input. Decisions could then take place.

5.3.2 The participatory right in morally controversial patents

In terms of the human right to participate, this should be permitted to permeate the patenting process where it concerns morally controversial biotechnological

19 Ibid, 14067.

20 Detlof von Winterfeldt, 'Bridging the Gap Between Science and Decision Making' *PNAS* 20 August 2013, vol. 110, suppl. 3, 14055, 14060.

21 Thomas Dietz, 'Bridging Values and Deliberation to Science Communication' *PNAS* 20 August 2013, vol. 110, suppl. 3 14081.

22 Ibid, 14084.

patents. Perhaps guidance can be sought from the United Nations' Committee on Economic, Social and Cultural Rights. When commenting on Article 15(1)(c) of the International Convention on Economic, Social and Cultural Rights, they observed that intellectual property rights are used to encourage creation and invention along with preserving their works for society's benefit. Human rights are fundamental to the person.[23] While intellectual property rights are temporally limited, human rights are not[24] and effectively, the latter trump the former.

It has been the contention of this book that the issue of morality in patent law is unsettled and that the current framework by which it is decided is unsatisfactory because patent office employees have no tools with which to arbitrate morality. It is contended that no one can really have expertise but that everyone has an interest and, therefore, should at least have the right to participate in the decision-making process. Many arguments could be made against the proposed reform model of this book and the next section will address and seek to answer some of these anticipated concerns.

5.4 Objections

Objection 1: There are other ways of dealing with the problems in applying the morality bar: this model is not needed. Reform can be brought about through legislation, judicial activism or patent office practice.

Answer: Every solution to a problem will produce a different outcome and the normative claim of this book is that all the publics *should* be given a chance to be involved in this decision-making process and to influence the outcome. Legislative reform could achieve more clarity, judicial activism may establish precedents over time and patent office reform could achieve more transparency. As this book seeks, however, to ensure inclusivity, representation and participation, the result will not be achieved through reform from within the system, hence the reliance on participatory and deliberative mechanisms.

Objection 2: The publics are disinterested, therefore there is no justification for the envisaged reform.

Answer: We currently have no way of assessing this, although the polls and surveys advanced as evidence by Greenpeace in *Plant Genetic System* suggest that there is interest in this issue, even if it has not been heeded. Among cohorts of the population that are educated on this matter, there is plenty of concern as seen from the variety of NGOs, civil society groups and individuals prepared to oppose patents. The state along with the news media should educate us more. We are

23 Office of the High Commissioner for Human Rights, Committee on Economic, Social and Cultural Rights, *General Comment No. 17: Article 15(1)(c) – Right of everyone to benefit from the protection of the moral and material interests resulting from any scientific, literary or artistic production of which he or she is the author*, introduction and basic principles para 2 (E/C. 12/GC/17), (Geneva, 12 January 2006) http://tbinternet.ohchr.org/_layouts/treatybodyexternal/TBSearch.aspx?Lang=en&TreatyID=9&DocTypeID=11 (accessed 5 March 2019).

24 Ibid para 2.

much more likely to die from a disease that could be treated by a therapy developed from a patented invention than in a terrorist attack but this is not reflected in public communications.

Objection 3: This book is advocating a very paternalistic approach, which smacks of a nanny state. If people don't want to engage, they should be left alone. Being overly protective goes against the trend in international governance where the state apparatus is being reduced in the age of austerity.

Answer: Part of the normative claim of this book that the state *should* be more proactive in engaging the public, but not mandate participation, in line with the Universal Declaration of Human Rights, Article 21 and also the Universal Declaration on Bioethics and Human Rights, Article 23. The state is currently very paternalistic in manipulating data, news and finance but not too generous with information and this model would redress this balance in the context of patents.

Objection 4: The right to participate was never intended to be used in this area, or if it was, it was not intended to engage with individuals over NGOs.

Answer: This is not necessarily true in light of the Universal Declaration on Bioethics and Human Rights which encourages states to engage with groups such as NGOs on the issue. The right to participate in the Universal Declaration of Human Rights is an individual right and this is reflected in the Brazilian and other constitutions that interpret the right to participate as an individual, as well as a collective right. It is also a right which is currently evolving so its ontology is not fixed.

Objection 5: Some elite democrats argue that many people have insufficient cognitive capacity to understand these very complex issues and they are best left to experts who can be trusted to decide for them.

Answer: It is becoming less acceptable to speak ill of people who are less privileged than us, whether by class, age, disability, education or other perceived disadvantage. We live in an era when our definition of capacity is changing. It behoves us to communicate better and to work harder to include others who do not look, sound or behave like us rather than excluding them because we have judged negatively their right to participate on our own subjective standards. This would also include bidirectional engagement in addition to unidirectional effective communication.

Objection 6: The right to participate is fine for budgets, but will not work in other areas as the issues are far too complex. You cannot translate systems, whether legal or political.

Answer: The reform proposed in this book is not a legal transplant – it is a study of a democratic practice, an extraction of its principles to an abstract level and their subsequent application to an area of patent law which some legal academics believe is in need of reform. Academics such as Sampaio recommends the adaptation of the participatory budgetary process to the issue of climate change in Denver where he argues if the citizens could influence decisions about investments, the process would be legitimated. An environmental scheme in Denver known as the Greenprint Denver Plan, has as one of its guiding principles to broaden its reach through strategic partnerships.[25] This shows that participatory principles can be applied elsewhere. Moreover, legal transplants can be very successful and a good example is the Ombudsman, which originated in Sweden.

Objection 7: Some academics may argue that this sort of model would be cost prohibitive. It may also be unduly time-consuming and inefficient.

Answer: This is difficult to calculate and depends on what metrics are being used. The cost of medical care for an ageing population whose illnesses may be treated by patentable medicine may be much higher. A "stitch in time may save nine" approach may require some initial expenditure to avoid much great expense at a later stage.

The model may, of course, involve a substantial cost and be less temporally efficient as compared with the current regime. Substantial investment both in terms of monetary and other resources would certainly have to be made at the outset and ongoing training would require oversight. However, cost should not be a reason to fail to implement the recommended model and it is argued that such are the benefits of the reform, that any costs accrued should be borne. The increased costs would be outweighed by the improvements in the decision-making process.

Objection 8: A public vote would be a huge deterrent to industry and it will hold back research. Many patents are sought after research has commenced and this represents a significant investment by private firms. They would not be comfortable being subject to public whimsy.

Answer: At present, the application of the morality bar leaves firms or researchers in very uncertain terrain as they cannot predict how decisions may be made. The *WARF* and *Technion* cases are good examples as is the *Brüstle* case in the Court of Justice of the European Union (CJEU) where human dignity concerns have started to occupy centre stage as the EU Charter starts to eclipse the European Convention on Human Rights in the Court's jurisprudence. Concepts of human dignity in the Charter, for instance, were relied upon in *Brüstle* and this may also affect judgments from the EPO and its boards, given its willingness to align closely with legal developments in the EU.[26] Public engagement would afford patent applicants the opportunity to justify their monopoly to the publics. If their invention merits a patent, they can learn how to convey this. If it holds great promise but is morally dubious, there will still be a need to weigh up the ethical qualms and decide outcomes. How this is done and by whom is the focus of this book. Moreover, perhaps more publicly funded research should take place, putting less of a risk burden on the private sector.

Objection 9: The publics cannot be trusted, any debate on morality will be hijacked by special interest groups and descend into populism.

25 R Silveira da Rocha Sampaio, 'Regulating Climate Change Risk at the Local Level – the Denver Experience: Greenprint or Greenwash?' (2010) 17 *Mo Envtl L & Pol'y Rev* 356, 387.

26 The Biotech Directive 1998 was effectively incorporated into the EPC and major departures in patent decisions at the EPO have not occurred.

Answer: The reason for indicating throughout this book that a deliberative and participatory paradigm entwined with education, communication and engagement is proposed is to avoid the populism, sabotage and extremism which can sometimes permeate public debate. The design of such debates will be crucial. They will have to avoid any attempt to shape public views and information must be impartial and multi-faceted. As public moneys would be used in such campaigns, restraint can be put on any expenditure which favours one argument over another.[27] Otherwise decisions could be open to challenge.

Objection 10: Participation rates in the budgetary processes are too low to justify reform of the nature proposed.

Answer: Participation in Brazil, as seen in Chapter Four, averages between 2 and 7 per cent and it has also been shown that while up to 10 per cent of the population may have participated at one stage, some participation is fleeting. However, the Portuguese administration in Ovar achieved a rate of 25 per cent by the use of gamification and other technologies could help to encourage further participation and make it more worthwhile. These figures show that participation rates can vary greatly, depending on the manner in which public participation is organised. While the level of engagement on issues to do with morality in biotechnological patent grants remains to be seen, the Portuguese experiment suggests that different technologies can have a significant effect on the electorate's interest.

Objection 11: There is nothing new here – the criticism of the patent system as not being inclusive could be applied across the board, as there is nothing special about patents.

Answer: There *is* something special about patents because of the fact that monopoly and property rights are allocated to an invention which has already been sanctioned so we are dealing with a separate regulatory regime. It may be that there is a case for more deliberative participation in a whole host of different areas that lack democratic inclusion and accountability to which this book can make a significant contribution in terms of its abstract principles. Moreover, the approach that this book takes to the problem of the democratic deficit in the decision-making process of morally controversial patent grants is original in that it seeks a Latin American paradigm as a guiding principle.

Objection 12: There is no way that the EPO will consider this reform. It would require amending the EPC and as can be seen from the incorporation of the Biotech Directive into the EPC, there is a reluctance to engage in legislative reform where a diplomatic conference has to be convened.

Answer: Whether or not the EPO considers such reform will depend on the manner in which it is presented and on the extent to which it is receptive to criticism. Industries whose patent applications have been unsuccessful may be persuaded to publicise their research activities and may well relish an opportunity to convince the publics of the merits of monopoly. Moreover, NGOs may relish the opportunity to benefit from a more participatory process as may individuals.

27 *McKenna v An Taoiseach* [1995] Ir Rep 10.

Objection 13: The participatory model would be extremely disruptive and could become viral, with everyone wanting a say on everything.

Answer: The participatory budget has spread extensively around the world and participation is now part of the zeitgeist. It may be that its time has come: as participation becomes more widespread, so too will positive and negative experiences be built up and efficient, low cost, truly representative models will serve as exemplars of how to engage an enthusiastic population in matters of deep concern. For the purposes of this book, patent system reform in morally controversial biotechnological inventions is deemed necessary by some academics to be nigh. It has been the aim of this book not just to criticise the functioning of the system but, in particular, to identify a way in which this might be done and also to anticipate some of the hitches than can be expected along the way. Furthermore, this model would be kept under review and would be subject to adjustment over time.

5.5 Conclusion

This chapter has established a model structure of how the proposal of the book, which is a public vote within the EPO on the availability of patents for morally controversial biotechnological inventions should be conducted. It has identified a potential procedure by which existing structures and personnel such as the EPO and its officials remain in place but their functions alter. It adds a permanent patent ethics committee to the bodies involved to ensure that moral issues are identified and it sketches how public information, deliberation and the vote can be administered. It envisages hurdles if heed is not paid to experience which shows that there is an array of means to carry out public education and deliberation and that some models are more successful than others. Best practice should be followed throughout and administrators of this decision-making process should be receptive to criticism and suggested improvements, based on good practice elsewhere. The EPO can initially decide to run a pilot so that logistics can be estimated prior to rolling out the scheme. While not aiming to be a panacea to cure all ills involved in the current decision-making process, the model proposed in this book is not just theoretical but is grounded in real examples to test its viability. The conclusion of the book is that the solution proposed can address the qualms about opacity, lack of transparency and a democratic deficit in the current decision-making process on morally controversial biotechnological inventions.

This book adopted a pluralistic methodology of doctrinal, socio-legal and interdisciplinary methods to achieve a critique, analysis and proposal for reform of the decision-making process involved in morally controversial patent applications at the EPO. It gave a chronological account of relevant legislation and discussed key cases and literature which pointed to tensions in the arbitration of the morality bar. Reform from within the system of legislation, case law or patent office practice was examined but it was found that reforming these artefacts would not address the democratic deficit. Ethics committees were also considered but as the research problem of the book was to find a way to increase inclusion, universal rather than elite discourse was favoured. The book then embarked on a scrutiny of deliberative democracy in which various small-scale devices are used to articulate a voice but the nexus between this voice and policy change is not in evidence. Having established, however, that deliberation can occur among myriad groups and that debate can be constructive, the human right to participate was identified as a potential grounding for public inclusivity. A model of participatory budgeting was used as an example of the practice of deliberative participation in Brazil where budgeting is both discursive and participatory. A case study of the participatory budget was carried out and principles which could be used to establish a framework for participation in morally controversial biotechnological patents were identified. These principles were then mapped onto the intricacies of patenting and a blueprint for a three-stage process of engagement and voting was designed. Some of its weaknesses were identified and discussed, showing that radical reform can be enunciated when we cast our nets wide and seek to learn from countries which were themselves inspired by political devices such as popular councils from the Russian revolution. Brazil adapted these models to its own environs, eschewing a strong centralised state role in the deployment of participatory budgeting and instead developed a matrix between grassroots groups and top-down institutions.

This book did not confine itself to conducting a critique: instead, it developed an original architecture, identifying and extracting principles from a long-standing participatory practice – as it happens, in the area of budgeting – and applied it to the EPO's fraught decision-making process in morally controversial biotechnological patents, extending and crafting the ideas of academics who argued that the participatory budgeting principles could be used in other realms. This work crystallises these ideas in the domain of patent law for the first time, making it a significant contribution to knowledge and addressing a chasm in the literature between law, science, political science, sociology and philosophy. Its originality also consists in the drawing up of a feasible paradigm for a universal suffrage for morally controversial biotechnological patents.

Index